Appreciation for *The Combat Trauma Healing M*

"America's Warriors returning from deployments and from com
a myriad of ways – as are their families. Many will seek care, co
Our Lord told us in Mark 12:30 to 'Love the Lord your God with all your heart, with all your soul, with all
your mind, and with all your strength' – reminding us that we human beings have to pay attention to our
emotional, spiritual, and mental, as well as our physical needs. This manual is a superb resource in helping
our Warriors and families, and helping counselors and caring communities to assist them, especially in
dealing with their unseen wounds and in ministering to their emotional and spiritual needs."

Major General (Retired) Kenneth L. Farmer, Jr., M.D., U.S. Army

"This outstanding manual provides a wealth of material for the care of our military Reserve Components
warriors who often return home without the ready infrastructure of a military base. It needs to be in the
hands of every religious congregation across America as they seek to serve those in their communities who
suffer PTSD as a result of serving their country in war."

Chaplain (Brigadier General, Retired) Douglas E. Lee, U.S. Army

"I wish I had this (The CTHM) 15 years ago."

Arizona National Guard Desert Storm Veteran

"I have used *the Combat Trauma Healing Manual* in the past with great success. Not only does it describe
the 'what' and 'why' that surrounds stress and combat stress, but also details a focused Christ-centered plan
of 'how' to overcome. This positive and inspiring manual is one of the only tools that I've seen be successful
in helping to overcome the effects of PTSD."

Major, Company Commander, U.S. Army

"I was sent a copy of *The Combat Trauma Healing Manual*. This is the best workbook that I have seen in my
thirteen years of ministering to veterans."

State Coordinator for Point Man International Ministries

"*The Combat Trauma Healing Manual* is a wonderful resource for the Christian Pastor who truly wants to
understand and help combat veterans and their families. The traumatic experience of combat can leave
painful scars in the mind, body and spirit of a warrior. Physical injuries obviously have life altering results
that soldiers and their families must cope with for the rest of their lives. The psychological and spiritual
injuries of war are often not as visible, but they are just as real. This book integrates what we know from
science, medicine, and Biblical faith to bring healing to the wounded soul and hope for a fulfilling and
meaningful Christian life. Because it is designed as a workbook, it provides a step-by-step process to
address critical issues, allowing time for reflection and prayer to process the deep emotions that are a
natural part of the internal battle often resulting from the wounds of war."

Keith Ethridge M.Div., former Navy Chaplain

"*The Combat Trauma Healing Manual* is a labor of love that I have seen touch many military families, and
we are still at the beginning of reaching out to our brothers and sisters in pain. I have seen this book open
the eyes of so many that have been hurting for so long and have not known how to deal with their post-
traumatic stress. With God as our cornerstone and *The Combat Trauma Healing Manual* as our instrument,
God has given us the tools we need so that others may find his love and heal their wounded souls."

Gene Birdwell, Executive Director,
The Post-Traumatic Stress Disorder Foundation of America

Returning Warriors Finding Spiritual Healing through the CTHM

These comments and requests have been selected from messages to Cru Military and from comments on Amazon.com:

Excellent resource for someone with PTSD: I bought this for a friend of mine who as PTSD. He has been through several programs at VA and personal counseling that didn't really help him. He expressed a desire for something that was spiritually based since he is a Christian and he has thanked me many times for buying this workbook for him. He says it has helped him more than anything else he has done. He now has a passion for starting a veterans group to work through this book. An excellent resource for the returning combat veteran who has difficulty re-integrating into civilian life.

Amazing method for treating PTSD: I am a disabled vet with PTSD from service in Iraq. Ten years late, I am still battling with things that I did and saw over there. This book has helped me put much of it to rest. That is something to talk about. If you are someone or know someone that suffers from PTSD from combat, this is the book for them.

A terrific manual for more than just PTSD sufferers: This manual was required for my PTSD class at LU. What a gem to assist in spiritual healing! The chapters were just long enough to complete in about 15-20 minutes, the content is extremely informative, and the scriptural references were awesome! Although this focuses on symptoms of PTSD, I believe that anyone who has ever experienced deep soul wounds can benefit from the contents of this workbook, and recommend that this become a library fixture.

My son returned from Iraq last year and has lost everything. His wife, his son and he is now living with us. We are struggling to find a way to help him. Our hearts break for him each day. My mother has been listening to you this week and I know that this is an answer to our prayers. So thank you for caring for our young men and our families. May God bless this ministry the need is great!

I am a disabled Army Vet who thanks you for your ministry. God is using you to start the healing process in my life also. Thanks.

Thank you for your ministry. Being a disabled vet from the Vietnam era myself I have interest in helping others find comfort in Jesus Christ.

This guide is very challenging to refocus your attention on combat experiences, but I do recommend to anyone seeking a biblical approach to help regain control over your symptoms by allowing the Lord to heal through this manual.

Good workbook, but no workbook can replace good therapy: This is a good workbook. The writer does seem to understand what trauma is like (although it is different for everyone). This is NOT a replacement for therapy.

Although religious based I am working my way through the book. Is good so far.

Amazon Reviews for "When War Comes Home"

Thank you so much for writing this book! I'm am on the first chapter and it's amazing! I feel like I could be reading my own story! I'm not alone! There are personal stories, explanations of what's going on, and questions you can answer that help you reflect. Ordinarily, I'd skip these and fast read through it. I'm taking my time. If I'm too tired to answer in that moment, I put the book down and come back to it later. This is helping me see things differently. I'm excited to see what happens next! I can't thank you enough!!!

This manual is so excellent. As a wife of a soldier who has PTSD from combat and childhood abuse, this manual has been a wonderful resource. I recently finished a spouse support group that used this manual as a guide and it was a life saver. This manual is so well rounded, and addresses many issues that may not come up in a mainstream Christian atmosphere. I do appreciate that it is faith-based, but does not shy away from gritty topics. As a nurse, I have researched the topic of PTSD thoroughly and this book covers most of the physical components and treatment, while also addressing the needs of the support person, faith and military repercussions. Very well done: would recommend it to anyone with a spouse or family member who has PTSD. Although it comes from a combat standpoint, there are many aspects to it that could pertain to the needs of any support person living with a person with PTSD, regardless of the cause.

Amazon Review for the children's books: "My Hero's Home!!," "Helping My Hero!!," and "My Hero is Hurting!!"

I was very impressed with how user friendly these three resources were. In *My Hero's Home*, the author uses the story of Carrie and Cody's family as she deals with ,What happened to my daddy, what am I doing wrong, daddy?, why are you so sad, daddy?, should I say, "I'm sorry"?, I'm scared, who can help me?, God ,I need you, who are my friends? I am God's child, should I pray? , how can we help daddy?, how can we help each other?, where are we going?(Page3, *My Hero's Home*). The chapters are short, just two pages and full of practical help. The author shares a brief story, a verse that relates, key words and their definition, activities the child can do and a prayer. The appendix in *My Hero's Home* includes activities, templates and Parent's Pages (Pages 35-63, *My Hero's Home*).

In *Helping My Hero*, the author shares and explains what the grief cycle is (Page 26, *Helping My Hero*).She also answers tough questions, such as, "Why did Sara's dad point a gun at her mom? (Page 43, *Helping My Hero*). In My Hero Hurts, the teenage workbook, the author goes into great depth to explain what is happening in the military family. She answers questions such as, What can cause the wounds of war?, What causes PTSD?, What happens to the whole body because of trauma?, What are the symptoms of PTSD, What is the difference between PTSD and Traumatic Brain Injury (TBI)?, What are the symptoms of TBI? And five things Military teens want to understand (Pages 1-16, *My Hero is Hurting!*). The appendix for *My Hero is Hurting* includes a homecoming checklist, more questions for the family sit-down talk guide and more verses for prayer (Pages 126-127, *My Hero is Hurting*). These books are amazingly full of practical tools! I would highly recommend these books to military families who are dealing with PTSD !

THE COMBAT TRAUMA HEALING MANUAL

CHRIST-CENTERED SOLUTIONS FOR COMBAT TRAUMA

BY CHRIS ADSIT

MILITARY

The Combat Trauma Healing Manual: Christ-centered Solutions for Combat Trauma is part of the **Bridges to Healing Series**.
Also in the series: *When War Comes Home: Christ-centered Healing for Wives of Combat Veterans;*
The Combat Trauma Healing Manual and When War Comes Home Leader's Guides for Group Discussion; and, coming soon,
a new series for children who have a parent dealing with Combat Trauma.

Published by Military Ministry Press, part of Cru Military, a division of Campus Crusade for Christ, Inc.
Cru Military, 100 Lake Hart Dr., Orlando FL 32832.
This printing includes a new cover, textual edits and a new introduction. For more information about Cru Military, please visit our web site at www.crumilitary.org or call 1-800-444-6006.

All Scripture quotations, unless otherwise indicated, are taken from the *New American Standard Bible.*
Copyright © 1960, 1962, 1963, 1968, 1971, 1972, 1973, 1975, 1977 by the Lockman Foundaton. Used by permission.
Other versions of The Bible used are:
Amp = THE AMPLIFIED BIBLE, Old Testament. Copyright © 1965, 1987 by the Zondervan Corporation.
The Ampli ied New Testament copyright © 1958, 1987 by the Lockman Foundation. Used by
permission. All rights reserved.
Msg = THE MESSAGE. Copyright © by Eugene H. Peterson, 1993, 1994, 1995. Used by permission of
NavPress Publishing Group. All rights reserved.
NIV = the *Holy Bible, New International Version®.* Copyright © 1973, 1978, 1984 by International Bible
Society. Used by permission of Zondervan Publishing House. All rights reserved.
NKJV = the *New King James Version.* Copyright © 1979, 1980, 1982 by Thomas Nelson, Inc. Used by
permission. All rights reserved.
NLT = the *Holy Bible, New Living Translation.* Copyright © 1971, 2004. Used by permission of Tyndale
House Publishers, Inc., Wheaton, IL 60189. All rights reserved.

DISCLAIMER
This book is not a substitute for appropriate medical or psychological care for those experiencing significant emotional pain or whose ability to function at home, school or work is impaired. Chronic or extreme stress may cause a wide assortment of physical and psychological problems. Some may require evaluation and treatment by medical or mental health professionals. When in doubt, seek advice from a professional.

ISBN 978-1-4196-7820-2
Printed in the United States of America

To everything there is a season, a time for every purpose under heaven:

. . . A time to kill,

And a time to heal . . .

– Ecclesiastes 3:1-3 (NKJV)

Your time to kill is passed.

Your time to heal has come.

TABLE OF CONTENTS

ACKNOWLEDGEMENTS

About the author:

Christopher B. Adsit (Chris) is a graduate of Colorado State University in Biological Sciences and has been on the staff of Campus Crusade for Christ since 1974. For his first fifteen years he ministered with Athletes in Action, competing in the decathlon and achieving All-American honors. In 1991 he founded Disciplemakers International, a ministry of Campus Crusade for Christ. During that period he wrote *Personal Disciplemaking* and *Connecting With God*, publications used by many Bible colleges and seminaries. In 2005 Chris began serving as Cru Military's (formerly Military Ministry) Associate National Director of Disciplemaking. Chris is currently the National Director of Branches Of Valor International. He lives in Eugene, Oregon with wife Rahnella. They have four grown children.

The following were contributing writers to this manual:

Rahnella Adsit, President/CEO, Branches of Valor

Colonel Nancy Davis, USAF, Retired, MS (counseling), MS (psychology), Stephen Minister, Cru Military PTSD Task Force

Colonel Paul Davis, Ph.D., USAF, Retired; Cru Military PTSD Task Force

Major General Robert F. Dees, US Army, Retired

Glenn Gritzon, MA, MABC, Church Relations Representative, FamilyLife Ministry

Nate Self, former Captain, US Army Rangers; Co-founder and Director of Development of The Prævius Group, Inc.

Karen Watkins, Cru Military

Research Assistants: **Ann Christianson, Jamie Christianson, Elizabeth Pearson**

Illustrations by **Sandy Silverthorn**

And we want to extend a special debt of gratitude to:

Bruce Cutshall, former Army National Guard Medical Platoon Sergeant of 2/162 HHC during Operation Iraqi Freedom, March 2004 to April 2005 – PTSD victor.

Andrea J. Westfall, former US Army Reserves Staff Sergeant and combat zone flight medic before and during Operation Iraqi Freedom, August 2002 to May 2003 – PTSD victor.

Thank you for your service to our country, for your inspiration to all of us with Cru Military, and for your contributions to the writing of this manual.

❋　❋　❋　❋　❋

We are thankful for the crucial input we received from the following people either directly or through their writing or speaking:

Dr. Neil T. Anderson. Founder and President Emeritus of Freedom In Christ Ministries. Anderson's books on spiritual warfare, including *Victory Over the Darkness* and *The Bondage Breaker* were obviously very helpful to us on the subject of spiritual warfare, but also on the issue of self-identity.

Dr. Larry Crabb. A leading psychologist, author, Bible teacher and seminar speaker; founder and director of New Way Ministries; serves as a Spiritual Director for the American Association of Christian Counselors and Distinguished Scholar-in-Residence of Colorado Christian University. Among Dr. Crabb's many helpful books, *Shattered Dreams* was of special aid to us as we prepared this manual.

Dr. Laura Mae Gardner. Board Vice Chairman and International Coordinator for Member Care for Wycliffe Bible Translators; presenter of "PTSD: A Biblical Approach to Helping Veterans, Victims and Survivors" at the Fellowship of Christian Military Ministries 3/27/07 at Fort Carson, CO. Thank you for your passion and insights on this subject.

"Chaplain Ray" Giunta. Encouragement Pastor at Central Christian Church, Las Vegas, NV and Senior Chaplain at We Care Ministries. Ray and his wife Cathy have been involved in crisis intervention during disasters from Oklahoma City to 9/11 to Katrina and everything in between. Their excellent book *Grief Recovery Workbook* was a great resource for us as we assembled several of the Steps in this manual.

Robert Hicks. Cofounder of Life Counseling Services in Philadelphia; Professor of History at Belhaven College/Orlando; Wing Chaplain for the 187th Fighter Wing of the Air National Guard; Consultant for the Air Force Air University. He is an Air Force Reserve specialist dealing with traumatic stress and frequently teaches at military schools and conferences. His book *Failure To Scream* provided a great deal of insight regarding the symptoms of PTSD and the necessity of debriefing and communicating one's traumatic experiences.

Patience Mason. Married to a Vietnam War veteran (Robert Mason, author of *Chickenhawk*) who suffered from severe PTSD long before it was formally identified as a disorder by the APA. She has spent over thirty years researching PTSD and written extensively on the subject on the internet (www.patiencepress.com) and in print: *Recovering From The War.*

Dr. Aphrodite Matsakis. After years of experience with the Veterans Administration Medical Center in Washington D.C., she is now the Clinical Coordinator of the Vietnam Veteran's Outreach Center in Silver Springs, MD. We benefited greatly from her many excellent books on the subject of Combat Trauma including *I Can't Get Over It: A Handbook for Trauma Survivors; Trust After Trauma: A Guide to Relationships for Survivors and Those Who Love Them* and *Post-Traumatic Stress Disorder: A Complete Treatment Guide.*

Patricia K. Miersma RN, MN, CS. MASH nurse in Vietnam; currently working with Wycliffe in crisis intervention and counseling in Africa. Co-Author of *Healing the Wounds of Trauma* and presenter of "Combat Trauma: Readiness, Resilience & Recovery" at the Fellowship of Christian Military Ministries 3/27/07 at Fort Carson, CO. The experiences she gained in her years of working with Africans who were the victims of ethnic cleansing have proven to be helpful and inspirational to us.

Dr. H. Norman Wright, MFCC, CTS. Has served as a professor and department head at both Biola University and Talbot Theological Seminary, maintained a private counseling practice for 30 years, and written over 70 books on crisis, trauma and grief, including *The New Guide to Crisis & Trauma Counseling; Recovering From Losses in Life* and *Experiencing Grief.* We have benefited greatly from his research, experience and personal encouragement.

❋   ❋   ❋   ❋   ❋

BEFORE YOU BEGIN...

If you are a veteran struggling with Combat Trauma – especially with Post-Traumatic Stress Disorder – we want you to know that we of Cru Military are very grateful for your service and sacrifice for our country and that our hearts go out to you because of the difficulties you are currently experiencing. We, and many others in our global network, have prayed for you and are continuing to do so.

We know that one of your primary objectives in life right now is to establish some stability, peace and strength in your life once again. We are certain that the One who created you, Who has walked by your side your whole life (whether you knew it or not), and Who loved you enough to take your bullet when He was crucified on Calvary stands ready to help you.

Many people think that Christianity is merely a "religion" and we're sorry to say that it has degenerated to that in many parts of the country and the world. But at its core Christianity is a *relationship* with the living God made possible through His Son, Jesus Christ. Many of us in Cru Military were "religious people" for years before we understood how to enter into an actual relationship with Jesus Christ. Others of us were very far from Him most of our lives.

But from the day that we made the decision to invite Christ into our lives as Lord and Savior, our relationship with God became personal, alive and... not boring! And, most importantly, each of us has seen that as we pursued this relationship with God we were able to experience His specific guidance, comfort, healing and joy. We're not saying that our lives became a moonlight cruise on calm seas. But we *are* saying that with Him now at the helm, He has brought us through every storm we've encountered, *better and stronger* each time.

God is many things, but one of His primary characteristics is that He is our *Healer.* There are many approaches to PTSD therapy that can be beneficial to you. They can equip you with coping strategies, behavior modification and cognitive therapy. But God wants to bring about your *healing.*

In this manual, we have integrated strategies endorsed by most mental health professionals in the military and private practice. But underlying it all are the strategies endorsed by God Himself right out of His message to mankind: the Bible.

If you have not yet begun a relationship with Jesus Christ, then you won't be able to experience the most effective benefits from this manual. If that's the case, we urge you to first take a few minutes to read through Appendix A, starting on page 153 to learn how to enter into a personal relationship with your Healer. It – and He – will make all the difference in the world.

> *For whatever is born of God overcomes the world; and this is the victory that has overcome the world – our faith. Who is the one who overcomes the world, but he who believes that Jesus is the Son of God?*

– 1 John 5:4,5

❁ ❁ ❁ ❁ ❁

INTRODUCTION

Recently I was talking to a group of veterans, most of whom had been in combat. Many were struggling with the symptoms of combat trauma: nightmares, hypervigilance, flashbacks, sleep difficulties, anxiety in crowds, anger, substance abuse, homicidal and suicidal thoughts, etc. All of them felt a strong sense of imprisonment because, in fact, they were all inmates at a maximum security state penitentiary. But that's beside the point. Each of them was looking for answers to the daily despair and frustration stemming from their past trauma – and this would have been the case regardless of which side of the prison bars they lived on.

I shared with them that the medical and mental health communities have a good understanding of what causes Post-traumatic Stress Disorder (PTSD) and they provide a number of helpful suggestions on how a person can cope with the alarming symptoms produced by this condition. I also told them they could go far beyond "coping." They could actually experience *healing*. God has said in the Bible, *"For I, the Lord, am your healer"* (Exodus 15:26). I shared a number of other Scriptures where God offers help to those who have been victimized, traumatized or wounded, and where He spells out how to obtain that help.

During this part of the evening, one of the inmates in the front row got up and walked resolutely out of the room.

When the presentation was over, he returned and talked with me very politely.

"I liked what you had to say about PTSD and all, but I left when you started talking about God and the Bible."

"Oh? Why did that make you leave?" I asked.

"Because I don't believe in God or the Bible. I didn't come to the meeting tonight to hear about religion and I think you should have left that part out."

I thought for a moment, and then asked him, "How could I leave out the most important element in the whole process? There have been quite a few studies which have shown that when trauma sufferers have a connection with God, they get better much quicker. We've seen it with the Resiliency Groups we've started, too. Wouldn't I be doing a disservice to everyone here if I kept that part a secret?"

Now it was his turn to think. "I see your point. But I still don't think you should quote the Bible. Just say something like, 'A wise man once said…' and then quote it."

Well, I didn't want to get into an argument with a convicted murderer who likely had PTSD, so I told him I'd think about it. We parted on friendly terms. And I did think about it – for about five seconds.

By the sixth second I knew for sure I could not compromise on this issue. Several factors will prove to be helpful when introduced to a trauma sufferer's environment. But there is one factor – the God factor – that can shift the healing process into high gear. God created us, "stitched us together" in our mothers' womb, and accompanied us along every step and every mile of our life journeys. He is intimately acquainted with every detail that makes us who we are. He was with us when we went through hell on the battlefield and He knows how to counter every aspect of our affliction. How could I downplay that?

FREEDOM. One doesn't need prison walls to feel trapped by the present effects of past traumatic experiences. But Jesus said that He had truth to share that would set us free – from any kind of bondage. So no, we won't be trying to hide the Christian nature of this manual. We don't mean to offend anyone who is of a different faith-persuasion than we are, but all we can offer is what we know works. We will quote many "wise men" in this book, but when the direct source of the wisdom is God as He is revealed in the Bible, we intend to honestly acknowledge that fact.

NORMAL. Our objective in this manual is to help you set up a healing environment in which God can have optimal access to your body, mind, soul and spirit for the purpose of healing. We have no doubt that your deepest desire is to simply return to how things were before you went into battle – to be "normal" again. But here is the difficult truth: Because of the life-changing trauma you have encountered, it simply will not be possible to get back to *that* normal. God wants to help you integrate your past trauma into your present reality, move you forward, make you stronger, more stable, more mature, better able to deal with stress and trials, and to use you to help others who are struggling. He wants to move you to a "New Normal" which will be even better than the old one.

INTENTIONALITY. Reaching that new normal will only happen if you actively partner with God and be intentional in this pursuit. PTSD commonly makes people passive. They give up. They're tired of fighting. They want to just "wish" the disorder away. This mindset will ensure that nothing changes. But if you can make proactive choices and take the steps outlined in this manual – slowly, steadily, at your own pace, and daily looking to God for help – you will see significant improvement. You'll get out of it what you put into it. If you dabble in it, try it for a few weeks or a few pages, disregard its suggestions or bail out if your world doesn't immediately turn into moonlight and calm seas, your time between the covers of this manual will be in vain. However if you decide *right now* to push through to the end, regardless of the difficulties, roadblocks and fears you might encounter, it will be worth it.

NO SOLO OPS. Frankly, not many people with severe Combat Trauma will be able to work through this manual alone. It will direct your mind and soul to places where you don't really want to go – but where you *must* go if you want to heal. If you are alone, it's easy to cop out. We humans usually seek the path of least resistance. But if you are with some battle buddies, men or women who will encourage you, pull you up when you're down, watch your six, search with you for answers and also look to *you* for support and insight, it's much more likely you will be successful in your pursuit.

Try to find two, three or more buddies who would like to go through the manual together as a "Resiliency Group." Ask your chaplain, pastor or a lay-leader if they would lead it. A free, downloadable leader's guide is available at www.crumilitary.org/ptsd-healing.

THE HEALER. Know this: *This manual will not heal you.* Your "R Group" buddies will not heal you nor will the leader. Studying the Bible, praying, going to church – none of these pursuits will heal you. But each of them is a strong element of an environment in which God can work to provide direct healing of your visible and invisible wounds. *He is the Healer!*

A wise man (whose name was Jesus) once said, *"These things I have spoken to you, so that in Me you may have peace. In the world you have tribulation, but take courage; I have overcome the world"* (John 16:33). Don't miss the two promises there: tribulation in the world and peace with Jesus the Overcomer. You've experienced the first one already. It's time to see that second promise fulfilled.

Chris Adsit

✳   ✳   ✳   ✳   ✳

PROLOGUE

CASUALTIES AND SURVIVORS OF TAKUR GHAR

I had a beautiful wife and two healthy sons. I was an All-American youngster, a quarterback, a West Pointer, and a combat hero. For valor in Afghanistan, I was the President's guest at the 2003 State of the Union Address. As a symbol of respect and appreciation, my men gave me a COLT .45 pistol, a World War II edition with parkerized plastic grips.

"Leaders like you come along once in a lifetime," they said.

That was five years ago.

Today, my pistol is rusted, my medals are misplaced, and my uniforms don't fit. I don't even wear a uniform anymore – I've been discharged from the Army. And yet, I still fight. I fight in a war of my own, battling an unseen enemy. I dream of combat every night, I see the faces of those I lost under my command, my anger rages. My shrapnel wounds have scarred over, but my emotional and spiritual wounds are still open. I led a battle I'd been training for my whole life – and it changed everything.

My story has been much publicized in the media, but for two contrary reasons: a *Dateline* special about my leadership against harrowing odds in battle, and a front-page *Wall Street Journal* feature on being unable to cope with the aftermath of war. How could I show so much personal courage and proven fortitude in combat and now be losing the battle for my own mind?

✻   ✻   ✻

As a boy, I dreamed of becoming a soldier. In my elementary logic, I thought war was a man's God-given burden to bear in life – only fair, since women had to endure the pain of childbirth. As a teen I worked on a ranch in Crawford, Texas – running horses, herding cattle, and mending fences. My family and faith were strong, I excelled in school and in sports, and I had a sweetheart named Julie. My future was promising. In choosing a college, I zeroed in on the biggest challenge I could find: West Point. When I received my appointment to the Academy, my mother saw her greatest fear realized: Her son would become a soldier. The only comfort she took was in knowing I'd be joining a peacetime Army. After four years of education and military training, I graduated, commissioned in the Army, and got married to Julie – all in a span of two weeks. Life was moving fast for us.

As an eager Infantry officer, I immediately deployed to Kosovo, where I gained respect as a leader of soldiers. I dealt with death up close and personal as we tried to prevent ethnic cleansing and intimidation. After several dangerous situations, I came to believe that God was in control of everything, and that included my safety. I believed I would be physically safe as long as God had a plan for me. Some of my soldiers showed indicators of emotional and psychological stress in the environment, but I believed my relationship with God was protecting me from even mental, emotional, and psychological harm. The Academy's Superintendent touted my experiences as a model of responsibility and competence on my mission in Kosovo. Vice President Al Gore even used me as an example in his commencement address to the West Point Class of 2000 of how recent graduates were shining in strategic assignments like Kosovo and Bosnia. God was blessing my time in the Army through successful missions and favor with commanders.

Already experienced at leading soldiers, I was selected to serve in the Army's elite 75th Ranger Regiment as a platoon leader. I felt humbled, nearly uncomfortable to have been selected, but found comfort in Psalm 75:6-7 (AMP): *"For not from the east nor from the west nor from the south come promotion and lifting up. But God is the Judge! He puts down one and lifts up another."* With that encouragement, I felt confident that God was responsible for my selection. I trained hard to lead America's sons, and before long, Julie and I were pregnant with a baby boy of our own. All was well in my life. Then, one month before Caleb was born, al Qaeda terrorists attacked the United States on September 11. That was it. I knew that in my job, in my unit, I was sure to deploy to war – and soon. On New Year's Eve, 2001, I set boots on the ground in Afghanistan, joining a special operations task force with the mission to kill or capture al Qaeda's top leaders.

After three months of fruitless preparation in Afghanistan, my Rangers and I were anxious to make a difference in the War. Then, I answered a call that resulted in my becoming the most decorated officer in the Global War on Terror.

A Navy SEAL was missing – his name was Neil Roberts. Neil was also the father of a baby boy – one whom he'd never see again. Neil had fallen from his helicopter on top of a mountain in Southeastern Afghanistan. He wasn't hurt – he fell maybe 10 feet and into a blanket of powdery snow. But he wasn't safe. Nor was he alone. Neil was quickly surrounded by al Qaeda fighters. As they closed in on him, a small group of US Army Rangers 150 miles away received an order: Get him out.

I was given command of the mission to rescue Neil Roberts. Neither I nor my Rangers knew who Neil was, but we lived by a creed – a creed that expected us to give our lives in order to save another. None of us expected to die, but we had a promise to keep.

On that night, March 3, 2002, our promise to leave no man behind would be tested. I had been leading the platoon of Rangers for 18 months, and earlier that evening I had led them in a Bible study. Contemplating the Psalms, we Rangers were facing our fears, reaching out to God, knowing that we looked death in the face every day. We were in the midst of a spiritual revival. Some said we had become a "Christian Band of Brothers."

Our faith was also tested that night. As we flew to find Neil, we were ambushed and shot down in our helicopter in the snowy mountains, just feet away from the missing SEAL. Four of us were dead within seconds, including men on my left and right. Our rescue mission quickly became a matter of survival, as we were surrounded and outgunned at over 10,000 feet. Despite the overwhelming fire, I felt that God was protecting me through the experience, and I didn't explicitly fear for my life. However, I did think of my wife and son, how they would be affected if I didn't come home. Bleeding, outnumbered and alone, I led my Rangers the next 15 hours in a desperate battle against encroaching al Qaeda fighters – reeling from a staggering number of casualties, calling in multiple danger-close air strikes, and fending off the enemy at close range. Our application of skill and determination ultimately resulted in the enemy's demise and the successful recovery of the missing SEAL, but not without a price. We got Neil Roberts' body out at the cost of six American lives.

> *Greater love has no one than this: to lay down one's life for one's friends.*
> **– Jesus Christ, John 15:13 (NIV)**

For my command and courage under fire in what came to be known as the Battle of Takur Ghar (translated "Tall Mountain"), I was awarded the Silver Star, Bronze Star, and Purple Heart. Our story was featured in newspapers, books and NBC's *DATELINE*. We were celebrated and examined as a model of exemplary combat action within the Army and without. Cadets began to study my actions in the battle at my alma mater and commissioning source, West Point. I became the most recent embodiment of the Academy's saying that, "Much of the history we teach was made by those we taught." The Army used my story as a vignette in its field manual on leadership. But beneath it all, under the armor and the decorations, beyond the praise and the attention, my deep unseen wounds began to fester.

I first began to see a difference in myself when I was attending a 6-month Army educational course. I didn't want to talk with my peers, I felt angry at times and I wanted to underachieve. However, I felt drawn back to combat.

Within a month of the course, I was in Iraq, where the stresses of combat, the nature of the enemy, and my continued isolation from others led to an onset of intense fear. I began to doubt God's ability to protect me. I began having intense nightmares concerning my family's safety. I knew that after three dangerous deployments, I was stacking the odds against my survival. My fear crushed my faith. I slid backwards into a dark season of running from God – devoid of prayer, fellowship and time in the Word. I decided to act on my own. I decided to leave the Army.

I was a 25-year-old father who led rough-and-tumble Rangers first to spiritual revival and then to victory in the most valorous day in Special Operations history, but I quietly resigned from the Army, a casualty in the war for the human spirit.

❊   ❊   ❊

My family and I thought leaving the Army would remove me from the dangers of war. I had survived combat and had come home, safe at last. Now I could focus on being a parent and a husband. But upon leaving the Army, I entered a different kind of fight: the war for my own heart and mind. I went face-to-face with my memories, with the horrors and stresses of combat – and lost.

I rejected my family and my faith. I isolated myself, refusing to talk about the details of combat with those I loved the most. Nightmares of war and death haunted me. I gained weight and struggled with my job. Questions and doubts ravaged my mind. *Why did I survive and my men die? Why did they send me there? Why does God allow such terrible wars to happen? Why can't I feel anything?* Ashamed of the man I had become and unable to reconcile war, I reached a breaking point. I had led Americans in the highest battle ever fought; I toiled close-up with battle-hardened Chechens, Uzbeks, and Arabs; I was highly praised and decorated for leadership under fire – yet I anguished in the aftermath of war. As a prisoner of an unseen enemy, I asked myself one more question: *How should I kill myself?* I realized I was about to lose everything: my marriage, my family, even my life. I had led a daring rescue mission and found myself in dire need of rescuing. I had fought to keep a promise – to never leave a fallen comrade – but who would keep that promise to me?

The answer to that question is clear: God. I laid broken in front of my Savior, Jesus Christ. I began to look for encouragement in the Bible and it was there. God used a small group of heroes – my family, along with a few Christian brothers – to seek out and rescue the man I once was. They pulled me out of the clutches of despair and walked with me along the path of healing. They found a Christian counselor – a retired Army chaplain – to minister to me. They helped me get help at the Veterans Affairs hospital. They listened. Their abiding love, their forbearance and their constant care made a difference for me. But most importantly, my return to faith in God resulted in my recovery from PTSD.

I found a deeper appreciation for God's sovereignty, His willingness to suffer with us, and the power of forgiveness. I believed once again that I had nothing to fear, and I recognized fear was a tool in Satan's disassembling of my faith. I saw examples in the Bible of God's redemptive power – that whatever Satan meant for evil, God has used for good (Genesis 50:20). I saw that war was part of God's plan, that the Lord is a Warrior (Exodus 15:3), that even King David suffered the effects of killing and combat, and that God could restore everything in me, that He would replace the years I had lost (Joel 2:25,26). Just as Ezekiel 37:1-14 explains, God has the power to take my old, dry bones off the valley floor, to make them stand erect, to make them regenerate flesh and sinews, and most importantly, to breathe life into them again.

God has given me opportunities to minister to others through my experiences. These opportunities have reinforced to me that no matter how badly I foul up my life, and no matter how tight a grasp Satan may think he has on me, God can take any circumstance and use it to His glory. I know God's plan for me includes using all my mistakes, my pain, my brokenness to minister to those in similar circumstances. He wastes nothing. He's given me opportunities to minister to veterans in my own church, to my close friends who still lead soldiers in Afghanistan and Iraq, to former service members across the world, and to churches. I pray that this message to you is one of the ways God can use my hard-fought and hard-learned lessons in walking with Him – to your edification and to His glory.

Mine is a story of survival, both on the battlefield and at home, and of eventual revival of faith in my heart. It is a story of healing and restoration, valuable spiritual lessons learned, the gracious forgiveness of my family and service borne from suffering. I still carry scars from battle, both physical and emotional, but the scars are reminders of what God has done and what God is doing in my life. My road to recovery is not over, and He promises to complete the good work in me – so I continue to work out my salvation with fear and trembling in His awesome shadow. In the end, my story displays that the most powerful sacrifices were made by those who entered my pain – and ultimately, by my Savior, who kept his promise to me: to never leave a fallen comrade.

> *For He Himself has said, "I will never desert you, nor will I ever forsake you,"*
> *so that we confidently say, "The Lord is my helper, I will not be afraid. What will*
> *man do to me?"* — **Hebrews 13:5-6**

Nathan Self
Former Captain, U.S. Army
Author of *Two Wars*

STEP 1: WHERE WAS GOD?

UNDERSTANDING THE SPIRITUAL CONTEXT OF YOUR TRAUMA

He was only twenty years old. Let's call him Mike.

Just like Nate Self, whom you just read about, Mike loved America. Mike loved people. He wanted to defend America against the atrocities of terrorism so he joined the Army. His compassionate heart prompted him to become a medic.

His training was brief and intense, and he was quickly declared qualified to be a combat medic. Now he found himself in a traffic circle in Fallujah along with several of his newly-forged closest friends, checking identification papers.

Mike was looking right at his best friend, chatting, when two things happened at the same instant. A puff of pink mist erupted from his friend's upper torso just above his body armor and the single crack of a sniper's rifle pierced the morning heat.

The bullet, entering a relatively inconsequential spot just below his collarbone, traveled a destructive path through his upper torso ricocheting several times off the inside of his Kevlar vest to conduct its fatal business.

Mike sprang into action, ripping off his friend's vest, trying to find the wounds and stop the bleeding. But there was nothing he could do. It took less than a minute. Last words: "... sister... my sister..."

Less than an hour later, Mike's CO was in his face. "You're lying! This couldn't have been a single shot from a sniper! They're not that good! What were you doing?! Why didn't you move faster to save my soldier?!"

"It was at that moment," Mike will tell you, "I knew there was no God."

❀ ❀ ❀ ❀ ❀

? How about you? What are your thoughts at this moment about the existence of God?

When a person experiences a horrible event, when evil triumphs, when the innocent are harmed, when a random, unexpected incident results in destruction and death, it's a natural human tendency to ask, "Where was God? Why didn't He prevent this?" It's natural and *normal*. Nate and Mike both asked, in their own ways.

Since you're reading this book we're going to assume that you have lived through a horror of some sort, probably related to combat. Didn't you wonder where God was when it was happening? Didn't you question His existence or His ability? Maybe you knew He was *somewhere*, doing *something*, but you shook your fist at heaven and cursed Him because He wasn't *there* doing what you needed when you needed it. It's okay. You're not alone. Some of the most godly, faith-filled men and women in history have done the same, more or less. Even the Son of God cried out from the murderous cross...

My God! My God! Why have You forsaken Me?

— **Matthew 27:46**

What do you know about God? Since He's infinite, it's hard to know a *lot* about God, but we're very sure about a few things. For instance, those who have walked with God very closely for a long, long time tell us that He is "supremely-good" and "supremely-powerful." But wait a minute. If God is supremely-good, He certainly wouldn't want bad things to happen. And if He's supremely-powerful, He certainly would be able to do what He wants – and keep bad things from happening.

So… why do so many bad things happen in a world ruled by a God who is so good and so powerful?

Here's why…

"For God so loved the world…" You've heard that line before, right? God loves the world – and God loves *you* – at a depth and with an intensity that exceeds our understanding by infinity. His love isn't the sentimental, syrupy love that we see in the movies or daydream about. It's a love that is wise, selfless and freeing. It has eternity in mind, not just the here-and-now.

"Control freaks" are also characterized by depth and intensity. But they don't care about you – they have their own agenda. God is the opposite of a control freak. He is not going to force you to do anything. He will not impose His will on you. He's not interested in a group of puppets who will do what He says when He pulls the right strings. He *loves* you and what He wants more than anything in all the universe is *your* love, sent back to Him of your own free will. If we are forced, it's not love at all. It's *physics*: simple action and reaction.

So God – from the very beginning – has deeply desired that we'll decide on our own to respond positively to His loving overtures. Love cannot be coerced.

❋　❋　❋　❋　❋

Put an "X" on the line below that describes best how you feel toward God right now.

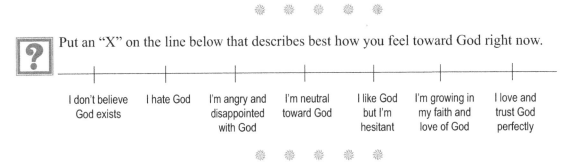

| I don't believe God exists | I hate God | I'm angry and disappointed with God | I'm neutral toward God | I like God but I'm hesitant | I'm growing in my faith and love of God | I love and trust God perfectly |

❋　❋　❋　❋　❋

"We do not want this man to reign over us!" That was Jesus telling a story in Luke 19 about how He was going to be rejected as King.

The story came true a few days later. *"Away with Him! Away with Him! Crucify Him! We have no king but Caesar!"* The people didn't want God – or His Son – as their ruler, so they killed Him. But this was nothing new. People have been rejecting God's rule in their affairs since the time of Adam and Eve. Mankind said "No" to God at the first opportunity and we've been saying "No" ever since. God has been reaching out in love, saying, "May I be your Covering, your Guide, your Guardrails, your Sustainer, your Companion, your Comforter?" And every one of us at one time or another has said, "No, You may not. I would prefer to be the Captain of my own soul. Leave me alone. I'll do as I please."

God didn't change His mind about respecting our free will. He granted our wish. He backed off. But not very far. Always there, always ready to respond, always reaching out – but out of our way. "We don't need Him – we can handle things just fine by ourselves."

How are we doing? Are we humans indeed handling things just fine, doing as we please? Consider just the last half of the 20th century. After six million Jews and six million Christians and gypsies were exterminated by the Nazis during World War II, the world vowed "We will *never* let that happen again." And yet between 1958 and 1961, Mao Zedong orchestrated the starvation deaths of at least twenty million Chinese as the world watched from the sidelines. In 1972, intake ducts in the dams of the Nile were plugged with the bodies of more than 300,000 Ugandans whom Idi Amin murdered with impunity. Between 1975 and 1978, Pol Pot executed two million of his own Cambodian people, and the rest of humanity remained disinterested. Did anyone try to stop Saddam Hussein from gassing thousands of Kurdish families in 1984? During three months of 1994 the world stood idle while the Hutu people hacked 800,000 Tutsis to death in Rwanda. Today, armed militia in Sudan, Congo and Somalia rape and murder tens of thousands and have turned more than two million people into refugees. We could go on. Suffice it to say that more innocent men, women and children have been murdered through genocide in the 20th century than have been killed in all previous wars.

But this is not a recent development. According to historian Will Durant, there have only been 268 of the past 3,421 years when a major war wasn't raging somewhere on earth.[1] Man is at the helm and things are *not* getting better.

"It was at that moment I knew there was no God."

We can understand Mike's deep frustration and despair. He was fed up with the horror and injustice of it all, and by gosh, the buck has to stop somewhere! We can all identify with Mike at some level. But isn't it ironic? We tell God to get lost and then blame *Him* for our unimaginable inhumanity toward each other. We have done this to ourselves. While we were supposedly captaining our souls and the souls of others with care and compassion – but without God – many used their power to enslave, torment and murder. They did as they pleased.

As one Jewish prisoner of Auschwitz remarked to his friend, "Where is God?" The other, pondering their sadistic guards and the unresponsive world, replied, "Where is man?"[2]

✽   ✽   ✽   ✽   ✽

Write down one incident that occurred while you were at war that demonstrates man's inhumanity toward their fellow man (you might think of *many*, but just choose one).

_____

_____

_____

✽   ✽   ✽   ✽   ✽

You've been downrange. You have seen things that no person should ever have to see. You've seen your friends get maimed or die. You've seen dead children. People have tried to kill you. You've fought and fought and fought way past the time you were ready to drop from exhaustion. You may have had to kill or be killed. You may have killed without justification.

And now, even though you've left the theater of war, you can't shake it. The anxiety, the anger, the hypervigilance, the dreams, the hair-trigger rage, the depression – they're not getting better. Maybe they're getting worse.

Here's the most important thing you need to know about what you are currently experiencing:

YOUR CONDITION IS DUE TO THE SINFUL ACTIONS OF EVIL MEN – NOT GOD.

"Where *was* God, then? Where was He when I got shot? Where was He when that IED flipped our Humvee killing my best friend? Did He go AWOL? Is He a deserter?" It might have felt like that, but He was right there with you. Backed off, but ready to act and stepping in at just the right moment. Weeping over your dead friends just as He wept at the tomb of His friend, Lazarus (John 11:30-36). Biding His time until the day He will judge and eliminate all evil and those who practice it. But in the meantime He is walking beside you and anguishing over the pain you are experiencing.

And *protecting* you. Have you ever considered that? You are well aware of the bullets and shrapnel – both literal and otherwise – that got through to wound you. Do you know about all the ones He deflected to keep you alive? One thing's for sure: if you belong to Him, there were many. But you won't find out about them until heaven. He was there though, right with you, perfectly harmonizing your will, His will, your attacker's will and the circumstances to keep you alive, equip you better for eternity and bring glory to Himself – God's supernatural juggling act.

But why didn't He at least keep your buddy alive? We'll never know this side of heaven. There are too many variables for us to try to figure it out. It's like a camel spider trying to understand a computer. It – and we – simply don't have the equipment to figure those things out.

We keep trying anyway, however. That's our nature. The Bible says that God put eternity in our hearts (Ecclesiastes 3:11). Because of this, we *know* there's something beyond this crazy life. We *long* for it. It makes us conclude that the present evil and suffering are *not right;* yet, we're utterly immersed in it. And "no answers" frustrates the heck out of us.

Here's a question that will help lead you to at least *some* answers:

ARE YOU SURE YOU KNOW WHO YOUR ENEMY IS?

Any War College worth its salt will tell you that a primary factor in securing victory in combat is this: Knowing Your Enemy. If you're a combat veteran, you know that it was sometimes difficult to figure out who your enemy was when you were over there, wasn't it? They looked just like the friendlies. They blended right in. But you know how deadly it was when you or your buddies *didn't* correctly identify your enemies.

Those enemies wanted to take your physical life, but you have other enemies who have more eternal objectives. Your thoughts, your spiritual and emotional health, your priorities, your plans, your allegiances, your productivity, your family, your heritage and your body are the disputed territories. Our *real* enemies aren't even human.

> *For our struggle is not against flesh and blood, but against the rulers, against the powers, against the world forces of this darkness, against the spiritual forces of wickedness in the heavenly places.*
>
> **– Ephesians 6:12**

 Who, or what, do you think the preceding verse is talking about?

There is a real being known as Satan who has existed for thousands of years. He was once the Number One angel in God's kingdom, beautiful, intelligent and as powerful as they come. Back then his name was Lucifer – "Star of the Morning." Just like us humans, he had a free will. But he also had an audacious, prideful ambition: to take God's place. So before man had even been created, the Bible reports that he led a rebellion of one-third of the angels, attempting a cosmic coup – which he lost. As a result, he and all his cohorts were cast out of the Kingdom of Heaven onto the earth, and turned from angels into demons. (You can read about this in Ezekiel 28:12-19 and Isaiah 14:12-17.)

Satan *still* thinks he can overthrow God, and he and his network of spiritual combatants are continuing his assault even today. He hates God with a passion that surpasses anything a human has ever imagined. He hates God's creation, and most of all, he hates humans – because of how much God loves them. Satan and his demons gained permission to enter and deeply influence the minds of people like Hitler, Stalin, Lenin, Pol Pot and others, who in turn unleash devilish oppression and wars on humanity. He seeks defectors from God's army that he can induct into his own. Human armies have their objectives, but many of them are subordinate to Satan's goals. He is just using them.

He has objectives involving presidents, dictators and nations. But he also has objectives for each and every one of us. If he can't use you, he'll seek to eliminate you. *"Be of sober spirit, be on the alert. Your adversary, the devil, prowls around like a roaring lion, seeking someone to devour"* (1 Peter 5:8). Don't miss this: he doesn't want to trip you up, make you feel bad, bum you out or hurt your feelings. He wants to *devour* you, and he won't quit trying until he's accomplished this ultimate objective.

He almost succeeded with Nate Self, bringing him to the point of asking, "How should I kill myself?"

He will use any weakness we have, any experience we've gone through, any vulnerability he can discover to fulfill his mission for us. You can be positive that he will use your traumatic combat experience to find the open spots in your armor. He's got his eye on that place just above your vest, under your collarbone.

He is our enemy. Not God.

It's not the war that will do you in. It's what your spiritual adversary will do with what you experienced in combat that could. But there are counter-measures. You'll learn much more about this in Step 8: *How Do I Fight? – Rebuilding Your Defenses.*

ARE YOU SURE YOU KNOW WHO YOUR ALLY IS?

Have you ever heard the term "the fog of war"? Heard it – you've probably *lived* it. In the midst of combat when all hell's breaking loose, you know it's sometimes difficult to discern who's friend, who's foe, which way is safety and which way is death. In the Bible, Israel's greatest leader – King David – was a world-class warrior. He had personally led, fought in, survived and won dozens of campaigns during his forty years as king. But one thing he was never fogged about was who his #1 ally was. He *always* knew where to turn for aid.

Each of the Scripture passages below highlights a time when David was facing unbeatable foes, desperate situations and deadly consequences. But in each case, his foundational mindset and supreme confidence was that Almighty God, the Commander of the Hosts of Heaven, would rescue him, strengthen him and give him victory over his enemies.

Here he is as a mere teenager, facing 9'8" Goliath of Gath, champion of the Philistines, while all the other soldiers of Israel stood back and wet their armor…

> *You come to me with a sword, a spear, and a javelin, but I come to you in the name of the Lord of hosts, the God of the armies of Israel, whom you have taunted. This day the Lord will deliver you up into my hands, and I will strike you down and remove your head from you. And I will give the dead bodies of the army of the Philistines this day to the birds of the sky and the wild beasts of the earth, that all the earth may know that there is a God in Israel, and that all this assembly may know that the Lord does not deliver by sword or by spear; for the battle is the Lord's and He will give you into our hands.*
>
> **– 1 Samuel 17:45-47**

 What character qualities were manifested in David because of his confidence in God?

Now he's leading the armies of Israel in battle. He is the "theocratic warrior," an instrument of war in the hand of God. Not many can claim that position, but David could. God was not only his ally, but his battle-buddy *and* his commander-in-chief…

Arise, O Lord, in Your anger; lift up Yourself against the rage of my adversaries, and arouse Yourself for me; You have appointed judgment... O let the evil of the wicked come to an end, but establish the righteous; for the righteous God tries the hearts and minds. My shield is with God, who saves the upright in heart. God is a righteous judge, and a God who has indignation every day.

– Psalm 7:6,9-11

Check the statement that you think is correct:_

❑ David was a blood-thirsty killer with an imperialist agenda and a lust for power.

❑ David saw himself as a servant of God – and he looked to Him to set the agenda, issue the orders and produce the outcome of the battle.

But don't get the idea that David's life was all smooth sailing and victory parades. Many times, before the dawn of God's deliverance, he went through some very dark nights...

But You, O God, the Lord, deal kindly with me for Your name's sake; because Your lovingkindness is good, deliver me; for I am afflicted and needy, and my heart is wounded within me. I am passing like a shadow when it lengthens; I am shaken off like the locust... Help me, O Lord my God; save me according to Your lovingkindness. And let them know that this is Your hand; You, Lord, have done it.

– Psalm 109:21-27

How would you describe David's frame of mind as he wrote this?

_____

What was his attitude toward God?

_____

❄ ❄ ❄ ❄ ❄

Have you ever watched a bunch of chicks with their mother hen? When danger comes, they instantly scurry toward their mother, who lifts her wings and gathers her babies underneath for protection. Could you imagine a wolf bounding into the chicken yard and one of the chicks running *away* from the hen and *toward* the wolf? That would be one very stupid – or confused – chick. And one very happy wolf.

And yet so many humans, when problems bound into their lives, decide to run *away* from the Supreme Problem Solver of the universe, rather than toward Him.

Why do you think that is?

_____

_____

In which direction are you running right now – toward God or away from Him? Why?

_____

_____

WHAT'S GOD GOT TO DO WITH ANYTHING?
HE CAN'T KNOW WHAT I'M EXPERIENCING. HE'S IMMUNE!

Oh, really? Here's something to chew on. Applied to any other so-called "god" on the planet, that statement could be true. Fake gods are always depicted as transcendent, all-powerful, above the wretched company of mere mortals, not limited by the things that limit us, pain-free, trauma-free, sorrow-free. Except for the God of the Bible.

He is the only god who has suffered.

The theology of the Trinity is difficult for *anybody* to have a firm grasp on, but Jesus Christ was the physical manifestation of God. God the Father, God the Son and God the Holy Spirit – one in essence but three in identity and function. When Jesus showed up in Bethlehem, it was God Himself packed into that tiny little body lying in that dirty animal feeding trough. The baby grew into a boy and then into a man. Along the way, He suffered many things – everything that the rest of us humans do – and He learned from them. The only thing He didn't experience was guilt, because He never sinned.

Then He was rejected, scorned, falsely convicted, whipped, beaten beyond recognition, mocked, tortured and crucified. God was willing to endure this in order to pay the penalty that He Himself had set to atone for our sinful lives.

This is how our loving God defeats evil. He took it into Himself, experienced it at its worst, and then triumphed over it in the resurrection. He has earned the right to say, "I know *exactly* what you're going through."

> No one can ever go so low that God in Jesus has not gone lower. What other faith has at its heart a writhing body, torn flesh, shameful desertion and disgrace, anguished desolation, and a darkness that can be felt? God liberates not by removing suffering from us, but by sharing it with us. Jesus is 'God-who-suffers-with-us.'[3]
>
> – **Os Guinness**, philosopher, survivor of the Henan famine in China, 1943

> Jesus was not crucified in a cathedral between two candles, but on a cross between two thieves; on the town garbage heap; at a crossroad so cosmopolitan they had to write his title in Hebrew and in Greek and in Latin, at the kind of place where cynics talk smut, and soldiers gamble. Because that is where He died. And that is what He died about.[4]
>
> – **George Macleod of Iona**, clergyman and Scottish soldier in WWI

> I found out that God is not in a nice, neat package with a bow on it like I had been taught in my Sunday school classes growing up. In Iraq, I experienced reality. I experienced God in that reality. And He had His sleeves rolled up, He was in the dirt with me. He was getting sandblasted with me. He was right there with me.
>
> – **Andrea Westfall**, former sergeant and flight medic with the Oregon National Guard

❋ ❋ ❋ ❋ ❋

SUFFERING HAPPENS. CAN ANY GOOD COME OUT OF IT?

If you've ever been an athlete, if you've ever had a dream, if you've ever pursued excellence in *anything*, then you know that not only *can* suffering produce good results, it's practically a requirement.

The same is true in the Kingdom of God. We're not saying that God has *caused* the trauma that you have encountered. It's been devastating, costly and very difficult – but it's not a total loss. In fact, over time God will *use* it to accomplish extraordinarily good things in your life – if you will let Him.

 What truth or principle about God and our adversity can you discover from each of the following passages? Write your observations down after each Scripture.

> *And we know that God causes all things to work together for good to those who love God, to those who are called according to His purpose.*
>
> – **Romans 8:28**

Blessed be the God and Father of our Lord Jesus Christ, the Father of mercies and God of all comfort, who comforts us in all our affliction so that we will be able to comfort those who are in any affliction with the comfort with which we ourselves are comforted by God.

–2 Corinthians 1:3,4

For God, who said, "Let light shine out of darkness," made His light shine in our hearts to give us the light of the knowledge of the glory of God in the face of Christ. But we have this treasure in jars of clay to show that this all-surpassing power is from God and not from us.

–2 Corinthians 4:6,7 (NIV)

[Joseph, great-grandson of Abraham, had two sons while he lived in exile in Egypt – where he eventually became the second most powerful man in the world.] *Joseph named the firstborn Manasseh, "For," he said, "God has made me forget all my trouble and all my father's household." He named the second Ephraim, "For," he said, "God has made me fruitful in the land of my affliction."*

–Genesis 41:51,52

❋ ❋ ❋ ❋ ❋

? Be honest. Right now, today, do you think knowing and experiencing God at a much deeper level might eventually make your current level of anxiety and pain worth it?

❋ ❋ ❋ ❋ ❋

CONCLUSION

Does cold exist? Yes and no. We've all been cold and if you've pulled guard duty during a Korean winter, you *really* know cold! But cold is merely the absence of heat. We can measure heat with a thermometer, but cold is defined only by how hot it isn't.

Does darkness exist? Again, yes and no. We all *think* we've seen darkness, but actually we've not seen it at all. Darkness is only the absence of light. No one can measure darkness, but light is easily measured by various instruments.

Does evil exist? We've all seen evil. You are marked by its scars. But just as cold is the absence of heat and darkness is the absence of light, evil exists only in the absence of God. As the Christian theologian C. S. Lewis once said, there are only two places in the universe where God does not exist: in some human governments and in some human hearts. He was speaking metaphorically, but the point is that wherever God is not vitally present, evil pours in propelled by dark forces of demons and men.

Just as heat overcomes cold and light dispels darkness, the presence of God drives out evil. The trauma you experienced was because of evil. Its continuing effect is because of evil. Only as you allow the light and heat of God to enter those wounded areas will you be able to experience His healing and His victory.

He loves you with an infinite love. He has loved you since before you were born; since the day He created the earth. He loved you when you were in combat. He knows everything about you. He knew ahead of time what you were going to experience and knows how to heal you. He may not do it as fast as you'd like or in the manner that you'd prefer, but He'll do it perfectly – if you will let Him.

Nate Self and his Ranger platoon came back for Neil Roberts stranded on top of Takur Ghar. Later, God came back for Nate. Now He's come back for you.

※　※　※　※　※

PRAYER SEED

Father, you know how much I hurt. You know the depth of my anxiety, fear, anger and confusion. You know how much I just want to be normal again! Please hear my prayer, asking for Your help. Forgive me for not giving You full access to my life up to this point. I know now that I can't fix this. But You made me. You know what to do. So I ask You to lead me out of my darkness into Your light. Help me to cooperate with You in this process. Give me patience and the ability to see Your hand at work in my life. Increase my faith. Thank You that You would not leave me behind. Amen.

※　※　※

---

[1] Quote from Will Durant found at www.brainyquotes.com.
[2] Quote from Os Guiness in *Unspeakable,* p. 46.
[3] Quote from Os Guinness in *Unspeakable,* pp. 147, 148.
[4] Quote from George Macleod in *Unspeakable,* p. 148.

STEP 2: WHAT HAPPENED TO ME?

UNDERSTANDING THE PHYSICAL/PSYCHOLOGICAL CONTEXT OF YOUR TRAUMA

YOUR TRAUMA'S ROOT OF HONOR

Edmund Burke wrote, "The only thing necessary for evil to triumph is for good men to do nothing." *You* – as opposed to so many on our planet today – *did something.* You joined the military and decided to fight evil directly – eyeball-to-eyeball. Like young David in the Bible *running* to engage Goliath in a battle to the death, you ran to where the evil was breaking out, also ready to fight to the death.

Maybe you joined prior to 9/11 in a relatively peaceful time – for the college money? – and didn't really anticipate that you were going to see combat. Or maybe it was specifically *because* of that twenty-first century "day of infamy" that you made the decision to stand in the gap for our country. Maybe you were drafted during the Vietnam War era. Whatever the case, when you were ordered to get on that plane for Kuwait, Iraq, Afghanistan, Somalia, Bosnia, Croatia, Vietnam, South Korea, Normandy or wherever Uncle Sam decided to send you, *you went.* You went through hell over there so that we could continue to live in heaven over here. Your efforts have kept evil from triumphing.

And your country – whether they're very good at expressing it or not – is very grateful for the sacrifices you have made. "Thank you" – it seems like such a lightweight expression for all you've done.

Now the parades are over (if you *had* any parades). Your duty is safely stateside or your uniform is hung up in the closet. The back-slapping is becoming less and less frequent. But you still have those… sacrifices. At this point, you probably hold two primary thoughts concerning the unanticipated symptoms those sacrifices have brought you:

> PTSD is a disorder of warriors, not men and women who were weak or cowardly but … who followed orders and who at a young age put their feelings aside and performed unimaginable tasks … PTSD is a disorder of a good warrior."
>
> – Anonymous disabled Marine[1]

1. I don't know how or why I got them.
2. I want them gone.

This Step will try to address that first thought. The rest of the book will help you with the second one.

❀ ❀ ❀ ❀ ❀

? Take a moment and consider … A sacrifice generally means "something was given up." Because of your experiences in combat, what are some of the things you have given up (or that were taken from you)?

_____

_____

_____

_____

❀ ❀ ❀ ❀ ❀

COMBAT TRAUMA AND PTSD

"Combat Trauma" (officially called "Deployment-Related Stress" by the Army) describes a spectrum of distressing reactions a troop may have to the trauma of combat. These reactions could include anything from the normal, relatively mild tensions associated with the transition from deployment back to home and family life (Reintegration Issues), all the way up to severe conditions known as Acute Stress Disorder (ASD) and Posttraumatic Stress Disorder (PTSD). ASD and PTSD occur in those who have been exposed to a traumatic combat-related event (or series of events) which involved actual or threatened death or serious injury and caused an emotional reaction involving intense fear, panic, helplessness or horror. The symptoms for both disorders are: (1) a persistent re-experiencing of the event(s) through nightmares, intrusive thoughts or dissociative episodes, (2) obsessive avoidance of any stimuli associated with the event(s), and (3) feeling "keyed-up" (aroused, angry, sleepless, jumpy) at all times.[2] The difference between these two disorders is how long the symptoms persist: one month for ASD, no time limit for PTSD.

By the way, you didn't have to experience direct combat to develop Combat Trauma symptoms. You may have been a logistics officer, a truck driver, a mail deliverer, never experienced a firefight, and still came back traumatized – which could be very puzzling to you. In most modern wars, *there is no safe place!* You were conscious of the fact that any moment could be your last. Mortar rounds frequently fell inside the Green Zone in Baghdad. Improvised Explosive Devices (IEDs) killed many truck drivers and mailmen. Seemingly friendly civilians or their vehicles could be wired to explode at an opportune time. You knew this, and for months you were constantly on edge and on high alert, 24/7. This accumulation of stress and anxiety can result in Combat Trauma.

The following graphic presents this **spectrum of Combat Trauma**.[3]

MILD					SEVERE
Pre-Deployment, Deployment and Reintegration Issues	Combat/Operational Stress Reactions	Adjustment Disorders	Acute Stress Disorder	Posttraumatic Stress Disorder	

Combat Trauma sufferers toward the left end of the spectrum will usually exhibit fewer symptoms and typically improve without significant treatment. Those at the right end of the spectrum exhibit profound symptoms which persist for at least a month, maybe years, and – if untreated – a lifetime. These symptoms may not begin to surface for months or years after the traumatic event(s).

❋ ❋ ❋ ❋ ❋

 Put an "X" on the line above which you feel represents where you are right now on the spectrum. You don't have to know the definitions of each designation on the line – just estimate where you fit on the "mild" to "severe" continuum.

❋ ❋ ❋ ❋ ❋

SECONDARY TRAUMA

When a serviceman comes home from war suffering from PTSD, how he or she interacts with the family is very different from before. Anger, over-reacting, paranoia, fits of rage, disinterest in sex, lethargy, substance abuse – these and other symptoms may become the new context of family life. The symptoms of the PTSD sufferer can end up traumatizing the spouse. This is called "Secondary Trauma." The spouse can begin to manifest the same PTSD symptoms as the combat veteran (or sometimes different ones) and will need the same care. Secondary Trauma can show up in their children as well.

Posttraumatic Stress Disorder has been called "the signature injury" of Operation Enduring Freedom (Afghanistan) and Operation Iraqi Freedom. This is the ailment that most people have heard about and is probably the one that you are most worried about. Though people who are more to the left on the line above *will* be helped by what is shared in this manual, our intention is to target PTSD. It's a good principle: if you have to fight a gang, go for the biggest, baddest dude first. That's what PTSD is and, just like the gang bully, if we fight it correctly, it will go *down!*

PTSD ISN'T NEW

PTSD has been called by many terms over the centuries, which makes it clear that it's a disorder not unique to modern wars, but common to all wars. During the latter half of the 1600s, the Swiss observed a consistent set of symptoms in some of their solders and called it "nostalgia." German doctors of the same period used the term *Heimweh* and the French called it *maladie du pays*. Both terms are roughly translated as "homesickness." The Spanish called it *estar roto,* "to be broken." During America's Civil War it was called "soldier's heart." They called it "shell shocked" in World War I, "combat fatigue" in WWII, and "war neurosis" during the Korean war. In the 1970s they coined the phrase "Vietnam Veterans Syndrome."

> Whenever Robert Reiter is asked when he left Viet Nam, he answers, 'Last night. It will be that way till my soul leaves this old body.' When the survivor cannot leave war's expectations, values, and losses behind, it becomes the eternal present. This frozen war consciousness is the condition we call post-traumatic stress disorder.
> – Dr. Edward Tick[4]

Each of these terms shows facets of the disorder. The soldier's heart *does* get profoundly altered by war. Nostalgia and homesickness describe the desperate longing of a PTSD sufferer to leave the chaos of the battle and return to the safety of home. Emotionally something is indeed broken inside these wounded warriors, resulting in various psychological neuroses – a familiar, persistent syndrome of symptoms. No doubt, you can identify with many of these facets.

It wasn't until 1980 that the American Psychiatric Association formally identified, named and defined Posttraumatic Stress Disorder, and it's been in the official diagnostic manuals of the medical profession since that time. More and more research is constantly being done on this mystifying disorder. But here is the first thing that you need to know – which *all* the experts agree upon:

Posttraumatic Stress Disorder is a natural reaction to an unnatural event.

Natural. It may be difficult for you to imagine that your anxiety-riddled behavior – which is so different from how you were before – could be "natural," but that's exactly the case. Your symptoms are what we would *expect* from someone who experienced what you did. They are common to hundreds of thousands – perhaps millions – of other courageous men and women who have fought in wars down through the centuries. For a person who saw, smelled, felt, heard and tasted the things you did, it's natural.

And you are far from an isolated case. It is estimated there are over 400,000 Vietnam war veterans who suffer from PTSD – undiagnosed and untreated. Some put the number as high as one million. In a recent report by the Veterans Health Administration 38 percent of OIF/OEF veterans (100,580 troops) who have sought care were diagnosed with PTSD or other mental heath issues.[5] This doesn't include the ones who *haven't* sought care (it is estimated that only 23 percent seek treatment [6]). You are most definitely *not* alone.

If this information is new to you, let us spell it out:

- PTSD is not rare or an aberration – it's a natural response to an unnatural stressor.
- Hundreds of thousands of men and women are in the same boat you are.
- It is *normal* to be affected by combat.
- It is *normal* to be affected by pain, atrocity, horror and gore.
- Facing death changes a person.
- It would be *abnormal* if you *weren't* affected.
- It shows that you are human and that what happened downrange matters to you.

Here is the next thing that you *must* know:

You are not weak, weird or cowardly. You have been wounded.

What can cause a wound? We normally think of physical implements, like a knife or a bullet. But one can receive "soul wounds" that are as bad as or worse than physical wounds, affecting you deeper and lasting longer than anything a gun could produce. And we're not talking sentimental psychobabble here – this is as real as it gets. You know. You're living it.

The word "trauma" is from a Greek word which means "a wounding." When applied to the physical realm, it refers to an event in which some external force has damaged a part of your body. The normal defense mechanisms (such as the skin, muscle, skull, internal bone framing, etc.) were unable to prevent the injury. For a while, you won't be able to function the way you used to because of the wounding. The punch that knocked the wind out of you will keep you doubled over for a few moments. The cast on your leg will prevent you from walking normally.

In a similar fashion, we can receive psychological wounds that incapacitate us. Events can get past our normal defenses and severely disrupt our emotions, our souls and spirits, our faith, our self-identity, our confidence, our trust in other humans, our sense of security and even our will to live. After this, we won't be able to cope, think, react, plan and function in the ways we used to – at least not for a while.

If you pulled a buddy out of a Humvee that had just been hit by an RPG and saw that his leg had been broken and his foot pointed the wrong way, would you expect him to get up and run to safety? Not likely. Even if you knew he had been a track star in high school. In the same way, neither you nor anyone else should expect that you can simply deny your *very real* wounds and take off running at full speed. You need time and treatment to bring about the healing. For you to try to get on that track and run too early – whether we're talking about physically or spiritually – will only deepen your wound and prolong your convalescence.

❄   ❄   ❄   ❄   ❄

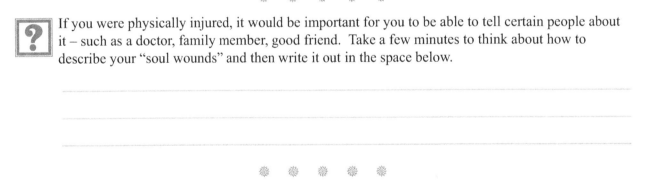
If you were physically injured, it would be important for you to be able to tell certain people about it – such as a doctor, family member, good friend. Take a few minutes to think about how to describe your "soul wounds" and then write it out in the space below.

❄   ❄   ❄   ❄   ❄

WHAT CAUSES PTSD?

Not just combat. A psychological shock or any kind of horrific event that makes a person think they could be severely injured or killed *can* trigger PTSD. We emphasize *can* because it doesn't mean it necessarily will. One study determined that approximately 75 percent of Americans have had a traumatic experience significant enough to cause PTSD, but only about 10 to 25 percent of those actually develop the disorder.[7] Experts do not fully agree as to why some do and some don't, but it seems that the *intensity* of the experience or multiple experiences has a lot to do with it. In addition, if a person has been traumatized at a younger age (physical or sexual abuse, abandonment, kidnapping, assault, etc.) it increases their likelihood of developing PTSD as an adult.

Experiences that can produce PTSD are combat, sexual and physical assault, being held hostage, terrorism, torture, natural and man-made disasters, accidents, receiving a diagnosis of a life-threatening illness, violating one's conscience by engaging in mutilation or other violations of the Law of Armed Conflict or the killing of innocents (accidentally or on purpose) in life-threatening situations. Even witnessing threatening, mutilating or deadly events or hearing about them happening to a family member or other close associate can cause PTSD. It can be especially severe or long-lasting when the trauma comes from an intentional human act, rather than from an accident or a natural disaster.

❋　❋　❋　❋　❋

Did you ever experience any of the events listed in the previous paragraph besides combat?

_____

_____

❋　❋　❋　❋　❋

THE PHYSIOLOGY, PSYCHOLOGY AND THEOLOGY OF PTSD

One of God's top design priorities when He created us was that we be equipped to defend ourselves and survive in a wide variety of dangerous situations. To this end, He equipped us with an amazing set of response mechanism.

> I will praise You, for I am fearfully and wonderfully made; marvelous are Your works, and that my soul knows very well.
> – Psalm 139:14 (NKJV)

Our brains are divided into two halves. The left side is our analytical side. It scrutinizes incoming information logically, thinks rationally, explicitly, in concrete terms. It is on this side that we store practical information, our ability to speak, read, write, spell and do math. This side remembers names and craves precision.

If our left side is more like a "computer," our right side is more like a "photo album." This side remembers faces and craves rapport and relationship. It's our emotional side. It is intuitive, spontaneous, experience-oriented, artistic, creative. It stores emotions. We dream on this side of our brain. And very importantly, this is the "alarm" side of our brain.

Beneath these two halves is our "lower brain" or brain stem. This part of our brain controls all automatic life functions, such as our breathing, digestion and heartbeat. The lower brain always trumps the two halves of our higher brain. Doesn't matter how logical it may seem or how passionately you might want to do it, you can't make your heart stop beating just by thinking about it. You can hold your breath for a little while, but before long your lower brain once again asserts its dominance.

The Science of Trauma Reactions. When we encounter something that we feel threatens our life, a cascade of hormonal reactions is triggered. A nerve shoots a message to our adrenal glands to dump adrenaline and noradrenaline into our bloodstream, causing our heart to beat faster, our lungs to pump harder and getting the rest of the body ready to either fight, fly or freeze. Our pupils dilate, giving us tunnel vision so we can focus on the threat and not be distracted by peripheral action. Thousands of small muscles in our arms and legs constrict, sending blood away from our skin and into our muscles for quick movement – and so that if our extremities are wounded, we won't bleed as badly. Our blood sugar and free fatty acids instantly ramp up, giving us more energy. At the same time, up to 70 percent of our brain-bound oxygen is quickly shunted into our muscles so we can run, kick or punch like we never had before. Additional hormones give us uncommon strength and quickness. Our perception of time is altered – a ten-minute firefight seems like it only took a minute.

But something happens deep inside our brains, too. Our right-brain alarm goes off and drowns out the logical analysis of our left brain. It screams, "Less thinking, more action!!" It also starts taking pictures like mad – the noradrenalin heightens the emotional aspects of the situation making it more vivid and notable. Very strong and clear memories are being recorded, probably so that we will remember this event and avoid it in the future.[8]

At this point, our lower brain takes over. It's live-or-die time. With this organ in control, nothing else matters. It automatically directs the rest of the body in very complex but focused ways to do whatever it takes to survive. Patience Mason, who is married to a Vietnam War veteran and has written extensively on PTSD, describes this behavior eloquently and realistically…

> Whatever it takes! This is not a polite, well-behaved part of us. It [urinates] and [defecates] in its fear. It scratches and bites and goes berserk, beating people to death with the rifle-butt when the bullets are gone. It kicks and gouges. It runs out on its friends, trampling whoever gets in its way. It cowers, unable to get up or to fight, unable to protect those it loves. It may freeze or follow orders that are against all the survivor personally believes in. Survivors may feel shock or shame over what this part of them did.[9]

Research has shown that your body will exhibit these built-in survival techniques no matter what your race or gender is, whether you come from a privileged background or the ghetto, whether you are mentally slow or highly intelligent, whether you come from a happy family or a broken one, whether you're a cheerful person or a total pessimist. But it's important to know two things:

1. God gave you this reactive pathway so that you would be able to do whatever was necessary to survive. It kept you alive. God knows that when our lives are threatened this behavior needs to come out or we could die. At that point, all the rationality, dignity, intelligence and decorum in the world is absolutely useless.

2. No matter how hard you might have tried, you couldn't have stopped this reaction. Can you stop your heartbeat? No. Neither are we able to control ourselves when our brains have clicked into this mode.

❅ ❅ ❅ ❅ ❅

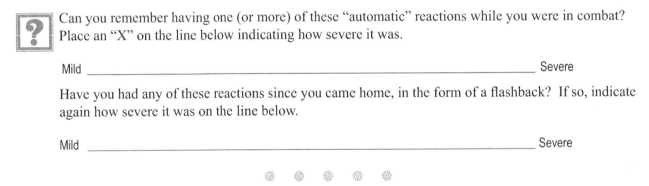

Can you remember having one (or more) of these "automatic" reactions while you were in combat? Place an "X" on the line below indicating how severe it was.

Mild _____ Severe

Have you had any of these reactions since you came home, in the form of a flashback? If so, indicate again how severe it was on the line below.

Mild _____ Severe

❅ ❅ ❅ ❅ ❅

PTSD PERSISTENCE

"Ok," you say, "The crisis is over now. I survived. What happened wasn't pretty, but the score ended up Me – 1, The Grave – 0. So why can't I move on? Why do I keep reliving what happened?"

Often, a trauma survivor can go through a short period of decompression and processing and return pretty close to "normal." But if the traumatizing event was exceptionally violent and life-threatening or if there were multiple episodes, the brain stays "stuck" in this crisis-alert mode.

Think of it in terms of walking across a frozen lake. As you walk, you feel confident and enjoy sliding on the ice. You might even do a few aerial leaps and spins like the skaters on TV, just for fun. Suddenly you hear a loud pop and you notice the ice is cracking under your feet. You instantly freeze. Your arms reflexively shoot out from your sides for balance and your feet spread wide to distribute your weight. Your muscles are now tight, your shoulders bunched up, your eyes are the size of softballs and you begin to take very small, careful steps back the way you came. After about twenty yards, you're beyond where the cracks were. Do you think you'd go bounding merrily the rest of the way to shore? You'd probably remain on high alert the rest of the way, because you are now aware that the ice *could* give way beneath you at any time.

After a traumatic event, your brain knows that it just had an incredibly close call, and it is determined to be ready to react if the danger comes by again. Good idea – except if it gets stuck in that mode, which is essentially what PTSD is. It's like the ice-walker tiptoeing two miles of sidewalk to get home.

The shock physically alters parts of your brain. Your reactive pathways modify, your brain chemistry changes and becomes hypersensitive, overreacting to normal stimuli. Your hippocampus – the part of your brain that interprets and calms your emotional responses – shrinks and works less effectively. Your left and right brain hemispheres have trouble communicating and balancing each other – so you're either all emotion and unordered, or you are emotionless, cold, withdrawn and not much fun to be around. Sometimes each of them inside of five minutes.

And whenever your brain senses that it's getting near the "scene of the crime" via some sensory trigger (a smell, a sound, a sight, a memory), it quickly opens up the photo album it created during the earlier traumatic event and puts on an intense slide and video show to re-instruct you that you don't want to go there again! "Are you *nuts!??* We almost *bought* it when we were there last time!! Get away!!" The technical term for this is "re-experiencing."

The opening of the photo album can also have another function. It's a flare being sent up by the trauma survivor's inner self alerting the outside world that he's been through more than he can handle and he needs help dealing with it. We humans aren't meant to suffer our traumas alone and not bother anybody else about them. We are an *interdependent* species, ordained so by our Creator. We need each other. And if our "outer self" won't take action, our "inner self" will keep up the pressure until we do. By the way, it seems to work. More PTSD sufferers finally decide to seek help due to their re-experiencing symptoms than any other reason.

❋   ❋   ❋   ❋   ❋

? Three questions: (1) Have you talked much with anybody about your traumatic combat experience(s)? (2) If not, why not? (3) Are you open to talking more about it if the right person was willing to listen?

_____

_____

❋   ❋   ❋   ❋   ❋

PTSD SYMPTOMS

Since the American Psychiatric Association defined Posttraumatic Stress Disorder in 1980, and with additional research done since then, experts seem to agree that there are three classic categories of symptoms that characterize this disorder. Read through the list that follows and put an "X" in the box of any symptoms that you have experienced in the past or are currently experiencing. If your experience of a symptom is mild or very infrequent, give it a light, small "x." The more intense or more frequent the symptom, enlarge and darken the "**X**."

SYMPTOMS

1. Re-experiencing Symptoms Memories and images of the traumatic events may intrude into the minds of those with PTSD. They occur suddenly without obvious cause. They are often accompanied by intense emotions, such as grief, guilt, fear or anger. Sometimes they can be so vivid a person believes the trauma is actually reoccurring.[10]

In the past but not now / Experiencing currently

In the past but not now	Experiencing currently	
❑	❑	Nightmares, night terrors
❑	❑	Sleepwalking, sleep fighting
❑	❑	Unwanted daytime memories, images, thoughts, daydreams
❑	❑	Flashbacks, feeling like you're reliving the traumatic event
❑	❑	Fixated on war experience, living in the past

27

❑ ❑ Somatic flashbacks (physical pain or a medical condition emerges, linked to the feelings or bodily states associated with the traumatic event)

❑ ❑ Spontaneous psychotic episodes (the world vanishes and you're suddenly somewhere else, experiencing some sort of trauma)

❑ ❑ Panic attacks, undefined dread or fear

❑ ❑ Phobias (what kind?)

2. Avoidance Symptoms Traumatized individuals attempt to avoid situations, people or events that remind them of their trauma. They feel numb, emotionless, withdrawing into themselves trying to shut out the painful memories and feelings. Friends and family feel rejected by them, as they are unable to show appropriate affection and emotion.

❑ ❑ Avoiding anyone or anything that reminds you of the traumatic event

❑ ❑ Physical/emotional reaction to things that remind you of the traumatic event

❑ ❑ Self-isolating, dread of social interaction

❑ ❑ Anxiety in crowds, traffic

❑ ❑ Despair, depression, sadness, emptiness, loneliness

❑ ❑ Inability to trust others

❑ ❑ Very reluctant to talk about your traumatic event

❑ ❑ Lack of interest or motivation regarding employment, recreation, former hobbies, sex, exercise

❑ ❑ Relationships that were once close and even intimate are now strained, cold, distant, requiring too much energy to maintain

❑ ❑ Emotional numbness, flat, can't get happy or sad, "dead" inside

❑ ❑ Substance abuse to "numb" yourself (drugs, alcohol, food)

❑ ❑ Suicidal thoughts

❑ ❑ Suicide attempts

❑ ❑ Physical fatigue

❑ ❑ Neglect/abandon personal care, hygiene, nutrition, exercise

3. Arousal Symptoms Fearing further trauma, PTSD sufferers are always on the alert, on guard, jumpy, unable to sleep, angry, irritable. Many also have concentration and memory problems.

❑ ❑ Anger, irritability, "short fuse," fits of rage

❑ ❑ Hypervigilance (always on guard), always need to be armed with knife or gun; could also include "emotional" hypervigilance

❑ ❑ Easily startled, react to loud noises, jumpy

❑ ❑ Perimeter checks (get up in the night to check for threats)

❑ ❑ Substance abuse to "un-numb" yourself (drugs, alcohol, food)

❑ ❑ Reduced cognitive ability (slow thinking, confusion, poor problem-solving, concentration)

❑ ❑ Poor memory

❑ ❑ Trouble falling asleep or staying asleep, insomnia

❑ ❑ Night sweats

❑ ❑ Accelerated heart rate, rapid breathing, heart palpitations for no good reason

❑ ❑ Question/abandon faith, feeling of being betrayed or abandoned by God, mad at God

❑ ❑ Fear of becoming violent

❑ ❑ Becoming violent, provoking fights

❑ ❑ Homicidal thoughts

❑ ❑ Anniversary reaction (become anxious nearing the monthly or yearly anniversary of the traumatic event)

❑ ❑ Adrenalin junkie (taking risks, getting hyped-up)

❑ ❑ Self-mutilation, cutting, excessive tattooing

? What do you miss most about how your life was before you experienced your combat trauma?

_____

_____

_____

_____

❀   ❀   ❀   ❀   ❀

TRAUMATIC BRAIN INJURY

Medical professionals treating those who have been wounded in the recent conflicts in the Mideast tell us that many troops coming home with a diagnosis of PTSD actually have *Traumatic Brain Injury*. According to Amber Nicodemus, Executive Director of the Cognogenesis Brain Center in Colorado Springs, Colorado, these conditions exhibit many of the same symptoms, hence the confusion.

Traumatic Brain Injury (TBI) is usually the result of a sudden, violent blow to the head. The skull can often withstand a forceful, external impact without fracturing – but a blow such as this can launch the brain on an internal collision with the skull. The result, an injured brain inside an intact skull, is known as a "closed-head injury."

A brain injury may also occur when a projectile, such as a bullet, rock or fragment of a fractured skull, penetrates the brain. The severity of brain injuries can vary greatly, depending on the part of the brain affected and the extent of the damage. A mild brain injury may cause only temporary confusion and headache, but a serious one can be fatal.[11]

According to the Congressional Research Service, the number of war-related instances of Traumatic Brain Injuries has increased steadily since the Global War on Terror began in 2000. The number of TBI's sustained by our troops in 2009 was almost 28,000. All told, over 178,000 Incident Diagnoses of TBI have been logged since the beginning of the conflicts in Iraq and Afghanistan.[12]

Read over the list of TBI symptoms below, and you will see how some troops could be misdiagnosed with PTSD. The symptoms in bold print are the same ones you'll find on lists of PTSD symptoms.

TBI SIGNS & SYMPTOMS[13]

1. headaches
2. dizziness or vertigo
3. **memory problems**
4. balance problems
5. ringing in ears
6. **sleep problems**
7. **poor word recall**
8. difficulty reading
9. **difficulty concentrating**
10. **slowed cognitive thinking**
11. visual disturbances
12. **irritability or anger outbursts**
13. **impulsivity**
14. lack of forethought
15. obsessive/compulsive behavior
16. inflexible in thought
17. **anxiety**
18. sensitivity to light, touch, sound
19. gets lost or becomes misdirected
20. **depression**
21. **negative attitude**
22. **antisocial or isolated**
23. slowed or impaired motor skills
24. **poor judgment**
25. speech problems
26. balance problems
27. seizures
28. loss of sense of taste or smell
29. **change in sexual drive or ability**
30. **avoidance behavior**
31. **restricted range of affect (e.g., unable to have loving feelings)**

Though we don't have the space to go into the subject of TBI in this manual, it's important for you to be aware of this alternative diagnosis. Only a healthcare professional can properly determine if you have TBI or PTSD, but if your symptoms seem to match the above list more closely than the previous list of symptoms for PTSD, you may want to investigate it. The treatment for the two disorders is *different*!

THE WAY OUT

According to memory expert Dr. Daniel Schacter, there are three basic types of memory:[14]

- **Procedural memory** – learned activities that we do automatically, like walking, bike riding, tying your shoe or spelling the word "cat."

- **Semantic memory** – involves remembering concepts, words, facts, data and other bits of knowledge, trivia, etc., like quoting the Lord's Prayer or the Pledge of Allegiance.

- **Episodic memory** – memory of an event that occurred in our lives, usually engaging the senses, including images, feelings, behaviors and meaning, like, "Remember the time we went body-surfing in Hawaii?"

Traumatic soul wounds are episodic memories – very negative ones, in dire need of processing and integration into our lives, values, beliefs and sense of well-being. One very effective way to release the unprocessed emotions of the past, heal traumatic memories and counteract some of the physiological consequences of your trauma, is to experience a *more powerful* episode, which involves Jesus Christ entering your episodic memories of your trauma experience. When this happens, images, senses, feelings, actions and meanings of the past are confronted, re-experienced, processed, released and overpowered by this new episode with Jesus.

Later in this manual (pages 62, 63), we'll be helping you set up and experience those "episodic encounters with Christ." A lot of the groundwork and preparation will involve faith, discipline, un-dramatic pursuits, some pain and work. It will involve time, commitment, and patience – with God, with yourself and with the process.

But you will experience healing. The trauma you experienced has changed you. You're not worse, just different. And as you cooperate with Christ as He works in you, you will absolutely end up better than ever! There is *much* to be hopeful about!

> For over three decades, I have studied victims of overwhelming stress – concentration camp survivors, POWs liberated from years of captivity, terrorized hostages. Repeatedly, I have been inspired by the countless cases that run counter to "expert" predictions. Instead of a pattern of deficit and defeat, there is one of coping and conquest. Indeed, rather than being devastated by their suffering, many survivors have actually used the experience to enrich their lives … Human beings have a magnificent ability to rebuild shattered lives, careers, and families, even as they wrestle with the bitterest of memories.
>
> – Dr. Julius Segal[15]

❋ ❋ ❋ ❋ ❋

If there's one thing you would like to include in your personal definition of how life will be when you are "healed," what would it be?

PTSD expert Dr. Aphrodite Matsakis divides the process of healing from severe trauma into three stages: Cognitive, Emotional and Empowerment.[16] Our intention is to cover these three stages in a non-linear fashion – as best we can in this small manual:

Cognitive Stage – Remembering the trauma and constructing it mentally

- Gaining a broad understanding of how things work in the Kingdom of God
- Identifying the facts about your trauma
- Deepening your faith and relationship with God
- Helping you reconstruct your identity based on God's truth
- Helping you construct an environment that will give God maximum access to your wounded soul

Emotional Stage – Feeling the feelings associated with the trauma

- Facing the episodic memories of your trauma and reintegrating it into your present reality with Christ's help
- Dealing with issues of forgiveness (needing to receive or needing to give)
- Identifying and eliminating bitterness
- Recognizing and dealing with repressed feelings caused by the trauma
- Understanding and entering into the grieving process

Empowerment Stage – Finding meaning in the trauma, redeeming it, mastering it and becoming a victor rather than a victim

- Healthy re-connection with your family, community
- Reaching out to others who are hurting
- Vital relationship with an "encourager" friend(s) ["Bridge people" are talked about in Step 9.]
- Victory over triggers and fears
- Setting healthy, achievable goals

We're not saying this process is going to be a smooth, uninterrupted flight path to the moon. There will be setbacks, slow times and detours. But stick with it! It will be worth it in the end. As Ralph Waldo Emerson once said:

Our greatest glory is not in never failing, but in rising up every time we fail.

And as God said in Proverbs 24:16 (NLT):

The godly may trip seven times, but they will get up again.
But one disaster is enough to overthrow the wicked.

Trauma is a thief. The self-defense mechanisms that God built into you were vital at the time your body and mind were attacked, but now – not so much. As a Marine, soldier, sailor, airman or coastguardsman, you sacrificed. But more has been taken from you than you bargained for. God wants to reimburse you for what has been taken, if you'll let Him:

Then I will make up to you for the years that the swarming locust has eaten... You will have plenty to eat and be satisfied, and praise the name of the Lord your God, who has dealt wondrously with you; then My people will never be put to shame.

– Joel 2:25,26

✺   ✺   ✺   ✺   ✺

PRAYER SEED

Heavenly Father, you know that my intentions were honorable when I joined the military. I trained hard. I was willing to sacrifice for the sake of others. I did the best I could on the field of battle. But I have been seriously wounded. I didn't know how seriously at the time. Now I do. I need your care and healing. This disorder is bigger than I am – but I know that You are bigger than it. Please come to my aid, show me the way out of this and bring health and restoration back into my life – body, mind and spirit. Amen.

❋ ❋ ❋

[1] Anonymous, from George Hill, in "Sharing the Struggles of a Friend," *The Gainesville Sun*, Nov. 10, 1993, quoted in Dr. Edward Tick, *War and the Soul,* p. 101.

[2] Adapted from American Psychiatric Association: *Diagnostic and Statistical Manual of Mental Disorders*, Fourth Edition, Text Revision (Washington, DC, American Psychiatric Association, 2000), p. 463.

[3] Combat Trauma Spectrum adapted from U.S. Army Center for Health Promotion & Preventive Medicine, *Redeployment Health Guide: A Service Member's Guide to Deployment-Related Stress Problems*, January, 2006.

[4] Dr. Edward Tick, *War and the Soul,* p. 99.

[5] Veterans Health Administration, Office of Public Health and Environmental Hazards, "Analysis of VA Health Care Utilization Among US Southwest Asian War Veterans: *Operation Iraqi Freedom Operation Enduring Freedom*," PowerPoint presentation, October, 2007.

[6] C. W. Hoge, et al. "Combat Duty in Iraq and Afghanistan, Mental Health Problems and Barriers to Care," *The New England Journal of Medicine*. Vol.351, No. 1, July 1, 2004.

[7] Donald Meichenbaum, *A Clinical Handbook/Practiced: Therapist Manual for Assessing and Treating Adults with Post-Traumatic Stress Disorder* [Institute Press, 1994], p.23.

[8] Observations from Dr. H. Norman Wright, *Crisis & Trauma Counseling*, p.198-205, and Patience H.G. Mason, www.patiencepress.com Post Traumatic Gazette, Issue 1, May/June 1995.

[9] Quote from Patience H. G. Mason www.patiencepress.com Post Traumatic Gazette, Issue 1 May/June 1995.

[10] Description of symptom categories from The Australian Centre for Posttraumatic Mental Health – www.acpmh.unimelb.edu.au

[11] Definition from Mayo Clinic: www.mayoclinic.com/health/traumatic-brain-injury/DS00

[12] Hannah Fischer, U.S. Military Casualty Statistics: Sept. 28, 2010. For the Congressional Research Service. www.fas.org/sgp/crs/natsec/RS22452.pdf.

[13] TBI symptoms from Brain Injury Association (www.biausa.org), Centers for Disease Control and Prevention (www.cdc.gov/ncipc/tbi), Dr. Daniel Amen, M.D. (www.amenclinics.com)

[14] Quote from Dr. Daniel Schacter in *Searching For Memory*, p. 18.

[15] Dr. Julius Segal, *Winning Life's Toughest Battles*, p. xii; quoted in Robert Hicks *Failure To Scream*, p. 79.

[16] Dr. Aphrodite Matsakis, *I Can't Get Over It*, p. 143.

STEP 3A: WHERE'S THE HOSPITAL?

CONSTRUCTING YOUR HEALING ENVIRONMENT

[THIS STEP IS COVERED IN TWO PARTS.]

"For I, the Lord, am your Healer."   – *Exodus 15:26*

Some people say that God is a crutch.
God is not a crutch. He's a whole dadgum hospital!
      – **Dr. J. Vernon McGee**

Robert Hicks is an Air Force Reserve specialist, counselor and expert on PTSD. In his book *Failure To Scream*, Hicks shares an experience he had as a young man assisting a famous neurosurgeon.

> At the end of the operation he asked if he could teach me anything about the brain. I asked, "What causes the brain to develop tumors?" He answered, "I don't know." Then I asked, "How does healing take place after we put the piece of skull back in place?" He laughed. "Listen," he said, "all I do here is take out the pieces of the brain that have died, and then God does the healing. *I just cooperate with the laws God has built into the human system.*" What a lesson from a humble yet brilliant man! I believe it is the same for psychological healing… We must cooperate with the laws that God has already ordained for proper human functioning. We are not the healers, but we can cooperate with the healing process.[1]

God has indeed ordained certain laws that will optimize your healing process. Two things are needed: you need to *know* the laws, and you need to *obey* the laws. Now these laws are not things like, "Go to church three times a week, carry a Bible with you at all times, shower in holy water and live a perfect life." The laws you'll be reading about here have to do with your relationship with God, and how you can cooperate with His healing process by giving Him optimal access to your wounded soul.

When it comes to seeking God's help, many people envision God as a drill sergeant with a clipboard and a check list, barking out orders and waiting to see if you'll respond correctly and measure up before you are considered worthy to advance to "Healed, First Class." In reality, it's more like you're an injured sapling and He's the weather, raining down life-giving water and energizing sunlight; bathing you with carbon dioxide for respiration; cool evenings and warm days for an invigorating rhythm; winds to strengthen your trunk. If the sapling wants to heal, it just needs to make sure it remains in the "weather." If it decides it doesn't like getting rained on or sun baked, pulls up its roots and takes up residence in a basement, it will never heal.

In the same way, God has set up a healing environment for you. The more you stay in contact with the elements of His "weather," the more healing you will experience.

THE ESSENCE OF HEALING

What are we looking for? When the subject of "healing" comes up, we usually think about doctors. A doctor will *do* something for you that will fix you up: set a bone, give you some antibiotic, remove your appendix. But they're not really *healing* you. They're just adjusting your environment in such a way that the normal healing processes that God has built into every person can proceed unhindered.

That's what we're attempting to do in this Step. Building on the foundation of Jesus Christ being your Lord and Savior (if you're still confused about this, see Appendix A which will describe how to begin a personal relationship with Christ), we want to share **five vital elements** that are crucial to your healing environment:

1. **The Holy Spirit – your divine power source**

2. **The Word of God – your divine food and weapon**

3. **Prayer – vital communication with your divine commander**

4. **The Christian Community – your divine Green Zone**

5. **Your Mindset – your spiritual battlemind for divine healing**

Their effect on you probably won't be as sudden as a syringe of adrenalin to a "code blue" heart. But what they *will* do is deepen your connection to the Healer, so that He can accomplish His healing work in you.

ELEMENT #1: THE HOLY SPIRIT – YOUR DIVINE POWER SOURCE

WHO IS THE HOLY SPIRIT?

The Bible presents God as a "Trinity" – three-in-one. That is, God is frequently affirmed to be the one-and-only God (Deuteronomy 6:4; Isaiah 43:10; John 17:3; 1 Corinthians 8:4), and yet there are three distinct "persons" who are referred to as God:

- God the Father – John 6:27

- · God the Son – John 20:26-28

- God the Holy Spirit – 1 Corinthians 3:16

One God presented in three different manifestations, each one with its separate and distinct function. All three have existed as a unit since before time began – never beginning, never ending. But each has had a different job.

In a way, God's different manifestations are like a platoon over in Iraq. That platoon could be named and described based on what they were doing when observed. When asked who they are, one Iraqi might say, "They're gunfighters, killing the terrorists who are trying to kill us." Another might say, "They're doctors, taking our wounded to a place where they can get fixed." Another might say, "They're entertainers, making our children laugh and giving them candy." Same platoon, different manifestations.

In a nutshell, the Holy Spirit's job is to live inside of us, empower us, comfort us, heal us and enable us to live a righteous and satisfying life, and to help us communicate with God.

 Study the following verses from the Bible and write down what you think it's saying about what the Holy Spirit does:

Jesus speaking: *"When He, the Spirit of truth, comes, He will guide you into all truth."*
– John 16:13

Jesus speaking: *"I will talk to the Father, and He'll provide you another Friend so that you will always have someone with you. This Friend is the Spirit of Truth. The godless world can't take Him in because it doesn't have eyes to see Him, doesn't know what to look for. But you know Him already because He has been staying with you, and will even be in you!"*

– John 14:16,17 (MSG)

Jesus speaking: *"You will receive power when the Holy Spirit comes on you; and you will be My witnesses in Jerusalem, and in all Judea and Samaria, and to the ends of the earth."*

– Acts 1:8 (NIV)

Paul writing: *"The Holy Spirit helps us in our weakness. For example, we don't know what God wants us to pray for. But the Holy Spirit prays for us with groanings that cannot be expressed in words."*

– Romans 8:26 (NLT)

THE INDWELLING OF THE HOLY SPIRIT

When you invited Jesus Christ into your life, He entered you in the form of His Holy Spirit. Once there, He's there permanently. This is called the "indwelling" of the Spirit. But what we shared with you in Step 1 about God not violating your free will still holds true. He's not going to *force* you to go His way on any subject. You can decide to disregard His fellowship, His counsel and His offers of help. The Bible says we can "quench" the Holy Spirit by our disinterest (1 Thessalonians 5:19). We can also "grieve" Him through our disobedience (Ephesians 4:30). We can make it so it's *just as if* He wasn't in our life. But He's always there – waiting for you to respond positively to Him.

THE FILLING OF THE HOLY SPIRIT

> *Don't be drunk with wine, because that will ruin your life. Instead, be filled with the Holy Spirit*
> **– Ephesians 5:18** (NLT)

In Ephesians 5:18, God gives us two commands, one positive, one negative. What are they?

1. _____

2. _____

To "be filled" with the Holy Spirit means to be controlled and empowered by Him. The point of the verse is that, just as alcohol can control us (in destructive ways), the Holy Spirit – if we will allow Him to – can control us in positive, constructive ways.

Three Kinds of People

The Natural Man – "Captain of my own soul!"

S = Self, sitting on the throne or control center of his or her life.

† = Christ, outside the life.

Circles = Activities, interests, priorities and plans in discord with God's.

This represents the **non-Christian** who doesn't have a relationship with God. As he tries to direct his own life in his finite and usually self-interested way, it often results in frustration, despair and discord with God's perfect plans for him.

The Spiritual Man – "Walking in faith and obedience."

S = Self dethroned, yielding to Christ's Lordship in his or her life.

† = Christ on the throne, guiding and empowering the Christian.

Circles = Activities, interests, priorities and plans in harmony with God's.

This represents a **Spirit-filled Christian** walking closely with God. Since Christ is all-powerful and all-knowing, He can ensure the Christian's life will harmonize with God's plans for him, resulting in love, joy, peace patience, kindness, goodness, faithfulness, gentleness, and self-control – among other things! No guarantee of a problem-free life, only one that is in harmony with God's plans for him or her.

The Carnal Man – "I'll take it from here, thanks."

S = Self back on the throne, trying to direct his or her life again.

† = Christ still in the life, but dethroned and not allowed to be Lord.

Circles = Activities, interests, priorities and plans in discord with God's.

This represents a **Carnal** or **Worldly Christian** who isn't walking with God. As he ignores or disobeys God's directions, his life falls into disarray. Comparing frustration levels, dead-ends and despair, it's difficult to tell the difference between the Carnal Christian's life and the non-Christian's life.

 Study the three diagrams and descriptions above. Which one would you say currently represents your life?

_____

Which one would you like to have represent your life?

_____

FIVE STEPS TO FILLING

1. DESIRE

Blessed are those who hunger and thirst for righteousness, for they shall be filled.
— **Matthew 5:6** (NKJV)

 What does Jesus say is required in order to be "filled"?

What would this "desire" look or feel like in your life?

Search your heart. Do you "hunger and thirst for righteousness"? Do you truly *want* Jesus Christ as your Lord, and the Holy Spirit as your Guide? Are you willing to obey what God tells you to do? Don't expect His power to flow unhindered if you're simply "going through the motions." God looks at the heart, and He knows your heart completely.

2. CONFESS

If we confess our sins, He is faithful and righteous to forgive us our sins and to cleanse us from all unrighteousness.
— **1 John 1:9**

The reason the Holy Spirit may be "quenched" in your life is because of sin – saying "No" to God and "Yes" to your unrighteous desires. In prayer, ask God to reveal the sins that have been disconnecting you from His plan and power. As He brings them to mind, agree with Him that those choices were wrong (that's the essence of confession). Ask Him to forgive you for each one.

We'll be taking a much more in-depth look at forgiveness in Step 6: *How Do I Move On?*

3. PRESENT

And do not present your members [body parts] *as instruments of unrighteousness to sin, but present yourselves to God as being alive from the dead, and your members as instruments of righteousness to God... For just as you presented your members as slaves of uncleanness, and of lawlessness leading to more lawlessness, so now present your members as slaves of righteousness for holiness.*
— **Romans 6:13,19** (NKJV)

 Do you think the "presenting" of ourselves spoken of in these verses involves a passive attitude or...

Most people associate slavery with demeaning oppression – and in most cases it is. In the spiritual realm, Satan desires to enslave you to his will, which will lead to destruction. But God wants you to be "enslaved" to *His* will for your *benefit*, leading to freedom from the things that tear you down, and a strong connection to the things that will build you up and bring you satisfaction, fulfillment and joy. He wants you to "pledge allegiance" to *His* flag.

A crucial insight is found in **Romans 6:16-18** (MSG):

You know well enough from your own experience that there are some acts of so-called freedom that destroy freedom. Offer yourselves to sin, for instance, and it's your last free act. But offer yourselves to the ways of God and the freedom never quits. All your lives you've let sin tell you what to do. But thank God you've started listening to a new master, one whose commands set you free to live openly in his freedom!"

4. ASK

So I say to you, ask, and it will be given to you; seek, and you will find; knock, and it will be opened to you. For everyone who asks, receives; and he who seeks, finds; and to him who knocks, it will be opened. Now suppose one of your fathers is asked by his son for a fish; he will not give him a snake instead of a fish, will he? Or if he is asked for an egg, he will not give him a scorpion, will he? If you then, being evil, know how to give good gifts to your children, how much more will your heavenly Father give the Holy Spirit to those who ask Him? — **Luke 11:9-13**

 What astounding, superhuman exploits does this passage say you need to perform in order to "persuade" God to give you what you need?

Remember what was said earlier about our free will? God won't compromise your privilege of choosing. Since you made a willful choice to depart from His will, you need to make a willful choice to get "reconnected."

5. THANK HIM IN FAITH

Therefore I tell you, whatever you ask for in prayer, believe that you have received it, and it will be yours. — **Mark 11:24** (NIV)

 Notice the past tense used? What does this verse say will happen if you believe that you have already received what you prayed for?

If you ask for something and believe you have received it, the normal thing to do next would be to say thank you! As Bible teacher Tommy Adkins once said, "Saying thanks is always a sign that you have 'faithed' God."

ASKING TO BE FILLED

When you pray to God, He isn't as concerned with your words as He is with the attitude of your heart. But sometimes it helps to express what is in your heart if someone else supplies the words for you. Here is a suggested prayer:

Dear Father, I need You. I hunger and thirst for Your righteousness, rather than for the garbage of the world. I want You to be my King and my Guide. But I confess that I have taken the throne of my life from Your control and have sinned against You. I've made many wrong choices. Please forgive me for this. I yield myself to You in obedience, desiring to serve You rather than myself or my enemy, the devil. Please fill me with Your Holy Spirit. I step down from the throne of my life and give it back to You. Based on Your promise, I have faith that You have heard my prayer and have filled me with Your Holy Spirit. Thank you! Amen.

 Does this prayer express the desire of your heart?

If you prayed the above prayer, or something similar, write the date in here:

❀ ❀ ❀ ❀ ❀

SO, AM I DONE WITH THIS NOW?

Well… no. It's an unfortunate but natural part of the human condition for us to periodically re-take the throne of our lives by asserting our will and ignoring God's will. As we grow spiritually, our objective is for this to happen less and less. In the meantime, we must be prepared to recognize when we have slipped into the "carnal" category, and take measures to once again be Spirit-filled. Remember: this doesn't mean we are no longer saved or that the Holy Spirit has left us, it simply means we've temporarily pushed Jesus Christ off the throne of our life and are trying to run things ourselves.

SPIRITUAL BREATHING

Here is an illustration that will help you understand what to do when you need to be "refilled." Think of it in terms of breathing. When you exhale, you rid your body of harmful carbon dioxide. When you inhale, you draw life-giving oxygen back into your body. Out with the bad, in with the good. A similar thing happens in the realm of the Spirit.

Exhale. When you become aware of sin in your life, it's time to take a spiritual breath. First, you must exhale by **confessing** your sin. The Greek word for "confession" is *homologeo,* which means "to say the same thing as." God's Spirit tells you your action was wrong, and you agree with Him – that's confession. And if you truly agree with Him about it, you will not only say so, you'll quit doing the thing that was grieving Him. That's what **"repentance"** is: "to stop, turn around and go back the other way."

Inhale. Now breathe in the life of the Holy Spirit by asking Him to once again take the throne of your life. By faith, ask Him to control, empower and guide you. When you make this request, you can *know* that He will immediately grant it, based on his command in Ephesians 5:18, and His promise in 1 John 5:14-15.

HOW OFTEN DO I DO THIS?

As often as you need to. It may be once a week, once a day, once an hour or even once every few minutes! The important thing is to not lose heart and give up in defeat. As a drowning man will struggle frantically to clear his lungs of water and breathe in oxygen, so we need to recognize the critical need to keep the Holy Spirit on the throne of our lives – confessing our sins and seeking His filling.

Spiritual breathing should become as natural and automatic as our physical breathing is. Each time you sense the conviction of the Holy Spirit, stop right then and take a spiritual breath. Some Christians have adopted the habit of starting out each day – even before getting out of bed – asking God if there is anything in them that is displeasing to Him, confessing it if there is, and then asking Him to fill them with His Holy Spirit.

❋ ❋ ❋ ❋ ❋

ELEMENT #2: THE WORD OF GOD – YOUR DIVINE FOOD AND WEAPON

When you received Jesus Christ into your life, you became a three-dimensional being, composed of a body, a soul and a spirit. We know that our physical bodies need to be fed. Most people are regularly reminded of it by hunger pangs. But our souls and our spirits also need nourishment. Our soul – our will, intellect, emotions, etc. – is nourished by things like truth, beauty, information and friendships. Our spirit – the part of us that relates to God – is fed by the words of God: the Bible. As Jesus said in Matthew 4:4 (NIV), *"Man does not live on bread alone, but on every word that comes from the mouth of God."* And as Peter wrote in 1 Peter 2:2 (NKJV), *"As newborn babes, desire the pure milk of the word, that you may grow thereby."*

A Christian who doesn't get a regular diet of God's Word will end up with an emaciated, weak and sickly spirit. Perhaps you've seen photos of people being liberated from Nazi concentration camps at the end of World War II. If we could take photos of the *spirits* of some Christians today, they would probably look very similar to the physical bodies of those poor men and women who had been deprived of proper nourishment for so long. Don't let this happen to you! Be sure that you're getting a steady diet of God's meat and potatoes!

❋ ❋ ❋ ❋ ❋

 Based on the two preceeding paragraphs, how would you complete this sentence? "The Bible is ..."

_____

_____

❋ ❋ ❋ ❋ ❋

BENEFITS OF READING THE BIBLE

 The following passages describe the benefits of studying and applying God's Word to your life. Write at least one benefit you observe in each passage.

God speaking to Joshua: *"Study this Book of Instruction continually. Meditate on it day and night so you will be sure to obey everything written in it. Only then will you prosper and succeed in all you do."*   **– Joshua 1:8 (NLT)**

_____

_____

King David writing: *"The law of his God is in his heart; his feet do not slip."*
    – Psalm 37:31 (NIV)

_____

_____

King David writing: *"How can a young man keep his way pure? By living according to Your word ... I have hidden Your word in my heart that I might not sin against You."*
    – Psalm 119:9,11 (NIV)

_____

_____

Jesus speaking: *"If you remain in Me and My words remain in you, ask whatever you wish, and it will be given you."*   **– John 15:7 (NIV)**

_____

_____

Jesus speaking: *"If you hold to My teaching, you are really my disciples. Then you will know the truth, and the truth will set you free."*   **– John 8:31,32 (NIV)**

_____

❋ ❋ ❋ ❋ ❋

Your Personal Plan

The following illustration shows that there are five ways a person can get a firm "grasp" on the Word of God. Called the "Word of God Hand Illustration"[1] and created by The Navigators, it demonstrates the importance of getting a balanced input of the different methods of taking the Bible into your life. If you try to grasp it with only one or two fingers, you won't hold it very well. But if you use all five fingers, your grasp of it will be strong.

1. Hearing – Listening to a sermon at church or on tape or CD; listening to audio recordings of the Bible being read; discussing the Bible with your friends.

2. Reading – Sitting down alone and reading a chapter or two of the Bible, perhaps when you first wake up or before you go to bed; reading when you're on a bus or train; in a waiting room; during lunch; when permitted to on guard duty.

3. Studying – More intense and focused activity than just reading; consulting commentaries; verse cross-referencing; outlining; answering questions; going slow and deep. Observation, Interpretation, Integration, Application.

4. Memorizing – Committing key verses of the Bible to memory. After 24 hours, you will remember: 5% of what you hear, 15% of what you read, 35% of what you study, but 100% of what you memorize. Running God's Word through your mind can affect your actions and *reactions*.

5. Meditating – Deliberately reflecting on God's Word, praying about it and considering how to apply it to your life. Just as your thumb can touch each of your four fingers, meditate on what you hear, read, study and memorize.

Personal Application

I will commit to a period of personal Bible intake (hear/read/study/memorize/meditate) lasting no less than _____ minutes, _____ day(s) a week, for the next _____ weeks, to start on _____ (date). I will ask _____ to check up on me, give me encouragement, and help me find answers to questions I come up with.

❋ ❋ ❋ ❋ ❋

Here's a good plan to follow as you study the Bible. Read through a chapter (the book of John is a good place to start, if you need a suggestion) and write down your thoughts and observations according to the **SPACE-Q** format:

S: Sins to confess

P: Promises to claim

A: Actions to avoid

C: Commands to obey

E: Examples to follow

Q: Questions I need answered

❋ ❋ ❋ ❋ ❋

TAKING THE SWORD

God's Word has another function: it's a **weapon**. In Ephesians 6:14-17, the Bible talks about the spiritual armor that is available to every believer: belt of truth, breastplate of righteousness, sandals of the preparation of the gospel, shield of faith, helmet of salvation… these are all defensive implements of war. But the final item mentioned is *"the sword of the Spirit, which is the Word of God."* This is *both* a defensive *and* an offensive weapon.

You can read a great account of how Jesus used God's Word in a battle with Satan in Matthew 4:1-11. Twice Satan launched an attacking temptation at Jesus. Twice He countered with a verse of Scripture – defensive moves. With the third attack, Jesus not only repelled the devil's assault, but sent him into hasty retreat with a counterattack using the sword of the Word. Hebrews 4:12 (NKJV) tells us that "The Word of God is living and powerful, and sharper than any two-edged sword…"

Learn how to use it.

A rifleman is intimately acquainted with every square millimeter of his weapon. Now it's time to begin a new training program to become as familiar with your new weapon – God's Word – as you were with your old one. It will keep you alive.

In Step 8: *How Do I Fight?* you'll be learning much more about spiritual warfare and how to defend yourself against the forces of darkness using God's Word.

PRAYER SEED

Father, I know that You love me – and I am thankful that You do. But I am wounded and I need Your healing. You are the Great Healer and so I'm coming to You. Help me to follow the laws of healing that You have established. I desire with all my heart to cooperate with You in this. Thank you for the gift of your Holy Spirit. May He control and empower me every day. May I never quench or grieve Him. Help me to give Him full access to every area of my life. Convict me whenever I sneak back onto the throne of my life. I know I can count on your forgiveness and correction when that happens. May I frequently and regularly come to your Word for nourishment, guidance and encouragement. Let me see my growth and strengthening as a result of its intake. Please motivate me to become intimately familiar with this new weapon of spiritual warfare. May I use it with skill and discernment. And may You be glorified in my life. Amen

---

[1] Robert Hicks, *Failure To Scream,* p. 164.

[2] William R. Bright, *Have You Made The Wonderful Discovery of the Spirit-Filled Life?* (Orlando, FL: Campus Crusade for Christ, 1966,1995). Illustrations used by permission.

[3] Word Hand Illustration, © 1976, The Navigators. Used by permission of NavPress, Colorado Springs, CO. All rights reserved.

STEP 3B: WHERE'S THE HOSPITAL?

CONSTRUCTING YOUR HEALING ENVIRONMENT

[THIS STEP IS THE SECOND OF TWO PARTS.]

There are three more crucial elements to your healing environment that still need to be considered …

ELEMENT #3: PRAYER – VITAL COMMUNICATION
WITH YOUR DIVINE COMMANDER

AMBUSH!

I was leading a patrol on foot in a neighborhood in eastern Ramadi – a place that supposedly had been "cleaned up" a couple weeks earlier. So we weren't too wired, kind of relaxed, actually. That's why it seemed so surreal when the first bullet ricocheted off the wall six inches above my head. We dove for whatever cover we could find as the neighborhood erupted with AK-47 fire. As quickly as we could, we returned fire and set up a not-very-effective perimeter. We were greatly outnumbered in both men and firepower. Somehow, they knew we were coming and they'd set us up.

As I scanned the area to gauge the threat, I could see my men glancing at me, desperately looking for orders. I began to think that maybe we could use a little help.

I quickly went through our options in my mind. Retreat wasn't one of them – we were pinned down. I really ought to think about contacting "Higher" and get them to send us a Quick Reaction Force. Six or eight fifty-cal-mounted Humvees would sure be a welcome addition to this party. A few Strykers would be nice. Maybe they've even got an AH-64 running combat air patrol in the neighborhood…

But then I thought, *Naaaah. We'll be fine. Besides, I don't like the guy running the radio today at HQ very much. And he's probably still sore about that disagreement we had the other night about the Steelers versus the Colts. He might be reluctant to put himself out for me. Or he might think I'm a big wuss, can't handle things by myself. Plus, my radio might not even be working. Maybe it's been shot up already. And what if everybody back at HQ is at chow right now? It'd just be a waste of time …*

"Looks like we're on our own here, guys," I yelled. "Keep shootin'!"

❋   ❋   ❋   ❋   ❋

That was obviously a fictitious scenario. *Every* troop outside the wire knows with 100% certainty he or she can rely on the team back at HQ to respond instantly to a call for backup. And they wouldn't hesitate to ask for it, unlike the dufus in the above story. Why would *anybody* – especially someone who is in some big-time trouble – not take advantage of any and all avenues of help and support available?

The ironic thing is that Christians do it all the time. We have been given this incredible communication system – instant contact with our Creator and Savior by simply talking or thinking – and we don't use it nearly enough. In fact, you can ask just about any Christian if they think they should be spending more or less time in prayer, and they will *always* answer "More!" Prayer is the Christian's "spiritual fire support," yet we seldom use it.

❋   ❋   ❋   ❋   ❋

Why do you think so many people are reluctant to spend much time in prayer?

_____

_____

❋ ❋ ❋ ❋ ❋

It could be that people don't have a clear idea of what prayer is for. Though God loves to answer the requests we make of Him in prayer, this isn't its only purpose. God is not a cosmic Santa Claus, existing only to grant us all of our desires and make us happy. We must never forget that Christianity is not supposed to be merely a religion or a philosophy of life. It is a *relationship* with our heavenly Father. And in any relationship, there must be communication. We don't always benefit directly from the communication itself, but the communication produces a deeper relationship, which opens the door to *all kinds* of benefits.

I talk to my wife on a very regular basis – because she's my best friend and I love her. We talk about *everything*. There's lots of give-and-take. Sometimes I talk and she listens, sometimes it's the other way around. Sometimes we don't even need words to communicate. Because of this, our relationship is very deep and satisfying for both of us.

But how would it be if the only time I ever spoke to her was to let her know what I wanted? She *does* want to know what I want – because she loves me – but she wants to know a lot more than that! Our relationship would be pretty shallow if all I ever did was issue my demands to her.

❋ ❋ ❋ ❋ ❋

 On a scale of one to ten, how much do you think God wants to hear from you?

_____

Not in the least	1	2	3	4	5	6	7	8	9	10	Very, very very much

 On a scale of one to ten, how much do you want to talk with God?

_____

Not in the least	1	2	3	4	5	6	7	8	9	10	Very, very very much

❋ ❋ ❋ ❋ ❋

WHAT DOES GOD WANT YOU TO PRAY ABOUT?

God loves you with a love that is as eternal, intense and pure as anything we can imagine, and more. Proverbs 15:8 says, "The prayer of the upright is His delight." And guess what – because of what Christ did on the cross for you, you are one of the "upright"! Imagine Jesus Christ, sitting by your bed when you wake up, saying, "Good morning! I love you! I can't wait to hear your delightful voice. Talk to Me, please!"

 Here are a few verses in the Bible that will give you some insight about the things God wants to hear about from you. After each verse write what is being prayed *for* or *about*.

Give us this day our daily bread. — **Matthew 6:11**

_____

_____

I love You, O Lord, my strength. The Lord is my rock and my fortress and my deliverer,
My God, my rock, in whom I take refuge; My shield and the horn of my salvation,
my stronghold.   **– Psalm 18:1-3**

In everything give thanks; for this is God's will for you in Christ Jesus.
                                                    – 1 Thessalonians 5:18

My God, my God, why have you abandoned me? Why are you so far away when I groan
for help?   **– Psalm 22:1,2** (NLT)

If we confess our sins, He is faithful and righteous to forgive us our sins and to cleanse us
from all unrighteousness.   **– 1 John 1:9**

Lead us not into temptation, but deliver us from the evil one.   **– Matthew 6:13**

Be anxious for nothing, but in everything by prayer and supplication with thanksgiving
let your requests be made known to God.   **– Philippians 4:6**

I WANT ANSWERS!!

God will answer *every* prayer that you pray in faith. Every one. But the thing to keep in mind is that, if we have submitted ourselves to Him as our King and Guide, He gets to decide *how* to answer our prayers. His answers will always be what's best for us and for His Kingdom. And since He's all-knowing, all-powerful and timeless, He ought to know!

- Sometimes He might answer our prayer "**No.** It wouldn't be good for you." Like the good father saying no to the toddler who wants to play with the nice, round hand grenade.

  For deeper study: *Examples of God saying "No" (even to His Son!):*
  2 Samuel 12:15-18; Matthew 26:37-42; 2 Corinthians 12:7-10.

- Sometimes He might answer our prayer "**Wait.** This would be a good thing for you, but not right now. Be patient. It's on the way." Like what I said to my fourteen-year old son when he wanted to borrow the car.

  For deeper study: *Examples of God saying "Wait": Genesis 15:2-5;*
  Genesis 50:24,25; Exodus 5:22,23; 6:6-8. In each case, the fulfillment of the
  promise happened many years later.

- Sometimes God might answer our prayer "**Yes!** This will be a *good* thing for you!" Like what I said to my wife when she asked, "How about a kiss?"

> **For deeper study:** *Examples of God saying "Yes": Psalm 32:5; 1 Samuel 1:11,19,20; 1 Chronicles 4:9,10; 2 Kings 6:15-18. In each case, God said "Yes" to their request.*

❄ ❄ ❄ ❄ ❄

Obviously, we would like to increase the percentage of "Yes" answers we get. Psalm 37:4 gives us some great insight on how to do this:

> *Delight yourself in the LORD;*
>   *And He will give you the desires of your heart.*

> Prayer is weakness plugged into strength. Prayer is saying, "I can't, but You can," and plugging into God's "I will."
> – Dr. Jack Taylor[1]

When the Lord is our delight, when our attitude toward Him is one of love, acceptance, submission and a quiet confidence that He always knows what's best for us, when we're willing to allow His will to be done rather than what we might prefer, this gives Him unhindered access to our souls and spirits so that our desires *will* line up with His before we even begin to pray. Then we'll be able to pray boldly the way Jesus prayed:

> *Nevertheless, not as I will, but as You will.*　　　　　**– Matthew 26:39b** (NKJV)

PERSONAL APPLICATION

I will commit to a period of personal prayer – either by myself or with others – lasting no less

than _____ minutes, _____ day(s) a week, for the next _____ weeks,

to start on _____ (date). I will ask _____ to check up on me,

give me encouragement, and help me find answers to questions I come up with.

PRAYER ASSIGNMENT

In Step 2, on page 29 you were asked this question: *If there's one thing you would like to include in your personal definition of how life will be when you are "healed," what would it be?* Assuming that you wrote something down (or at least, something came to your mind), begin today asking God if He would fulfill that desire for you. Ask Him *every day*. As Jesus advised us in Matthew 7:7 (NLT):

> *Keep on asking, and you will receive what you ask for. Keep on seeking, and you will find.*
> *Keep on knocking, and the door will be opened to you.*

❄ ❄ ❄ ❄ ❄

ELEMENT #4: THE CHRISTIAN COMMUNITY – YOUR DIVINE GREEN ZONE

You need a safe haven inside the wire. You need a place where you can rest, regroup, retrain, receive the latest intelligence and get ready to go out again. This is exactly what God created the Church for.

But PTSD sufferers tend to self-isolate, avoiding crowds *and* the Church. Why is that?

When a person goes off to war, he or she leaves behind a group of buddies who have spent lots of time together. The troop and his/her group's relationships have developed over a period of time and they know each other in unique ways. They are comfortable with each other's likes and dislikes, how they'll react in certain situations, what makes them laugh or get mad. They have similar priorities and goals, and they're OK with each other's hang-ups. They cut each other slack for the sake of the friendship. They respect each other – despite all the ribbing and sarcasm.

But things happened downrange that altered the troop's personality. Likes and dislikes changed. Reactions are different. Moods have shifted and the list of hang-ups has lengthened significantly. Any opposition or difficulty and boom! He just can't help it – he flies into a rage. Crowds make him anxious. Loud noises send him diving for cover. Overpasses or trash beside the road make him feel panicky. He doesn't want to go places where he might encounter those stressors anymore – even in his stateside Green Zone. He is very aware of the changes and strongly suspects his pre-deployment buddies are aware, too.

So, with all of this, he assumes he must seem very weird to his old friends and concludes that they could *never* understand what he went through, or who he is now. There can't be any respect left for him. And if his *friends* think he's weird, surely everyone else must too. Nobody likes feeling weird. So what action does he take? Simon and Garfunkel, writing during the Vietnam war, described the isolating troop's self-talk:

> Hiding in my room, safe within my womb,
> I touch no one and no one touches me.
> I am a rock.
> I am an island.
> And a rock feels no pain;
> And an island never cries.[2]

 On a scale of one to ten, how closely does the above scenario describe your experience?

Not in the least	1	2	3	4	5	6	7	8	9	10	Very, very very much

 What has made you the most discouraged about trying to reconnect with your old friends after you came back from the war?

_____

_____

_____

Social isolation may seem like your best option. It feels more comfortable at first, and it's easier than trying to deal with people who don't understand. But it's one of the worst moves you can make. Isolating yourself...

- severely diminishes your support network, which are human conduits to God
- robs you of emotional closeness to people you like and who care about you
- gives you more time to worry and feel lonely, helpless and depressed
- causes you to play into Satan's key tactic – isolate the prey, eliminate all avenues of support, turn up the heat, then offer destructive ways to "fix" problems
- keeps you from experiencing the *good* relationships that are energizing and healing
- makes your environment "encouragement neutral" – no minuses but no plusses either

In addition, this action goes against the basic design objective of our Creator. He made us to be a communal species. Companions were designed specifically *for* this kind of situation.

Two people are better off than one, for they can help each other succeed. If one person falls, the other can reach out and help. But someone who falls alone is in real trouble. Likewise, two people lying close together can keep each other warm. But how can one be warm alone? A person standing alone can be attacked and defeated, but two can stand back-to-back and conquer. Three are even better, for a triple-braided cord is not easily broken.

– Ecclesiastes 4:9-12 (NLT)

God invented the Church to be like an incubator – a place where His children can grow, get strong, get healed and become stable and independent. And who is supposed to supply all this beneficial stuff? The Spirit-filled Christians who occupy the church.

We're not necessarily talking about a building here – though that is often where "the Church" will be found. The Church is a living organism composed of Christians all over the world. The Bible refers to it as "The Body of Christ" as in, Christ is the head, and we are like His hands and feet, accomplishing His work on the planet. His intention is that we cooperate – and in so doing it's much more likely we'll accomplish His purposes. The Apostle Paul shows us how it all works in 1 Corinthians 12. Let's look at a few key verses to gain some insight:

God's various gifts are handed out everywhere; but they all originate in God's Spirit. God's various ministries are carried out everywhere; but they all originate in God's Spirit. God's various expressions of power are in action everywhere; but God himself is behind it all. Each person is given something to do that shows who God is: Everyone gets in on it, everyone benefits. All kinds of things are handed out by the Spirit, and to all kinds of people! The variety is wonderful:

- *wise counsel*
- *clear understanding*
- *simple trust*
- *healing the sick*
- *miraculous acts*
- *proclamation*
- *distinguishing between spirits*
- *tongues*
- *interpretation of tongues.*

All these gifts have a common origin, but are handed out one by one by the one Spirit of God. He decides who gets what, and when.   **– 1 Corinthians 12:4-11** (MSG)

The Main Point: The Holy Spirit gives every person – including *you* – some kind of a gift (or gifts) that he or she can use to help others with. He knows exactly which gifts each of us would be best suited for, and He expects us to use them for the good of His body! He distributes them, but He also continually energizes them. So, though the Spirit will accomplish a lot in your life by direct contact with you, He will also work on you through other gifted people.

I want you to think about how all this makes you more significant, not less. A body isn't just a single part blown up into something huge. It's all the different-but-similar parts arranged and functioning together. If Foot said, "I'm not elegant like Hand, embellished with rings; I guess I don't belong to this body," would that make it so? If Ear said, "I'm not beautiful like Eye, limpid and expressive; I don't deserve a place on the head," would you want to remove it from the body? If the body was all eye, how could it hear? If all ear, how could it smell? As it is, we see that God has carefully placed each part of the body right where he wanted it.

– 1 Corinthians 12:14-18 (MSG)

[?] What do you think the main point of the previous passage is?

_____

_____

The way God designed our bodies is a model for understanding our lives together as a church: every part dependent on every other part, the parts we mention and the parts we don't, the parts we see and the parts we don't. If one part hurts, every other part is involved in the hurt, and in the healing. If one part flourishes, every other part enters into the exuberance. **– 1 Corinthians 12:25,26** (MSG)

[?] What do you think the main point of the previous passage is?

_____

_____

❀ ❀ ❀ ❀ ❀

So "Church" is simply a community of Christians. It could be a formal congregation based in a building (the optimal environment here in America), or it could simply be a collection of your Christian friends who are looking after you and each other in love, motivated and directed by the Holy Spirit. Whatever its configuration, it is crucial that you be vitally connected with a group of believers who know and love you.

[?] Here are a few verses that describe what is supposed to happen when Christians form a community that is determined to make a place where God can help and heal. Write down what you observe in each verse:

Iron sharpens iron, so one man sharpens another. **– Proverbs 27:17**

_____

_____

Laugh with your happy friends when they're happy; share tears when they're down. Get along with each other; don't be stuck-up. Make friends with nobodies; don't be the great somebody. **– Romans 12:15,16** (MSG)

_____

_____

Those of us who are strong and able in the faith need to step in and lend a hand to those who falter, and not just do what is most convenient for us. Strength is for service, not status. Each one of us needs to look after the good of the people around us, asking ourselves, "How can I help?" **– Romans 15:1,2** (MSG)

_____

_____

But encourage one another day after day, as long as it is still called "Today," so that none of you will be hardened by the deceitfulness of sin.   **– Hebrews 3:13**

Let's not merely say that we love each other; let us show the truth by our actions.
    – 1 John 3:18 (NLT)

❀   ❀   ❀   ❀   ❀

WHAT HAPPENS UNDERGROUND?

Have you ever spent time in northern California and walked among the majestic redwood trees in the various parks there? These are the tallest and most massive trees on the planet, many of them ascending over 350 feet. Some are as old as 4,000 years. You can't help but to be awestruck by their strength, endurance and tenacity.

But think for a minute. Have you ever seen a redwood tree growing all by itself in the middle of a field? Probably not – unless the area around it was recently cleared by man. And if so, it won't stand there for long. God has ordained that redwood trees must always live in groves, because He is aware of their secret: *shallow root systems.*

Unlike many trees that have deep taproots, redwood root systems grow laterally, and cover a huge area to efficiently absorb the small amount rain that falls on their often rocky habitat. So, in order to keep from being blown over, redwoods *interlace* their roots below the surface, forming a solid platform that stretches for acres – even miles. When the storms blow through their valleys, they remain standing because they hold each other up!

This is an excellent picture of how the Christian community is supposed to be. The world can be a stormy place from time to time. As a combat veteran, you've been in some of the worse storms in history. Any Christian – even a non-vet – who tries to "go it alone" is vulnerable. It won't be long before he or she encounters difficulties that are more than they were designed to handle solo. This is why it is necessary for Christians to get involved in each other's lives, interlace their "roots" and hold each other up during the storms that come along.

❀   ❀   ❀   ❀   ❀

ELEMENT #5: YOUR MINDSET – SPIRITUAL BATTLEMIND
FOR DIVINE HEALING

To conclude this Step, we would like to give you one more prayer assignment. There are certain mindsets that are vital to creating a healing environment. If they are present, you will heal faster; if they're absent, it gets a bit iffy. No one can give them to you – no one but God, that is. If they're not already a part of your personality, or if they got burned out of you in battle, start asking God to supply them for you. It's as simple as asking, "Lord, give me courage." He'll give you what you need for today. But follow Jesus' advice to "Keep on asking" (Matthew 7:7).

COURAGE

Courage is not the absence of fear; it is the making of action in spite of fear.

– Dr. M. Scott Peck, *The Road Less Traveled*

If you are suffering from PTSD, every day can provide a new surge of fearful thoughts that threaten to shut you down and turn you into stone. This condition exists *not* because you are weak or cowardly, but because you are wounded, and your brain is not processing incoming stimuli properly. But with God's help, as He instills you with His courage to act in spite of your fears, you *can* conquer them (more on this in Step 10 in the section entitled *Facing Your Fears*, page 137).

You have problems. Lots of them. Why should *you* feel any reason to be courageous? Because you are vitally connected to the Supreme Problem-Solver of the Universe! And He says to you the same thing He said to Joshua, as he took over leadership of Israel after Moses died:

Have I not commanded you? Be strong and courageous! Do not tremble or be dismayed, for the Lord your God is with you wherever you go.

– Joshua 1:9

God *wants* to give you the courage to take action and become the man or woman that He desires you to become. He intends for your life to *matter*, despite – and possibly because of – the horrors of combat you suffered. He has a legacy in mind for you, but you need to have the courage to reach for it. If you reach, He will be sure you grasp it.

Do not let your fire go out, spark by irreplaceable spark, in the hopeless swamps of the approximate, the not-quite, the not-yet, the not-at-all. Do not let the hero in your soul perish, in lonely frustration for the life you deserved but have never been able to reach. Check your road and the nature of your battle. The world you desired can be won. It exists, it is real, it is possible, it is yours.

– Ayn Rand, Russian-born American novelist and philosopher

Success is never final. Failure is never fatal. It's the courage to continue that counts.

– Winston Churchill

INTENTIONALITY

As we mentioned earlier, your Combat Trauma is a wound. It's causing you pain and crippling you in some ways. Like any wound, you cannot deal with it by ignoring it. If you do, it will only fester and get worse. When you were in combat, you were a man or woman of *action*. You knew it was the only way to stay alive. To be passive could mean death. It's still true today.

Make at least one goal for each day. Combine your courage with your intentionality, and – as that great twentieth century marketing philosopher (Nike) once said – "Just Do It!"

You will miss 100% of the shots you never take.

– Wayne Gretzky, Hockey All-Star

Never grow a wishbone where your backbone ought to be.

– Clementine Paddleford, pilot and writer

When a man does not know what harbor he is heading for, no wind is the right wind.

– Seneca, ancient philosopher

OPTIMISM

Focus on your improvements rather than on your setbacks or stuck-points. You may lie awake at night and accusing thoughts begin to haunt you. "If only I'd done *that*! If only I hadn't done *that*!" With God's help, you can shift gears and begin thinking about the *good* things you did, the *right* decisions, the *positive* accomplishments. Your life might be characterized by "three steps forward, two steps back." So, focus on the cumulative total It doesn't matter how many times a football team is behind during the game – it's the final score that counts. And as the great sports philosopher Yogi Berra said, "It ain't over till it's over." And it ain't over for you. Your story is still being written. God has promised to bring you through this ordeal as a *winner*:

> *And we know that God causes everything to work together for the good of those who love God and are called according to his purpose for them. For God knew His people in advance, and He chose them to become like His Son, so that His Son would be the firstborn among many brothers and sisters. And having chosen them, He called them to come to Him. And having called them, He gave them right standing with Himself. And having given them right standing, He gave them His glory.*

> **– Romans 8:28-30** (NLT)

I am not a failure. I've just found 10,000 ways that won't work.

> –Thomas Edison, who estimates he tried 10,000 different substances before he discovered the lighting element for the incandescent bulb.

Optimist: A man who gets treed by a lion but enjoys the scenery.

> – Walter Winchell, newspaper and radio commentator

Optimism is a force multiplier.

> – General Colin Powell

PRAYER SEED

Thank You for Your provisions for my healing, Father. Thank You for your Holy Spirit and for Your Word. Thank You too for the opportunity to communicate with You any time, any place, through prayer. With the help of Your Holy Spirit, I'll do my best to delight in You, so that my desires will line up with Yours. I have confidence in the wisdom of Your answers to my requests. Thank You that You will say "Yes" to all of my requests that are in line with Your will and in my best interests. Thank You for the gifts You have given to Your body, the church. Sometimes I'm reluctant to break out of my isolation and make contact with them. I've seen that none of them is perfect, by any means. But I know I need their encouragement and support. Lead me to friends who will truly be Your conduits – those I can laugh with, mourn with, and count on through thick and thin. And please build into me those three crucial mindsets: courage, intentionality and optimism. May they reside in me, and help me to be receptive to everything You want to send my way. Amen.

---

[1] From *Evangelism Explosion* by Dr. James Kennedy [Tyndale, 1977], appendix A.
[2] *I am a Rock*, words and music by Paul Simon, from the album *Sounds of Silence*, released Januar, 1996

Step 4: How Did I Change?

Remembering What Happened

These things I remember, and I pour out my soul within me.   **– Psalm 42:4**

Numbness.
Not thinking about what happened.
Putting it out of your mind.
Stuffing it.
Turning it off with alcohol or drugs.

These actions are more comfortable than remembering. Easier. Remembering what happened while you were at war is painful, harder, stress-producing and absolutely no fun at all. So why do it?

Because it's pro-active. It's intentional. It's courageous. It will aid your healing.

When you experienced the horrors of war, your brain slipped into defensive mode in order to keep you alive (see Step 2). Many traumatic events that needed to be processed in your mind were put on the back burner for the time being – things that needed to be thought about, judged, responded to, emoted over, mourned, accepted or rejected, filed away properly. Your right brain took those videos of what was happening, and they're on your hard drive, along with all the soul-ripping emotions that went along with them. But they weren't meant to stay there. They're like computer viruses, disrupting your system at the most inconvenient times, leaking into other compartments of your hard drive and corrupting them. If they aren't discovered, brought out and dealt with, they'll get worse and the whole system will suffer. But if they *are* exposed to the light of God, their power over you can be weakened and removed.

Robert Hicks wrote *Failure To Scream* about the debilitating effect bottled up pain has on PTSD sufferers. What they went through *should* make a person scream in protest, pain, frustration and rage, but instead they stuff it in and don't deal with it. He wrote:

> What we have learned from the Vietnam experience is that denial and silence are not beneficial ways of coping. But talking about it, in some strange way, seems to be therapeutic. Naming and talking about our experiences, no matter how tragic, takes much of their control and power away … Silence and denial, no matter how subtle, only further break the heart and bring no healing to the scream.[1]

Ever had a splinter in your finger? It's not exactly life-threatening. But unless you're willing to do the work and dig it out, exposing it and the infection to the open air, that little thing will become a very big thing in your life, requiring all of your attention.

> *When I kept it all inside,*
> *   my bones turned to powder,*
> *   my words became daylong groans.*   **– Psalm 32:3 (MSG)**

We have no secrets from the all-knowing God. But sometimes, it's like part of our mind is trying to keep a secret from another part. We know what happened – heck, we were *there*. And yet, in some kind of deep, self-defensive, self-anesthetizing maneuver, we try to keep the painful truth from our conscious self – and thereby from the rest of the world. But this maneuver has long outlived its usefulness. As David Grossman, author of *On Killing*, wrote, "You're only as sick as your secrets."[2]

Getting the Secrets Out

God has written your story – you *are* His story. The Bible says, *"For we are God's workmanship, created in Christ Jesus to do good works, which God prepared in advance for us to do"* (Ephesians 2:10 (NIV)). In Greek (the original language of the New Testament) the word for "workmanship" is *poiema*, from which we get our English word "poem." You are a piece of God's creative writing.

"What?!" you might exclaim. "If that's the case, He's a horror-story writer! How could anyone say that God was the author of *my* difficult, confusing, pain-filled life?" God wasn't the author of the evil, as we examined in Step One. But as He wrote your life and saw the waves of evil that would hit you, He factored it all in ahead of time. He knew how He was going to keep you alive, He's planned how He's going restore you, and He's eager to see you walking in strength and confidence once again. He won't erase the pain, but He'll incorporate it into your body, soul and spirit and make you more like Jesus Christ than ever before.

In this Step we are proposing that you undertake a journaling project about your traumatic experience(s) to help with your healing. If you're already a writer-type, you are probably already looking forward to this exercise. If you're not, you're probably dreading it. In either case, you need to see it for what it is: therapeutic *work* – as in: *not play*. There's something about the process of crystallizing thoughts into words and then going through the physical action of putting them down on paper (or on a computer screen) that really helps a person pull out and organize his or her thoughts.

But before we dive in, let us share a few "rules:"

- Before you begin to write, spend a few moments in prayer, asking God to direct your thoughts and your writing. Ask Him to reveal any memories that will be useful in your healing process.

- If this exercise seems especially difficult for you, tell God that He will need to help you with it. He will. *The Lord is near to the brokenhearted and saves those who are crushed in spirit* (Psalm 34:18).

- Spend a few minutes getting relaxed and "centered" – that is, concentrate on eliminating thoughts and concerns that might crowd into your mind and keep you from thinking deeply about your past experiences. Take a few, deep, calming breaths, close your eyes, and let your thoughts drift back to that place and time.

- Imagine you are watching a television show about your traumatic experience.

- Don't get upset if you can't remember all the details. Memory loss is a common symptom of PTSD; so just do your best and don't worry about the rest. It could be that God knows that you're not quite ready to handle certain memories.

- Meditate on and be convinced of the following comforting facts from Dr. Aphrodite Matsakis' *I Can't Get Over It:*[3]

  ➤ You will not die, explode, disintegrate, or cease to function if you dare to remember.

  ➤ Remembering will not result in the memories recurring as real-life events.

  ➤ The memories will eventually diminish in intensity.

  ➤ Safety valve: You can always go back to dissociation, denial, numbing, or whatever methods you used before to keep from remembering. But for now, give this a shot.

- You don't have to try to do this all in one sitting. If you feel overwhelmed, take a break.

- We would like to help you better grasp your trauma – not cause *more* trauma. So if you start experiencing any of the following feelings or urges, it's time to STOP for a while:

  ➤ Faintness

  ➤ Hyperventilation

> ➢ Uncontrollable shivers

> ➢ Irregular heartbeat

> ➢ Losing touch with reality, flashbacks, hallucinations

> ➢ Disoriented, spacey

> ➢ Nausea, diarrhea, unexplainable pains

> ➢ Rage, violent behavior

> ➢ Desire to self-mutilate

> ➢ Thoughts of suicide or homicide

- You may choose to write on paper other than this manual, or on a computer. In doing this, you can later add to what you write today. Your memories of what happened to you will continue to sharpen and expand. Keep writing them down as you think of new things.

- Don't worry about the things your junior high English teach worried about – spelling, punctuation, penmanship, style, etc. Just write. You will not be graded.

- Consider using prompting objects that might help trigger some of your memories, such as photos, objects you carried with you in battle, your uniform, your medals, letters you received while you were there, a souvenir you brought home, music you listened to while there, etc.

- If you just don't think you're up to writing your story, consider recording it on a tape recorder.

❀　❀　❀　❀　❀

WARM UP

Let's start off with a warm-up exercise that doesn't have much to do with your war experience, but *does* have something to do with trauma, helping you connect with your past feelings and remembering how you coped with them before. Think back a few years. Write about one difficult event you experienced when you were in high school. It might have involved the death of a parent, friend, sibling or relative. Maybe your parents divorced, you were assaulted, your house burned down, you were jilted by the love-of-your-life, failing a class … What was it that wounded you so deeply back then?

_____

_____

What were some of the feelings you experienced during and after that episode?

_____

_____

What helped you deal with that event and the feelings it evoked?

_____

_____

How did that event help to make you the person you are today (a *positive* observation)?

_____

_____

A Long-Delayed Debriefing

In the past twenty-five years or so, we've learned a great deal about recovering from traumatic stress – whether we're talking about emergency workers after a catastrophe, rape victims, combat veterans, crash survivors – anyone. Two of the breakthroughs that just about all experts are agreed upon are (1) the victim needs to remember and talk about what they experienced, and (2) the sooner the better. As PTSD authority Patience Mason writes:

> "Today in many communities, after a crisis all the rescue workers are debriefed. They get to talk about what happened, what they saw, smelled, heard, felt, what they wanted to have happen and how it all turned out. Debriefing is what trauma work is about. You *don't* have to know every detail or relive every moment of trauma. As you talk [or write] about what happened to you and feel the feelings you had to suppress in order to live, you will relearn the broad variety of human feelings, because they have all been suppressed along with the painful ones. Recovery will help you understand yourself and be understood. This is a very healing experience for people who have felt like no one could ever understand what they have been through."[1]

The goal nowadays is that the trauma victim would experience this debriefing within seventy-two hours of their traumatic event. Well, for most of you reading this manual, that seventy-two hours is long gone. This makes the processing of your trauma a bit more difficult, but by *no means* impossible! With God's help, anything can be accomplished. Trust the Lord, and trust the process.

❋ ❋ ❋ ❋ ❋

Writing Your Story

This exercise will have three parts. Each part is crucial to the recounting of your story, so don't skip any of it! In **Part 1**, we'd like you to spend some time writing about what life was like before you went to war. Read over the following questions[2] to jog your thinking about what to write (don't attempt to answer *all* of them – just the ones that prompt your thinking):

- Where were you brought up?
- What did you look like?
- What did you enjoy most when you were young? What made you happy?
- How did you get along with your family?
- What was your biggest struggle then?
- What were your friends like?
- What did you like or not like about yourself?
- What did you believe about God then?
- What were you realistic about? Naïve about?
- What were your goals or dreams for yourself then?
- Can you think of a "theme" word or sentence for your life before combat?

Part 1: My Life Before Combat

[We encourage you to use additional paper if necessary – and we hope you do!]

That wasn't too difficult, was it? But now, **Part 2** will be a little more dicey. In this assignment, we want you to write about your traumatic experience – or experiences – in combat. If you're like most combat vets, you probably have many incidents that contributed to your current condition. Write about a few of the most painful. Or it could simply be that your entire deployment eventually wore you down, and you can't put your finger on a single causative incident. The accumulation of minor events over a long period of time can add up to a mountain of pain. Just describe how and when your PTSD symptoms began to bother you, how you responded, and how they built. As you write, your insights and associated emotions will follow.

In your writing, don't just recount the facts of the incident(s). Let your mind go back and remember the sensual and emotional details as well. What did you smell? What did you hear? What did you taste? Describe the heat, cold, sand. How did the experiences make you feel? What were your emotional reactions to the trauma? Dr. Aphrodite Matsakis writes about the necessity of "feeling" to your recovery:[1]

> For you to heal completely, the trauma must be reworked not only on the mental level, but on the emotional level as well. This necessitates two further processes:
>
> - First, the feelings generated by the trauma that were not felt at the time need to be identified.
>
> - Second, and more difficult, the feelings must be experienced, at least in part, on a gut level.
>
> The feelings trauma generates are perhaps the most powerful feelings known to human beings, among them fear, anger, grief and guilt. If you think you don't have these feelings, think again. Do you still have PTSD symptoms? Are you struggling with an addiction? Do you have headaches, backaches, stomach problems or other physical symptoms of unexplained origin?
>
> If so, this suggests that even though you may not want to deal with your feelings, your feelings are dealing with you.

You and your feelings need to get to know each other again. After the nation of Israel had been conquered by the Babylonians and taken in chains to Babylon (present day Iraq, by the way), their emotions were obviously quite high. But they didn't hold back experiencing and expressing them through their weeping, lethargy and their writing of this lament:

> *Beside the rivers of Babylon, we sat and wept*
> *   as we thought of Jerusalem.*
> *We put away our harps,*
> *   hanging them on the branches of poplar trees.*
> *For our captors demanded a song from us.*
> *   Our tormentors insisted on a joyful hymn:*
> *   "Sing us one of those songs of Jerusalem!"*

– Psalm 137:1-3 (NLT)

❈   ❈   ❈   ❈   ❈

As we mentioned, this won't be easy. Emotions that emerge due to loss or trauma are seldom pleasant. It will be uncomfortable and may even be painful. This is why you are to be *commended* for your willingness to do this hard work. You have made many sacrifices up to this point and we're asking you to make yet another one. But this sacrifice will be for your own sake, for your family, for your friends and for the sake of the Kingdom of God. Don't complete this writing exercise just because it was "assigned." Take it to heart and do it because of how it's going to help you. You'll get out of it only what you put into it.

PART 2: WHAT HAPPENED TO ME "OVER THERE"

[Again, you are encouraged to use additional paper if necessary.]

Sometimes remembering – especially remembering our periods of crisis – can be painful, but it is an emotionally corrective experience, like setting a bone. Feel like someone just wrenched your emotional femur? It's understandable, expected and normal. Sorry to put you through that. But as any orthopedic surgeon will tell you, there'll be no healing without the pain.

Part 3 shouldn't be as difficult. In this section, we would like for you to write a realistic account of your life at present – both the good stuff and the bad. You may be pretty satisfied with your current situation, if so, write down why. On the other hand, if you're suffering from PTSD, your life probably isn't exactly a sweet stroll down a rose-strewn path. Be open and honest – not only about the facts concerning your current status, but *also how you feel about them*. Here are some questions that we hope will stimulate your thinking:

- In what ways are you different from your pre-war self?

- What kind of work are you doing now, if any? Is this work satisfying or frustrating? Is it what you expected to be doing?

- How is your relationship with your spouse or significant other? Your children? Parents? Siblings?

- How is your relationship with your non-military pre-war friends?

- Do you still have contact with your battle buddies? If so, how is it when you get together?

- Have there been any incidents that really capture your current level of frustration, anger and pain since you returned from war?

- What are your most frustrating symptoms?

- What triggers you and what happens when you are triggered? How often does it happen?

- What makes you want to weep, pound the table, kick the wall?

- What is the significance of your combat experience to you?

- How different is your life now than how you thought it would be when you first joined the military? How does that make you feel?

- What are some *positive* things that are in your life at present? What gives you joy, hope, energy? What's fun? What do you look forward to doing?

Again, don't try to answer *all* the questions, just the ones you feel motivated to write about. But we *would* like for you to include that last item above for sure.

PART 3: MY LIFE SINCE COMBAT

[Please use additional paper as necessary.]

WHY?

Why have we done this exercise? Remember in Step 2 when we explained that traumatic soul wounds are "episodic memories" – very negative ones, in dire need of processing and integration into our lives, values, beliefs and sense of well-being? The process of healing these memories – and the subsequent reactions and symptoms that surface when they are accessed – involves experiencing them once again in a *safe* environment, and then bringing Jesus Christ into that traumatic event. As you experience this more powerful episode, it overpowers the fear-based, pain-filled memories and opens the door for God's healing to occur. Additionally, if there are spiritual forces at work binding you to that trauma and keeping you from experiencing victory, Christ's presence will break their hold. We'll talk more about that in Step 8: *How Do I Fight?* in the section on "open doors" and "footholds" (pages 112-114).

Battle buddy. Another element that can contribute to the overall therapeutic value of this exercise is to share it with a battle buddy – someone you trust, who understands you, and who wants to support you in your struggles. In Step 9, we refer to these people as "bridge people," because they are helping to bridge the gap between you and your Healer. You may want to have him or her right there with you as you are remembering and writing, or you may want to share what you wrote with them later. By sharing your traumatic events with a trusted companion, you're entering into yet another positive episodic experience which will aid your healing process.

INVITING JESUS INTO YOUR PAIN

Jesus Christ wants access to every area of your life – not to impose Himself and dominate you, but to bring healing and victory. Like a patrol in Fallujah searching from house to house, checking every nook, cranny and shadow for terrorists, He wants to enter even your darkest, most ominous corners in order to conquer the foes lurking there – whether they are physiological, psychological, philosophical or real spiritual entities.

> *He uncovers deep things out of darkness,*
> *And brings the shadow of death to light.*   **– Job 12:22** (NKJV)

This exercise was designed to help you remember and visualize – perhaps deeper than you have ever done before – the trauma you experienced. We know it was probably painful and stirred up a lot of emotions in you. As we've emphasized before, that's not all bad. This would be a perfect time for you to talk with God about how you feel right now, how you felt about what happened to you, and what you would like for Him to do for you. This would be a good time for you to bring Jesus into those dim, shadowy areas of your story, so that He might spotlight your enemies and bring His healing light to bear.

> *Even the darkness is not dark to You,*
> *And the night is as bright as the day.*
> *Darkness and light are alike to You.*   **– Psalm 139:12**

When you experienced your traumatic events, you were surrounded by chaos. In all likelihood, you thought you were about to die and it was difficult for you to think rationally. Your brain would allow you to think of only one thing: staying alive. You probably had no thought about where God was in the midst of the storm you were experiencing – but Jesus Christ was there, right at your side. Take a few moments alone and invite Him into your pain – He's not afraid of it. Ask Him to open your eyes, ears, heart and mind. Then visualize what you wrote in Part 2 above, and *see Him there.*

- Where is He standing?
- Where is He looking?
- What do you see Him doing?
- Is He touching you?

- Is He saying anything to you? Can you hear anything else?
- Is He giving you any smells or tastes?
- What does He want you to do?

He reveals deep and hidden things;
He knows what lies in darkness,
And light dwells with Him.

– Daniel 2:22 (NIV)

❀　❀　❀　❀　❀

This is a spiritual exercise that you should engage in frequently, if you're up to it. It requires courage, intentionality and optimism. It also requires practice. You may or may not have "seen" Jesus very vividly on your first attempt at this, but as you develop your spiritual muscles, you will experience a stronger connection with Him. Don't neglect the principles we shared in Steps 3A and 3B. They form the foundation for your deepening relationship with Him. And never forget that it is indeed a *relationship*. The story God is writing about you not only says that you know *about* Him, but that you *know Him*. You can know Him as deeply as the Apostle Paul did, in His power and glory as well as in His agony – which He has shared with you:

> *For my determined purpose is that I may know Him; that I may progressively become more deeply and intimately acquainted with Him, perceiving and recognizing and understanding the wonders of His Person more strongly and more clearly, and that I may in that same way come to know the power outflowing from His resurrection which it exerts over believers, and that I may so share His sufferings as to be continually transformed in spirit into His likeness even to His death.*

– Philippians 3:10 (AMP)

❀　❀　❀　❀　❀

PRAYER SEED

Father, what I experienced in combat was more than anyone should have to endure. It's affecting me still today. I don't know everything that went on during my episodes of life-threatening chaos – so much of it is a blur. But I do know by faith that You were there with me. You kept me alive for a reason. You protected me and brought me back home. Jesus, You know what it's like to experience pain, anguish, fear, torture, abandonment and death – at depths even lower than I can imagine. I sense Your brotherhood in that. Nothing I experienced, nothing I did could ever surprise You. I want to bring You into those dark and painful chapters of my story – past and present. Help me open those doors for You. Shine the light of Your presence into those black, horrendous places, and set me free. Amen.

❀　❀　❀

---

[1] Robert Hicks, *Failure To Scream*, p. 60-61.
[2] From Patience Mason's article "David Grossman: On Killing" in The Post-Traumatic Gazette (www.patiencepress.com), Vol. 4, No. 4 (Nov/Dec 1998).
[3] Dr. Aphrodite Matsakis, *I Can't Get Over It*, p. 154,155. Many of the principles in this section come from Matsakis' excellent book, pages 153 to 179.
[4] Patience Mason, The Post-Traumatic Gazette (www.patiencepress.com), Issue 1 (May/June 1995).
[5] Some of the questions taken from Dr. H. Norman Wright, *The New Guide to Crisis and Trauma Counseling*, p. 234.
[6] Dr. Aphrodite Matsakis, *I Can't Get Over It*, p. 168.

STEP 5: HOW CAN I STAND IT?

PROCESSING YOUR LOSS AND GRIEF

Resurrection is preceded by a violent death and a season in the grave.

Having been in war, you know something about violent death. So does Jesus – His was among the most violent ever. If you're reading this, odds are good that you have not personally died a violent death … or have you? Though your body is still functioning, there may be parts of your being that feel *real* dead. And it feels like they were killed violently. The gravestone has "PTSD" on it. And you are experiencing your season in the grave right now.

But there is hope. There is a *resurrection* scheduled for you. As Tony Campolo says, referring to the days of Jesus' crucifixion and resurrection: "It's Friday, but Sunday's coming!"

UNDERSTANDING GRIEF

"Chaplain Ray" Giunta writes: "Grief is the normal process of natural emotions and feelings which are uniquely experienced after any loss of any relationship."[1] Please note carefully the first characteristic listed: it is *normal*. It's built into us. God invented it. God experienced it. *Everybody* experiences it.

The word "grief" comes from the Latin verb meaning "to burden." That's exactly what grief feels like, doesn't it? A heavy load that you wish you could set down – but you can't.

Grief is always triggered by a **loss** of some sort – losing someone or something we had an attachment to. Grief has different levels and intensities. We grieve a little when our favorite shirt is ruined and we have to throw it away. We grieve a little more when our favorite team has its hopes dashed for championship glory. More profound grief comes when a beloved pet dies, when a cherished relationship ends, when dreams we've held for our futures evaporate, or when someone we love passes on.

But, as grief and trauma counselor Dr. H. Norman Wright tells us "Loss is not the enemy. Not facing its existence is."[2] Loss is the fuse that triggers the bomb. The loss has irretrievably passed – now comes the process of dealing with the crater that's left.

> Grief is neither a problem to be solved nor a problem to be overcome. It is a sacred expression of love … a sacred sorrow.
> — Dr. Gerald May, M.D.[3]

Name your loss. You have suffered many losses throughout your life – as we all have. But your time in combat likely brought about some new "lifetime lows" which you may have found difficult to deal with. In Step 4, you invested some hard work putting into words what happened to you. For this exercise, narrow your focus a bit, and write about what you *lost*, specifically. You could write about physical injuries that resulted in lost capabilities, lost friends, ambitions, dreams, self-identity, faith, love … whatever comes to your mind. By naming your loss, you'll be better able to accomplish the difficult work of grieving over it.

The Purpose of Grief

God built the grief response into us for the purpose of mentally, emotionally and spiritually *processing* loss-producing events, integrating those events into our altered world, and helping us move on to a state of greater strength, resourcefulness, resilience and faith. If we are not willing to face the grieving process, or if we try a short-cut, we're left adrift in our sea of pain, never reaching the shores of strengthening that the Lord intends for us.

As drill instructors love to mention to new recruits, "Pain is simply weakness leaving the body!" In a similar fashion, "Tears are a way God has provided for sadness to leave our body."[4] If we resist this mechanism, our sorrow may never lose its intensity.

When we grieve:

- We're authentically engaging the emotions that come with loss – rather than stuffing or denying them. As many grief experts say, "You can't heal what you can't feel."

- We're protesting the injustice of the loss, which we are truly convinced of – rather than acting like it was OK with us.

- We're expressing that we deeply wish that the loss had never occurred – rather than minimizing it.

- We're facing the devastating impact of the loss head on, absorbing it and eventually mastering it – rather than running from it, deflecting it or pretending it didn't happen, only to have its effects hit us again and again.

- We are allowing our right brain to replay the tapes of our traumatic episodic memories in a safe environment, thereby robbing them of their terror and integrating them into our rebuilding life.

- We're inviting Jesus to enter the dark forest of our pain, experience it with us, comfort us in the midst of it and walk us out the other side of it – rather than sitting passively alone and paralyzed at the edge.

When we refuse to grieve:

- Unresolved grief has been found to be a factor in the development of a wide range of psychological problems, including outbursts of rage, restlessness, depression, addiction, compulsion, anxiety and panic disorders.

- Unexpressed grief has been linked to the development or worsening of medical problems such as diabetes, heart disease, hypertension, cancer, asthma and a variety of allergies, rashes, aches and pains.[5]

- We are at odds with our body's built-in physiological processes to deal with a traumatic event.

- We are at odds with God's spiritual intentions to meet us in the midst of the fire of our trauma, missing out on His plans to deepen our faith and strengthen our relationship with Him.

What You Can Expect To Experience – "Normal" Grief

C.S. Lewis, one of the greatest Christian philosophers and teachers of the past century, had his own trek through the dark forest after his beloved wife Joy died of cancer. He kept a journal for many months after her death, and in it wrote the following:

> Grief still feels like fear. Perhaps, more strictly, like suspense. Or like waiting; just hanging about waiting for something to happen. It gives life a permanently provisional feeling. It doesn't seem worth starting anything. I can't settle down. I yawn, I fidget, I smoke too much. Up till this I always had too little time. Now there is nothing but time. Almost pure time, empty successiveness.[6]

As you read through the following list of symptoms, check any that you are experiencing.

❑ **Fear.** You may fear that your loss will occur again, that you won't be able to care for yourself, that you'll be alone, that your friends will reject you. If your loss involves the death of someone you were close to, you may have fears about where they are. You may fear that your current level of pain won't improve.

❑ **Anger.** It doesn't have to be logical. You could be mad at yourself, your circumstances, your friend who died, your CO who ordered you into battle, at God for allowing your trauma, the paperboy for bringing more bad news from the front, your neighbor for being intrusively helpful and caring. Your anger might always be seething just below the surface.

❑ **Rage.** You may yell, scream, slam doors, kick the trash can, kick the dog, punch the wall, punch your best friend, throw things, yank things off walls or out of the ground. Sometimes you feel better afterwards. Sometimes you don't.

❑ **Weeping.** You may cry. Then cry some more. And more. And just when you think you couldn't possibly have any more tears to cry, you cry some more. You may wail, scream, or just sit in a chair with your tears flooding down your shirt.

❑ **Guilt.** *If only I'd... What if... I should have...* Hindsight and Monday-morning quarter-backing could occupy all your thoughts for a while. You may blame yourself for what happened, even though you didn't cause it and couldn't do a thing about it.

❑ **Loneliness.** You may feel that no one can understand what you're going through now – and that no one wants to, either. People may indeed avoid you for a while – not because they don't hurt deeply for you, but because they just don't know what to do or say. So they choose the typical default setting: nothing.

❑ **Blaming.** *This is so unfair! Where's the justice? Who's going to pay for this? Somebody has to be held accountable!*

❑ **Running away/numbing.** You may look desperately for an escape hatch. *There must be a way out of this!* You may try drugs, alcohol, work, travel, ministry, sex, food, shopping – anything to get you away from your difficult environment.

❑ **Loss of appetite**	❑ **Feeling abandoned**
❑ **Loss of sexual desire**	❑ **Frustrated**
❑ **Dehydration**	❑ **Overly talkative**
❑ **Memory lags, mental short-circuits**	❑ **No desire to talk**
❑ **Unexplained aches and pains**	❑ **Feeling out of control**
❑ **Sleepiness, fatigue, lethargy**	❑ **Emotionally overloaded**
❑ **Sleeplessness**	❑ **No feelings at all**
❑ **Nightmares**	❑ **Others?**
❑ **Hyperactivity**	

This might sound strange to you, but the more boxes you checked, the better! It means that you are more fully engaging your grief. If you could only check a few of them you might be either denying your grief or deferring it – putting it off until later (of course, one other possibility is that you've already worked through a lot of your grief issues – if so, great!). In any case, healthy grieving will involve a number of the above symptoms simultaneously. If they persist for a long, long time (many months or years) it means something has "hung up" the process. But for now, it's *OK!* What you feel is normal and you need to welcome these feelings, not try to fend them off!

WHAT ABOUT "LOSS OF FAITH?"

In Step 1, we examined the question of how a loving, all-powerful God could allow His creatures to experience so much pain. A person may know the answer to that question. And yet, when your world is crashing around you, and you're one, huge tangled ball of emotions, excellent theology isn't always the greatest comfort. It's a pretty common response, based on a common assumption. As psychologist, counselor and educator Dr. Larry Crabb writes in his book *Shattered Dreams:*

> In our shallow, sensual way of looking at life, we tend to measure God's Presence by the kind of emotion we feel. Happy feelings that make us want to sing, we assume, are evidence that God's Spirit is present. We think a sense of lostness or confusion or struggle indicates His absence.[7]

Consider the paragraph written below by C.S. Lewis not long after his wife died. He didn't hesitate to communicate his disappointment with God as he tried to come to grips with the most shattering grief of his life:

> Meanwhile, where is God? … Go to Him when your need is desperate, when all other help is vain, and what do you find? A door slammed in your face, and a sound of bolting and double-bolting on the inside. After that, silence. You may as well turn away. The longer you wait, the more emphatic the silence will become. There are no lights in the windows. It might be an empty house. Was it ever inhabited? It seemed so once.[8]

❋   ❋   ❋   ❋   ❋

How closely can you identify with Lewis' "crisis of faith" expressed above?

_____

_____

_____

❋   ❋   ❋   ❋   ❋

C. S. Lewis' crisis didn't last forever. By the end of his journal, we read how he had come out the other side of the dark forest, with more clarity, more love, and stronger faith than ever before:

> Turned to God, my mind no longer meets that locked door; turned to Joy, it no longer meets that vacuum … There was no sudden, striking, and emotional transition. Like the warming of a room or the coming of daylight. When you first notice them they have already been going on for some time.[9]

God's secret work. As Dr. Larry Crabb has written: "When God seems most absent from us, He is doing His most important work in us. He vanishes from our sight to do what He could not do if we could see Him clearly."[10]

Remember when Jesus Christ hung on the cross, and cried out to His heavenly Father in confusion and despair, "My God! My God! Where are you?" God was silent. But it was at that exact moment that God the Father was closing the transaction that was the *number one reason* the Son had come to earth – reckoning His death as payment for our sins. And this is what brought Jesus the greatest joy of His eternal existence![11]

Pastor Ron Mehl describes what God is doing in your life while He seems absent:

> God is aware of your circumstances and moves among them.
> God is aware of your pain and monitors every second of it.
> God is aware of your emptiness and seeks to fill it in a manner beyond your dreams.

God is aware of your wounds and scars and knows how to draw forth a healing
    deeper than you can imagine.
Even when your situation seems out of control.
Even when you feel alone and afraid.
God works the night shift.[12]

WHAT YOU CAN EXPECT FROM OTHERS

When you have experienced a great trauma or loss and your grief is assumed and evident to all those around, you will be treated differently for a while. This is to be expected – but some treatment we receive is helpful and some we could do without. As C.S. Lewis expressed in his journal, "Perhaps the bereaved ought to be isolated in special settlements like lepers."[13]

The less-than-helpful things. Especially in the Western world, social taboos have been invented that make us try to avoid or deny any discomfort from loss. We look with disdain at the outpouring of grief in other cultures and accuse them of "lack of control." We don't realize that *we* are the foolish ones, holding in something that would better be let out.

But it's important to remember that your friends mean well. Their insensitivity is not because they intend to hurt you or prolong your grief – it's just that they're uninformed about what to do and how to help. When the following comments are shared, it's best to see the good hearts behind them. Smile if you can, say thanks and move on. But *don't follow their advice!* Check the ones you've heard…

- ❑ You need to put it behind you. Time to move on.
- ❑ Don't dwell in the past.
- ❑ You just need a good distraction.
- ❑ Think happy thoughts!
- ❑ Haven't you prayed about this yet?
- ❑ Don't "cave in" to your sorrow. Keep a stiff upper lip!
- ❑ You should be over this by now.
- ❑ What would Jesus do? (Counseling by cliché.)
- ❑ It's not as bad as it seems.
- ❑ Keep a grip on your emotions. Don't cry in front of *anyone*.
- ❑ Since you're a Christian, you shouldn't be grieving. Don't you know that God works everything out for the good?
- ❑ You'll feel better tomorrow.
- ❑ Hey! How 'bout those Seahawks? (In other words, let's talk about anything else but your grief.)
- ❑ Be strong for your kids – don't let them see you cry.
- ❑ How are you? (But they don't *really* want you to tell them too much.)
- ❑ You think *that's* bad? Let me tell you what happened to *me*.
- ❑ If you just had a little more faith, this wouldn't seem so bad.

The helpful things. There are going to be a few of your friends who are wise in the ways of grief – either because they've experienced it themselves, have been trained, are particularly intuitive or have read a lot of books! When you find these people, do whatever it takes to keep them around!

- When they ask, "How are you?" they really want to know, and they stick around for the answer.
- They're willing to give you their time, available when you need them.
- They'll sacrifice for you.
- They take the initiative with you; they reach out to you by calling you up, asking you out, including you in their lives.
- They're good listeners, non-judgmental, won't interrupt you to talk about themselves.
- They find out what you need and then go get it for you.

- They'll pray *for* you and pray *with* you.
- They won't mind if you cry, in fact they'll end up crying with you.
- They've got your back.

❋ ❋ ❋ ❋ ❋

 Who do you have in your circle of friends like this?

_____

_____

Prayer Assignment: If you can't think of anyone, start asking God to send someone like this to you or to open your eyes to a current acquaintance who can be that kind of a friend. Make this request of Him daily – keep on knocking![14]

❋ ❋ ❋ ❋ ❋

HOW NOT TO GRIEVE

We humans will sometimes do *anything* rather than to undertake the hard work of grief – then think we're accomplishing something. These actions may make us feel a little better temporarily, but it doesn't move us out of our despairing state. Following is a list of ways people attempt to cope with their situation without actually facing their grief – check any that you think you might do from time to time.[15]

- ❑ **Act out** – giving in to the pressure to misbehave.
- ❑ **Aim low** – to what seems more achievable.
- ❑ **Attack** – beat down what's threatening you.
- ❑ **Avoid** – stay away from anything that causes you stress.
- ❑ **Compensate** – make up for weakness in one area by gaining strength in another.
- ❑ **Deny** – refusing to acknowledge that the event occurred.
- ❑ **Displace** – shifting an intended action to a safer target (like kicking the dog).
- ❑ **Fantasize** – escaping reality to a world of unachievable wishes.
- ❑ **Idealize** – playing up the good points of a desired action and ignoring downsides.
- ❑ **Identify** – copying others to take on their desirable characteristics.
- ❑ **Intellectualize** – avoiding emotions by focusing on facts and logic.
- ❑ **Passive aggression** – getting your way by passive avoidance.
- ❑ **Project** – seeing your own undesirable characteristics in others.
- ❑ **Rationalize** – creating logical reasons for bad behavior.
- ❑ **Regress** – returning to a child state to avoid problems or responsibility.
- ❑ **Suppress** – consciously holding back unwanted urges while ignoring the root cause.
- ❑ **Trivialize** – making something small when it is really something big.

If you recognize any of these behavior patterns in yourself, you first need to see them for what they are: hoped-for shortcuts to restoration which won't get you there at all. **Suggestion**: show this list to a friend and ask them if they see you engaging in any of these behaviors. But don't "act out" and punch him if he or she notices some. He may end up "displacing" you.

Then, make it a matter of prayer. Ask God to help you realize when you're avoiding your grief work by falling into these habits, and to help you partner with Him in the process.

❋ ❋ ❋ ❋ ❋

HOW TO GRIEVE

Be aware of the process. It is a process, for sure. But it's not a *precise* process. Everyone will process their grief a bit differently than the next person. However, there are some generalized descriptions that are useful – kind of like milestones along a journey – to let you know that you are making progress. Or not.

Elizabeth Kübler-Ross was a Swiss physician who did groundbreaking research in the area of grief. Her book *On Death and Dying* has been a classic for decades. In her studies she found that there is a pattern that most people experience when they encounter a life changing trauma or crisis.

This cycle of emotional states is shown on the chart below. It demonstrates the roller-coaster ride of activity and passivity as the hurting person wriggles and dodges in their desperate efforts to cope with the trauma, avoid change and finally be reconciled to it.

The person starts out in a state of relative stability and then the bomb goes off. Over unspecified periods of time, he or she progresses through these stages:

- **Immobilization stage** – Shock; initial paralysis after being exposed to the crisis or trauma. It takes a while for the enormity to register and sink in. Jaw drops, breath catches, can't decide what to do next.

- **Denial stage** – Trying to avoid the inevitable. *No! This can't be happening!* Or, *It didn't affect me; it wasn't that bad.* Or even, *It never happened. You just imagined it.*

- **Anger stage** – Frustrated outpouring of bottled-up emotion. *Life sucks!!* Rage seething below the surface at all times; lashing out at anyone for the slightest reason; blaming others; sometimes cold, icy anger; self-isolating to avoid blowing up.

- **Bargaining stage** – Seeking in vain for a way out. Making promises to God if He'll fix things; setting conditions for healing, like: *When we pull out of Iraq and all my men are home, then I'll get well.*

- **Depression stage** – Final realization of the inevitable. A very sad time, but also the turning point, because the griever is finally resolved to the fact that he or she won't be able to restore life to the way it was. It's the staging area for victory.

- **Testing stage** – Seeking realistic solutions. *Maybe I should try getting out more. Maybe I should talk with someone about my situation. Maybe I should start exercising again. Maybe I should join that Bible study I heard about.*

- **Acceptance stage** – Finally finding the way forward. They are now fully acknowledging the trauma or crisis. *It was bad – real bad – but I survived. I'm going to make it. My world changed, but I can live in this new world. I could even prosper.*

THE KÜBLER-ROSS GRIEF CYCLE:

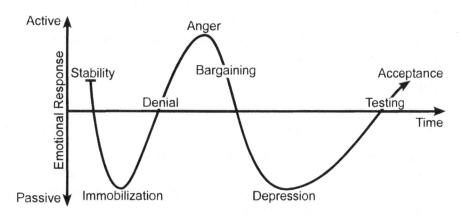

71

After you have read the descriptions of the above stages, think about where you might presently be in the Grief Cycle, and place an "X" on the appropriate place on the line. Two questions: How do you feel about where you are in the process currently? What do you think it's going to take to move you beyond your present stage?

_____

_____

_____

_____

_____

❀   ❀   ❀   ❀   ❀

A few words about the process. As mentioned before, it's not precise. You may not hit all of these stages. You may skip a stage and then go back to experience it later. You may whiz through one stage and sit in another stage for a long time. You may find yourself going back and forth between a couple of stages, or looping around to various stages willy-nilly. No one can say for sure how you will deal with your unique trauma, given your unique wiring.

Therefore, don't give in to the temptation to compare your grief process with someone else's. If you will keep your connections with God strong during this process, He will take you through it in a way that will maximize every stage and bring you through to the final stage as soon as possible.

How long will it take? Honestly, probably a lot longer than you'll like. In fact, if the trauma you experienced is severe enough, the grief will always be there. It won't be dominating your life like it currently is, but there will always be that hole where the lost person or thing or dream used to be. That ache won't go away. But that's not all bad – consider it a memorial to the depth of the love, attachment and value it (or they) held before the loss. And God will use it.

> *Blessed be the God and Father of our Lord Jesus Christ, the Father of mercies and God of all comfort, who comforts us in all our affliction so that we will be able to comfort those who are in any affliction with the comfort with which we ourselves are comforted by God.*
>
> **– 2 Corinthians 1:3,4**

❀   ❀   ❀   ❀   ❀

HOW TO HAVE A GOOD MOURNING

> *Blessed are those who mourn, for they shall be comforted.*   **– Matthew 5:4**

When we've experienced a traumatic event, grief is what we *feel*. Mourning is *what we do about it*. It is the action side of grief, the externalizing of our internal pain. And Jesus Christ – who knows *everything* – says that when we do it we are blessed and *will be* comforted. Here are a few principles to keep in mind as your work out your grief through mourning.

REMEMBER WHERE GOD IS

> *The Lord is near to the brokenhearted*
> *And saves those who are crushed in spirit.*   **– Psalm 34:18**

Because of your wound, you hold a special attraction to the Lord. You've got His attention. He is a compassionate God, always pulling for the underdog, ready to aid anyone who will let Him. *Count on that!* You can expect Him to be present and responsive to your needs during this time. He is like your best friend who says, "If you need anything, don't hesitate to ask!" And He means it.

Ask Jesus to enter your pain with you. Close your eyes and feel Him coming up behind you, wrapping His big arms around you and holding on tight. Let Him pull the pain out of your body, soul and spirit into His.

REMEMBER THE PAST AND REMAIN OPTIMISTIC

> How hopeless the naked wood of a fruit tree would look to us in February
> if we had never seen the marvel of springtime.

> – Lilias Trotter[16]

Though what you are currently enduring may be the worst experience you've ever had to slog your way through, it's not the *only* trauma you've known. Think back to all the times God has sustained you in the past. As Elisabeth Elliot wrote, whose missionary husband was murdered by primitive natives in Ecuador, "The death of wintertime is the necessary prelude to the resurrection of springtime."[17] Spring will come – as it always has for you.

We can make a distinction between the cliché, "Think happy thoughts!" and the admonition from the Apostle Paul to keep our minds focused on positive things:

> *Finally, brethren, whatever things are true, whatever things are noble, whatever things are just, whatever things are pure, whatever things are lovely, whatever things are of good report, if there is any virtue and if there is anything praiseworthy—meditate on these things.*

> **– Philippians 4:8** (NKJV)

AIM STEADILY AT FAITH'S TARGET

Ask yourself this question: "What do I have faith in?" How did you answer? Assuming you didn't say, "Nothing," perhaps it was like one of these:

- "That God will bring me out of this depression."
- "That my leg will heal."
- "That my husband won't leave me."
- "That I could quit drinking so much."
- "That I can get past my anger."

These are all great faith *goals* and excellent requests to make to God, but they aren't what you put your faith in. If you do – and they don't come about – what happens to your faith? The only answer to the question, "What do I have faith in?" should be "God." Whenever we tie our faith to our circumstances or to a particular desire, we take God off the throne of our life and set ourselves up for great disappointment. We are *lousy* at playing God! David Shepherd is a man of God who had suffered great setbacks when he wrote this letter to his friend Larry Crabb:

> Faith, as I am growing to understand it more, is about looking beyond my circumstances to a Person. To have faith in better circumstances, even in God creating better circumstances, is not true faith. I want to be the kind of man who can watch every dream go down in flames and still yearn to be intimately involved in kingdom living, intimately involved with my friend the King, and still be willing to take another risk just because it delights Him for me to do so. And my flesh shivers to think about it.[18]

As Thomas Merton wrote: "The real hope is not in something we think we can do, but in God, who is making something good out of it in some way we cannot see."[19] The essence of mature faith is to boldly express our fervent desires to God, and then leave them in His wise and benevolent hands – no matter what. He'll always do what's best.

DON'T TRY TO BE THE LONE RANGER

Grief is hard on a person and mourning is difficult work. Effective grief work is not done alone. Don't try to be the pillar of strength to everyone around you. You'll crumble. Be sure to find a few people that you know you can count on to be there for you when you need them. As Dr. Harold Ivan Smith, death and grief expert writes:

> Grievers cannot extricate themselves from their cistern called grief. They need a rope   Grievers need someone on the other end to pull. But they really need individuals to pad the ropes – not with pat answers or spiritual clichés or even Scripture promises but with hope.[20]

DO SOMETHING WITH YOUR ANGER

When anger is bottled up indefinitely, it morphs into bitterness. And, as we learned earlier, that bitterness will spread beyond the borders of your life. It's OK to be angry. It is a normal, reasonable emotion when we are confronted with unjust, hurtful or grievous events. It is recorded in the Bible that Jesus Himself became angry on a few occasions (Mark 3:1-5; Mark 10:14; John 2:13-16). But it's what we *do* with that anger that can lead to sin.

The Bible says in Ephesians 4:26 (NIV) ,"In your anger do not sin." When you feel the anger rising up within you, first remove yourself from the physical cause of your anger if you can (i.e., if it's a person, leave the room; a locational trigger, go somewhere else). It's like removing fuel from the fire. No fuel, no fire. Go out for a run; go to the gym and pound the heavy bag for a while; lift weights; dig a garden; chop down a tree; plant a tree; swim a few hundred laps. Or if you're able, do something truly constructive: go help someone who needs it; build something; go down to the church and see if they need help with anything.

 Plan ahead. What are some specific things you can do the next time you become angry?

GO WITH THE FLOW (OF TEARS)

Men normally find this harder than women, because – as many wives would testify – they tend to be right-brain-challenged! They seem to be reluctant to engage the strong emotions associated with grief. It has a lot to do with our society's programming: "Big boys don't cry." Maybe not – but big men *should* when it comes to grief.

King David beat a 9'8" giant in a fair fight, killed a lion and a bear in hand-to-hand combat as a boy, and collected the foreskins of two hundred Philistines as a dowry for his bride. He had a man under his command who single-handedly killed eight hundred men in one battle (that's in the days before automatic weapons, by the way); another who successfully defended a strategic position against the entire Philistine army; another who killed three hundred men in one battle with a *spear.* And David was *their boss.* We can rightfully assume he was "all man."

And yet, David did not hesitate to fully engage his emotions during times of grief:

> *I am worn out from groaning; all night long I flood my bed with weeping and drench my couch with tears.*   – **Psalm 6:6** (NIV)

> *I went about mourning as though for my friend or brother. I bowed my head in grief as though weeping for my mother.*   – **Psalm 35:14** (NIV)

I am exhausted from crying for help; my throat is parched. My eyes are swollen with weeping, waiting for my God to help me.   **– Psalm 69:3 (NLT)**

For I have eaten ashes like bread, and mingled my drink with weeping.   **– Psalm 102:9**

My soul weeps because of grief; strengthen me according to Your word. **– Psalm 119:28**

KEEP A GRIEF JOURNAL

Crisis care authority "Chaplain Ray" Giunta and his wife Cathy have assembled a very practical tool for those recovering from trauma called *The Grief Recovery Workbook.* In it they say, "To journal is to heal," and they urge their readers to regularly – daily – record their thoughts. "This may be the biggest favor you do yourself," they say.

He urges mourners to make this promise to themselves:

> I'm going to get my feelings out. I'm not going to be scared. I'm going to write down how I feel each day. I'm going to express what I'm discovering, how I'm responding to each new idea, how it helps or doesn't help, and where I am right now on the journey. I'll write at least a sentence or two each time I re-read the earlier entries and chapters, because each day is a new day and a new place on the road.[21]

In your journal, you could respond to these three statements suggested by Chaplain Ray:

- This is how I feel right now.
- This is what I've discovered today.
- This is what I still question today.

C.S. Lewis' grief journal, published as *A Grief Observed,* turned out to be extremely therapeutic to him and immensely helpful to all those grievers who have read it down through the years. And David's grief journal – scattered throughout the Psalms – has been a comfort and a guide to millions for centuries. Two great examples!

WRITE A LAMENT

A lament is a special kind of entry that you might find in a grief journal, or you might find it as a literary work all by itself. You find many laments in the Bible – in fact the whole book of Lamentations is a series of long laments by Jeremiah, the weeping prophet.

When a mourner writes a lament, they pour all of their emotion, frustrations, venom, vitriol, sadness, curses – everything *including* the kitchen sink – onto a piece of paper. They rail against their present circumstances. They don't hold back. Like Job (3:11-13 (MSG)):

> *Why didn't I die at birth, my first breath out of the womb my last?*
> *Why were there arms to rock me, and breasts for me to drink from?*
> *I could be resting in peace right now, asleep forever, feeling no pain.*

Or like Jeremiah (Lamentations 1:12):

> *Is it nothing to all you who pass this way? Look and see if there is any pain like my pain which was severely dealt out to me, which the Lord inflicted on the day of His fierce anger!*

Or even like our prime example of a griever, King David (Psalm 22:1,2 (NLT)):

> *My God, my God, why have You abandoned me?*
> *Why are You so far away when I groan for help?*
> *Every day I call to You, my God, but You do not answer.*
> *Every night You hear my voice, but I find no relief.*

Hey! This is the Bible! So apparently it's OK to talk like that! In a lament, it's "no holds barred." It's your opportunity to express your despair and anger, knowing that no one – not even God – is going to judge you. So let 'er rip!

And when you're done, read it over again. Read it to Jesus, giving Him all that anger, hurt, hate and despair. And He'll thank you for your honesty, absorb your anger and love you just as fiercely as He ever has.

❋ ❋ ❋ ❋ ❋

SIGNS THAT YOUR MOURNING IS WORKING

As the magnitude of trauma and its effects sink in, a person in crisis asks a lot of *"Why"* questions. *Why did this happen? Why did this have to happen to me? Why now? Why did I do that? Why did she do that? Why did God let this happen? Why won't this pain quit? Why must I suffer so deeply?* These questions are all normal, typical and expected. No one faults you for asking them.

What were (or are) some of the "Why" questions you've asked?

_____

_____

_____

As universal as they are, the frustration of the "Why" questions is that most of them will never be answered this side of heaven. We don't ask those questions lightly and we really do expect answers. But they just don't come.

When you start asking the *"How"* questions, that will be a good sign that you are making good progress. *How can I build new dreams? How can I move on? How can I deal with my pain and loss? How can I get back into the swing of things? How can I learn through what I've experienced?* These are all questions that *can* be answered. They look to the future, rather than the past. They spark action, rather than mere contemplation. They invite help from God and from others.

How can you change some of those "Why" questions you wrote above into "How" questions? What other "How" questions should you be asking?

_____

_____

_____

❋ ❋ ❋ ❋ ❋

GRIEF MEMORIALS

Researchers in the field of grief and mourning have learned that memorials play a very important role in starting the grief process and facilitating continued healing. That's why we have funerals and memorial services. That's why we have gravestones. That's why the Vietnam Veteran's Memorial Wall is so sacred and meaningful to all who visit it. These things are tangible experiences and symbols of our grief. We humans need them.

How can you memorialize the grief that's attached to your trauma? What can you do or construct that will provide a touchstone for your pain, something that will symbolize your loss? We're not talking about erecting a shrine in your dining room or anything – or maybe we are. This needs to be a personal gesture that you and God decide upon It could be as subtle as a smooth stone from Afghanistan in your pocket, a poem that you write and put up on the wall, or as obvious as the Taj Mahal. You and God decide.

Prayer Assignment: Ask God to give you a creative idea of how you could memorialize your grief and trauma.

❋ ❋ ❋ ❋ ❋

PRAYER SEED

Father, sometimes my grief is so burdensome, I think it's going to crush me into the ground. I want to be rid of it! It's like my worst enemy. But I need You to help me make it my friend. Help me to embrace it as part of my healing balm from You. Don't let me run from it or try to take shortcuts. Help me to face it head-on. But I cannot go there if You won't come with me. Please enter into my pain with me. Walk me through it. Take me out the other side whole, wiser, stronger and more like Jesus. Amen.

❋ ❋ ❋

[1] *Quote from "Chaplain Ray" Giunta in* Grief Recovery Workbook, *p. 63*

[2] *The New Guide to Crisis & Trauma Counseling* by Dr. H. Norman Wright, p. 64

[3] Quote from Dr. May found in *Ibid*, p. 87.

[4] Quote from Margaret Hill, Harriet Hill, Richard Baggé, Pat Miersma in *Healing The Wounds of Trauma*, p. 37

[5] This point and the one before it are from *I Can't Get Over It* by Dr. Aphrodite Matsakis, Ph.D., p. 202

[6] C.S. Lewis in *A Grief Observed*, p. 33.

[7] Dr. Larry Crabb in *Shattered Dreams*, p. 109

[8] C.S. Lewis in *A Grief Observed*, p. 5, 6.

[9] C.S. Lewis in *A Grief Observed*, p. 61, 62.

[10] Dr. Larry Crabb in *Shattered Dreams*, p. 157, 158

[11] Hebrews 12:2 (NIV) – "Let us fix our eyes on Jesus, the author and perfecter of our faith, who **for the joy set before him** endured the cross, scorning its shame, and sat down at the right hand of the throne of God."

[12] Written by the late Pastor Ron Mehl, who died in 2003 after a 23-year-long battle with leukemia. He was well-acquainted with the night shift. Quoted in *Experiencing Grief* by Dr. H. Norman Wright, p. 22.

[13] C.S. Lewis in *A Grief Observed*, p. 11.

[14] Matthew 7:7,8 (NLT) - *Keep on asking, and you will receive what you ask for. Keep on seeking, and you will find. Keep on knocking, and the door will be opened to you. For everyone who asks, receives. Everyone who seeks, finds. And to everyone who knocks, the door will be opened.*

[15] This partial list of coping mechanisms was taken from www.changingminds.org under the "Explanations/Behaviors/Coping" tab.

[16] Quote by Lilias Trotter, missionary to Africa from 1888 to 1928. Found in *A Path Through Suffering* by Elisabeth Elliot.

[17] Ibid, p. 41.

[18] Quote by David Shepherd in *Shattered Dreams* by Dr. Larry Crabb, p. 161.

[19] Quote by Thomas Merton in a letter to Jim Forest, director of the Fellowship of Reconciliation, quoted by Henri Nouwen in *Turn My Mourning Into Dancing*, p. 60.

[20] Quote by Dr. Harold Ivan Smith in *When Your People Are Grieving* [Beacon Hill Press, 2001], p. 38. Dr. Smith speaks widely on the subjects of grief and death, and conducts "grief gatherings" around the US.

[21] *Grief Recovery Workbook*, p. 15.

[22] Robert Hicks in *Failure To Scream*, p. 187.

STEP 6A: HOW DO I MOVE ON?

FORGIVENESS RECEIVED AND GIVEN

[THIS STEP IS COVERED IN TWO PARTS.]

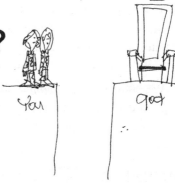

Though your sins are as scarlet, they will be as white as snow;
Though they are red like crimson, they will be like wool.

– Isaiah 1:18

Every saint has a past, every sinner a future.

– Oscar Wilde

WHY IS THIS CRUCIAL TO MOVING ON?

Our sins usually seem inconsequential when we first commit them – otherwise we wouldn't do them. And the immediate results often seem relatively harmless. But something is *always* going on behind the scene that isn't apparent, something that will have effects that will linger for a long time if not dealt with.

WHAT IS HAPPENING IS SEPARATION.

Every time we make the decision to go against one of God's laws, three separations potentially occur:

- A separation between you and God

- A separation between you and another person

- A separation between you and you

Between you and God. When we switch places with the Holy Spirit on the throne of our life in order to do something we know is wrong, we are quenching and grieving Him (1 Thessalonians 5:19; Ephesians 4:30). Isaiah 59:2 says *"But your iniquities have made a separation between you and your God, and your sins have hidden His face from you so that He does not hear."* This does not alter your eternal connection with God – you were born into His family when you received Christ as your Savior, and you can't get "unborn." The eternal life He gave you is indeed *eternal* and He loves you with an everlasting love (Jeremiah 31:3). But in terms of your experiential *relationship* with Him, it is strained. Much like when a husband and wife have a fight – they're still married, but their communication is clipped, awkward and cold. They live in the same house, but their hearts are separated. This is how it can feel between us and God.

Between you and another person. When we do something that injures another person in some way, this too results in alienation – like the couple in the previous paragraph. In Matthew 5:22-26, Jesus describes this split between people, and urges us to set everything else aside and be reconciled to our offended brother or sister – for our own good.

This works the other direction, too. When you are hurt by someone, you don't want to hang with them much anymore. You avoid them. Once burned, twice smart.

Between you and you. Sin also brings about a separation between who you are and who God is making you. In Ephesians 4:22-24, the Bible talks about our "old man" – corrupt, lustful, deceitful – and your "new man" – righteous, holy and honest. In Romans 7:14-24, no less a man than the Apostle Paul describes the war that rages between these two "men" in his soul. It's like having two dogs fighting inside of you – a good one and a bad one. The one you feed wins – and sin feeds the bad dog.

> **Materials needed for this Step:**
> *One glass jar with tightly fitting lid
> *One match or a lighter
> *Some masking tape
> *A pen

These separations are counter-productive to your healing. You *need* those life-giving connections to God and to other Spirit-filled friends. Without them, you're like that redwood tree growing in the open field, or that sheep wandering alone through the woods – vulnerable. And you need that unified, Christ-oriented control internally, so that you can receive and respond to His healing touch and direction.

What's needed is *reconciliation* – to God, to others, and to yourself. This is accomplished through forgiveness – received and given.

❋ ❋ ❋ ❋ ❋

ACCEPTING GOD'S FORGIVENESS

One of the greatest transactions that occurs in the universe is forgiveness from God.

God runs a tight ship. There are absolutes. There is right and wrong. There are laws which keep the universe and society running properly. If you break a law, it will break you. Example: there is a law (gravity) that says if you jump out of a plane, you will go down fast, land hard and hurt all over. Every time. That is, unless there is a law operating that supersedes the law of gravity, such as the law of the *parachute*.

Another example: With regards to eternal life, the Bible says that if you sin, you will die (Ezekiel 18:20). Why? Because in your natural, sin-prone state, you are separated from God, and if you step into eternity in that separated condition, you stay that way forever. That is, unless *that* law is superseded by the law of *forgiveness*.

WHAT DO YOU NEED TO BE FORGIVEN FOR?

Most people are prompted to seek God's forgiveness because they feel *guilty*. But there are two kinds of guilt, and you need to know which kind you are feeling, because one needs forgiveness and the other *doesn't*.

FALSE GUILT

As was mentioned earlier, we have an enemy who is seeking to devour us. One of his methods of doing this is to counterfeit the things of God, twist them, and use them for his destructive purposes. Guilt is good, invented by God. It's meant to let us know when we are doing something that's leading to separation of one sort or another, prompting us to go back to God for forgiveness and restoration. But Satan likes to give us guilt trips that have nothing to do with God's laws. His guilt does nothing but produce frustration and depression. This happens because there's no way to rid ourselves of the effects of that kind of guilt – unless we recognize it for what it is: *false*. Here are some examples of false guilt:[1]

- **Survivor's Guilt** – "I shouldn't have survived when others died." "If I'd suffered more, others would have suffered less." "If I had died, others might have lived."

- **Survivor's Euphoria Guilt** – "I feel so ashamed about it, but I can't help thinking, 'I'm so glad I didn't get killed!' How can I feel *good* when others died?"

- **Guilt Over Involuntary Flight/Fight/Freeze Response** – "I always thought I was so brave, but I just froze in my tracks! I couldn't move!" "When that guy jumped me and nearly killed me, I went berserk. I killed him, but couldn't stop beating him until his face was an unrecognizable pulp."

- **Guilt By Association** – "I'm a soldier; soldiers sometimes commit atrocities; I am among the atrocity-committers."

- **Competency Guilt** – "If only I had acted quicker, more skillfully or smarter, people wouldn't have suffered and died."

- **Catch-22 Guilt** (Forced to make a lose-lose choice) – "The woman looked like she had a bomb under her burqa. We kept yelling at her to stop, but she kept coming. If I didn't shoot her, she could blow up all my buddies. I shot her – but she had no bomb. How am I supposed to live with that?"

- **Helplessness Guilt** – "I wanted so badly to get my buddy out of the line of fire, but they had him pinned down. If only I could have gotten to him, he'd still be alive today."

- **Role and Responsibility Guilt** – "It was my responsibility to keep my men safe. Some of them died, so I didn't do my job. It's all my fault."

In each case listed above, there is *no guilt* as far as God and His laws are concerned, no moral factor in any of the decisions that were made. In each case the felt guilt was based on a false premise.

- You can't blame yourself because you lived while others died – you had nothing to do with that. There's no way you could have controlled all the conditions surrounding your traumatic events. The conclusions drawn are illogical and inaccurate.

- The euphoria over your survival is an involuntary function of your lower brain, as was your fight/ flight/freeze response – *involuntary*. As in: they were uncontrollable reflexes. They're *not* moral choices that you should be held accountable for.

- Guilt by association? As long as you didn't participate in atrocities, it's a huge thinking-error for you to punish yourself for it. You didn't do the crime, so why do the time?

- The "if onlys" of Competency, Catch-22 and Helplessness are irrelevant. In hindsight we may be able to see other options, but in the moment of crisis and the fog of war, you *can't* see them all. You did your best, and no one – at that moment under those conditions – should judge you for it. You could wish that some magical solution would have presented itself at the last moment – but it didn't. That's reality – not your fault.

- And leaders simply *can't* protect all those under their command all the time – there's a *war* going on. The potential for disaster surrounds a combatant all the time. Multiply that by the number of troops you commanded. Are you God, that you could control all of those variables simultaneously? Why would anyone think they could?

In all of these cases, it's normal to feel sad, angry and frustrated about how things turned out – but don't turn that emotion in on yourself. You weren't meant to take the hit for those very unfair and unfortunate events – so don't take it. Remember that you have a spiritual enemy who will try to manipulate the memories of those events in order to weaken and destroy you. Also remember what you heard all the time growing up: "Life isn't fair." It won't be until we get to heaven.

 Read over the list of false guilts above. Can you identify with one or more of those kinds of guilt? If so, write it down below. Do you still feel that it's legitimate to feel as you do? If so, why?

_____

_____

_____

The only way to deal with false guilt is to recognize its illogical, irrational basis, shine a spotlight on its source (Satan), and ask God to remove it from you. The guilt feelings may or may not lift immediately, but keep bringing it before God and let Him take that burden off your shoulders. It's not accomplishing anything. God doesn't mean for you to carry it – and *no one else* wants you to either.

REAL GUILT

For everyone has sinned; we all fall short of God's glorious standard.

– Romans 3:23 (NLT)

As you look back to your experiences while deployed, you may have done some things that were real, definite, no-kiddin' sins – not like the fake ones listed above. You may have broken some of the Top Ten found in Exodus 20:1-17. You may even have broken all ten and many more. There are two bits of good news you need to hear:

1. If you are feeling guilty about *those* sins, then it's because you are currently *not* quenching the Holy Spirit; you're sensitive to His conviction – that's *good!*

2. You're not alone – *all* of us have sinned; *every one of us* has done things that have set up separations between us and God. It's a fact of the human condition. And it's fixable.

All of us like sheep have gone astray,
   Each of us has turned to his own way;
      But the Lord has caused the iniquity of us all to fall on Him.

– Isaiah 53:6

Here's where we come to the "great transaction" talked about earlier. No matter how heinous our sins were, even "red like crimson," God can forgive them, and no longer hold you accountable for them – because Jesus was willing to be held accountable for them on the cross in our place. He was willing to exchange His perfect righteousness for our sins. He took them upon Himself, and then suffered the ultimate punishment for them: death. But then, to demonstrate His power over death and His eternal nature as God the Son, He rose again from the grave in strength and victory.

In order to have Jesus' sacrificial death apply to *your* sins, you need to take two steps:

1. CONFESS

As mentioned earlier, the word "confess" is from a Greek word that means, "to say the same thing as." God has told you what you did wrong, as in, "John, you stole that money." You confess by saying the same thing: "Yes, it's true. I stole that money and I agree it was wrong. Please forgive me." The Bible gives us a great promise concerning this:

If we confess our sins, He is faithful and righteous to forgive us our sins and to cleanse us from all unrighteousness. **– 1 John 1:9**

❊   ❊   ❊   ❊   ❊

 Math Test. What percentage of our unrighteousness has God promised to cleanse us from if we confess our sins to Him? _____ Which leaves how much *not* taken care of?_____

❊   ❊   ❊   ❊   ❊

Memorial Project #1

Grab a glass jar with a lid that can be screwed on tightly. Take a few minutes alone and present yourself before God. Ask Him to reveal to you any sins that are creating a separation between you and Him. Ask Him to be very specific about it. On a separate piece of paper (*not* in this manual), make a list of all the sins that He reveals to you.

When you're done with this, take your list and agree with Him regarding each thing you wrote down. When you're done, write "1 John 1:9" across the top of it in big, bold letters and numbers.

Then, take the paper and stuff it in the jar. Take it to a safe place (with no smoke alarms!) and light the paper on fire. Watch it burn and thank God as it symbolizes what He's doing to the list of sins that were being held against you.

After it's out and cooled down, screw the lid on, and put a piece of tape on the front. Write "1 John 1:9" and the date on the tape. Then put the ash jar somewhere to remind you of the "great transaction" God has accomplished for you. Whenever Satan tries to remind you of your sinfulness, bring out the "Memorial Jar" and remind *him* of what Jesus Christ did with your sins.

If you've been struggling with false guilt, write those on a list as well and burn them at the same time. Tell Satan he can't use those counterfeit accusations against you any more.

❀　❀　❀　❀　❀

2. REPENT

The word "repent" comes from the Greek word that means, "to turn around and go the other direction." While "confess" has to do with a transaction that takes place in the spiritual realm, "repent" has to do with action that needs to take place in *this* dimension. It's not enough to say, "Oops, sorry. I blew it. Forgive me," and then repeat the same act again and again. That's not true confession anyway, because if you were really agreeing with God that it was wrong, you would at least make the attempt to stop doing it.

Bottom line: God's not merely looking for your agreement with Him about your sins. He's interested in changed *action*. Your actions will validate your intentions. When this happens, it clears the way for God to bring His healing unhindered.

> *Therefore repent and return, so that your sins may be wiped away, in order that times of refreshing may come from the presence of the Lord.*　　**– Acts 3:19**

Confession and **repentance** won't be a once-and-for-all thing. The Memorial Jar you made commemorates a day when you drew a line in the sand and said, "From today on, I *know* that my sins are eliminated, and I am clean before God." It's going to make it a lot easier for you to do the maintenance necessary to keep Christ on the throne of your life, through regular "spiritual breathing" as needed (see Step 3A).

Restitution. In some cases, you may need to make restitution as part of your repentance. If you stole something, you need to return it or reimburse the victim for their loss. If you told a lie that damaged someone's reputation, you need to try to fix it. If you fathered a child through adultery, you need to support that child. If you broke a law, you may need to talk with God about turning yourself in. Forgiveness doesn't mean you are absolved of all responsibility attached to your sin. It means that it no longer separates you from God and clears the way for Him to work in your life. But part of your healing process may involve taking steps to make things right with other people.

❀　❀　❀　❀　❀

BUT YOU DON'T KNOW WHAT I'VE DONE...

Some people look at their sins and come to the conclusion that they are unforgivable. These pour souls live under a load of shame and self-condemnation that will eventually crush them. They're under that load *not* because God wants them there, but because their enemy does. This is "Industrial Strength False Guilt." Don't misunderstand – there is sin and therefore there is guilt, but the lie that it is *unforgivable* sin is what makes that guilt crushingly false.

To have the opinion that God is not willing or able to forgive their particular sin is a bit audacious, don't you think? They are deciding for God what He can or cannot do. They're saying that Jesus' death on the cross wasn't enough to pay for their sin. He's already told us in the Scripture at the beginning of this Step

(Isaiah 1:18 - paraphrased): *"No matter how bad your sins are, I can make you pure. No matter how low you've gone, I can go there and get you."* Do you really feel tough enough to say to the Almighty God of the universe, "Oh, no, you can't!"? If so, then you've either got "Industrial Strength Courage" or "Industrial Strength Foolishness." Probably the latter.

The Apostle Paul referred to himself as "chief among sinners" (1 Timothy 1:15). Here's why: Before he became a Christian, he had broken every one of the Ten Commandments – even though he was one of the greatest (non-Christian) religious leaders of the day. He threatened, chased, kidnapped, imprisoned, tortured and killed Christians, just because they were Christians. If he'd had the opportunity, he would have considered it a great honor to do the same to Jesus Christ Himself. But then he met Christ, and everything changed. That's why he could write with confidence:

> *Because of the sacrifice of the Messiah, His blood poured out on the altar of the Cross, we're a free people—free of penalties and punishments chalked up by all our misdeeds. And not just barely free, either. Abundantly free!*
>
> **– Ephesians 1:7,8** (MSG)

If God could forgive Paul, the world recordholder of sinners, He can certainly forgive *you!* If you haven't done the Memorial Jar exercise yet, do it now with the "unforgivable sins" that have been weighing you down. Thank Him for setting you "abundantly free"!

❋   ❋   ❋   ❋   ❋

 Can you think of any sin that would be unforgiveable? If so, write it down here. If you aren't going through this study with a mentor of some sort, ask someone who knows God and the Bible real well if they would agree with your assessment.

❋   ❋   ❋   ❋   ❋

SEEKING FORGIVENESS FROM OTHERS

In order to heal, each of us needs to experience both forgiveness from God and forgiveness from others that we may have hurt. For some people, the idea of admitting a wrong to another person and asking for their forgiveness would produce more anxiety than going on patrol in Fallujah with no helmet or flak jacket. But Jesus makes the point that this issue is so important that you should even put worshipping God on hold until you settle things:

> *This is how I want you to conduct yourself in these matters. If you enter your place of worship and, about to make an offering, you suddenly remember a grudge a friend has against you, abandon your offering, leave immediately, go to this friend and make things right. Then and only then, come back and work things out with God*
>
> **– Matthew 5:23,24** (MSG)

We'd like to share six steps you can take to help you in the process of seeking forgiveness from another.

1. ASK GOD TO SHOW YOU WHO YOU HAVE HURT.

Consider praying the prayer that David prayed:

> *Search me, O God, and know my heart; test me and know my anxious thoughts. Point out anything in me that offends you, and lead me along the path of everlasting life.*
>
> **– Psalm 139:23,24** (NLT)

If you're filled with the Holy Spirit, and if there *is* someone you've hurt, God will bring it to your mind pretty quickly. Be open to whatever He has to say to you.

 Has God brought one or more people to your mind? Write their name(s) here:

2. ASK GOD TO FORGIVE YOU FOR THE PAIN YOU INFLICTED.

This is like a "double sin." You've sinned against the person, but also against God for breaking one of His laws. Go through the process of confession and repentance regarding this incident. Get right with God first. *[**Note:** you don't have to fire up a Memorial Jar every time you confess a sin, by the way! That was a one-time symbolic act that depicts an on-going process in your life.]*

3. PRAY FOR THE ONE YOU'VE HURT.

If you've wounded someone either physically or emotionally, how do you think they feel toward you? You're probably not their favorite person on earth. So spend some time praying for that person, asking God to heal the wound that you caused. Ask Him to perform a miracle: that the hard feelings your wounded acquaintance probably holds toward you would be mitigated by God's supernatural love. Ask God to make a way for you to meet with him or her with a minimum of misunderstanding and vitriol. And ask God to make him or her receptive to your request for forgiveness.

4. TAKE THE INITIATIVE AND GO TO THE ONE YOU'VE HURT.

Here comes that walk through Fallujah in your underwear! But God will give you the courage to do it. He'll be right by your side in this, because He will be *very* pleased about what you're doing. It'll probably start with a phone call or an email. Let them know you want to talk to them about something, and try to get an appointment with them. If you can't get face-to-face, you'll have to deal with it over the phone, but talking in person is the best way to go. They'll probably know from the tone of your voice what it's about and that you feel bad about it.

 When will you take steps to contact each person whose name you wrote above?

5. IN HUMILITY, RECOUNT TO THE PERSON WHAT YOU DID AND ASK FOR FORGIVENESS.

You could say something along these lines: "Joe, remember that time that ... Well, I've thought a lot about what happened since then, and I want tell you that I'm sorry for what I did. I was wrong. Do you think you could forgive me?"

Don't try to put yourself in a better light, or try to explain or defend your actions. "I want you to know that the reason I said those things was because of what you said to me first." No. Now you're taking the spotlight off of *your* responsibility and pointing out theirs. That's between them and God, and you don't need to do God's job for Him. Just take responsibility for what *you* did. Go to them totally unarmed.

And don't say, "If what I did offended you, I'm sorry." No "ifs" about it. You did. God said so, and so did the damaged relationship. To say "if" is to say, "My actions may or may not have been wrong and offensive." That's no confession. You already know they were offensive.

6. Work on Rebuilding Trust with That Person.

They may or may not say they forgive you at that time   In either case, you can't expect your relationship to go immediately back to how it was before. You broke trust with that person. It's going to take some time to re-establish it. And it's going to take some initiative on your part to demonstrate that you meant what you said, and that you've changed. Ask God to give you some creative ideas about how to do that.

❋   ❋   ❋   ❋   ❋

What are some things you could do to rebuild a person's trust in you?

❋   ❋   ❋   ❋   ❋

Realistic and Unrealistic Expectations About Forgiveness

Forgetting. Deep hurts can rarely be wiped out of one's memory. In all likelihood, the person you wounded will always remember the wound – but they *can* look past it. Your hope is for forgiveness, not forgetting.

Forgiveness. They may not even be willing to forgive you at this point. Maybe later. But this is something you have no control over. As Nazi concentration camp survivor Simon Wiesenthal wrote, "Forgetting is something that time alone can take care of, but forgiveness is an act of volition, and only the sufferer is qualified to make the decision."[2] But if you obey God and take care of your obligation in this matter, it releases you from any further condemnation. You've done the right thing.

Realize that it might take the offended person a while to really forgive you from their heart. In fact, they may have to forgive you at deeper and deeper levels over a long period. Give them time, and in the interim, continue to work at rebuilding trust. Don't let yourself resent the person as they slowly process your wound and confession. "Why can't they get over this? I said I was sorry!" Healing takes time. The deeper the wound, the longer the convalescence. Whenever you start to feel impatient, just remember: You put that wound there.

Reconciliation. You may have done your best to mend fences between you and the one you hurt, and they may have forgiven you the best they could. But that doesn't mean that the two of you are going to be best pals from now on. You can only control what happens on your side of the ledger. Keep reaching out to them in love, keep praying for them and perhaps the Lord will do a miracle.

❋   ❋   ❋   ❋   ❋

Semi-conclusion. In this first half of Step 6, we've learned some important principles about forgiveness – seeking it from God and seeking it from people we have hurt. In the second half of Step 6, you'll be venturing into a realm that may be one of the most difficult you've ever entered, but one that holds enormous promise. It will examine how and why we should forgive those who have harmed us. Seem ridiculous? Hold your judgment until you've seen what we – and God's Word – have to say on the subject. You may just be blown away – in a *good* sense!

❋   ❋   ❋   ❋   ❋

PRAYER SEED

Father, thank You for being willing to forgive me for my many sins. Jesus, thank You for being willing to die on the cross and experience death instead of me – purchasing life for me. I can never repay you for that. You say in Your Word that even while I was still a sinner – running from You, disobeying You, with no interest in You whatsoever, You were willing to die for me.* Amazing! And even while belonging to You, I still sin – and You still love and forgive me, and draw me back to Yourself. I know I don't deserve it – no one does. That's what makes Your gift so incredible. Thank you. Father, give me the courage I'll need to seek forgiveness from others whom I have hurt in the past. Give me grace and favor in their eyes. Help me rebuild their trust Amen.

*Romans 5:6-8

❀   ❀   ❀

---

[1] *Dr. Aphrodite Matsakis, in her book* Trust After Trauma *has an excellent section that goes into great detail about these different types of false guilt, and offers exercises that will help a PTSD sufferer recognize them as false guilt and be released from them. Chapter 6 on "Guilt," pages 164-180.*

[2] Quote by Simon Wiesenthal, survivor of Nazi concentration camp in Lemberg, Poland, from his book *The Sunflower*. Quoted by Os Guinness in *Unspeakable,* p. 172.

STEP 6B: HOW DO I MOVE ON?

FORGIVENESS RECEIVED AND GIVEN

[THIS IS THE SECOND OF TWO PARTS.]

In Step 6A, we studied two important aspects of forgiveness: accepting God's forgiveness and seeking forgiveness from those we have hurt. There is one more major component to this study that needs to be considered…

FORGIVING THOSE WHO HAVE WOUNDED YOU

What does it mean to forgive someone who has brought crippling pain, trauma and difficulty into your life? The Greek word for "forgive" is *aphiemi,* which means "to release or set free." Here are some of the components of The International Forgiveness Institute's definition:[1]

- A merciful response to a moral injustice

- The foregoing of resentment or revenge when the wrongdoer's actions deserve it and giving the gifts of mercy, generosity and love when the wrongdoer does not deserve them

- A freely chosen gift (rather than a grim obligation)

- The overcoming of wrongdoing with good

Think you can do that? Set somebody free who deserves punishment? If we're honest, most of us would have to say no. It goes against the grain big-time. It seems to negate justice, fairness and righteousness and to give a pass to those who break the laws of God and man. The fact is it will take a miracle in the hearts of any of us to choose the route of forgiving. Good news: we belong to a miracle-working God!

 "Fight fire with fire." You've heard that one before, right? Before reading any further, write down whether or not you agree with that philosophy and why.

It probably depends on what real-life scenario you're applying it to. When fighting a forest fire, strategically placed back-fires rob a larger, advancing fire of fuel. We fight fire with fire in war all the time. If your enemy comes at you with tanks, match him with Warthogs. Meet force with force – it's the only language aggressors understand. If we back off, they fill the vacuum and evil triumphs.

But when it comes to interpersonal relationships, it does not apply. Fighting fire with fire only yields more fire.

> **"I don't get mad, I get even."**

> **"Go ahead, make my day."**

> **"Do ya feel lucky, punk? Well, do ya?"**

I know, I know. Those lines *do* stir the heart and get the adrenalin pumping in many of us who are action movie fans. And they may suggest an appropriate philosophy when dealing with a criminal, bully or terrorist (as long as you have superior firepower). But in the non-combat world, it leads to needless escalation of tension and no resolution of the problem. And it makes things worse for you.

Materials needed for this Step:
*Another glass jar with tightly fitting lid
*Another match or a lighter
*Some masking tape
*A pen

What alternative strategy does the Bible give us?

Do not be overcome by evil, but overcome evil with good.   **– Romans 12:21**

Setting backfires is an effective firefighting technique only under certain conditions. Firefighters generally prefer to use a substance that is the *opposite* of fire: *water.* That principle holds true here. If there's enough of it, water always puts out most kinds of fires. Likewise, if there is enough *good* and it's empowered by the Spirit of God – it is always going to be stronger than evil.

> Darkness cannot drive out darkness; only light can do that.
> Hate cannot drive out hate; only love can do that.
>
>   – Dr. Martin Luther King, Jr.

❄ ❄ ❄ ❄ ❄

AGAINST A SIMPLISTIC APPROACH...

There are different "intensities" of harm and woundings, and therefore different intensities of forgiveness required. When Sally makes a snide comment about how frumpy Janie looks in her new dress, that's one level. But the intensities take several quantum leaps when the offending incident involves a foreign insurgent sniper who ambushes a Marine in Tikrit, severely wounding his leg – which leads to an amputation. And in the same firefight, two of his buddies are killed as well. How easy will the ability to forgive come to that Marine?

The truths contained in this manual are foundational in helping a troop work through forgiveness issues attached to that level of pain and trauma. But the process might be augmented with the help of a PTSD support group or trained Christian therapist who can facilitate a deep-valley walk for him and Jesus Christ. In Step 9 we'll be giving you some input regarding how to seek out "bridge people" who could assist in this.

To lay the groundwork for this we would like to offer the Biblical principles concerning the **why** and **how** of forgiving those who have wounded us.

❄ ❄ ❄ ❄ ❄

WHY FORGIVE THOSE WHO HAVE WOUNDED ME?

1. FOR YOUR OWN GOOD

Poison oak thrives in the Pacific Northwest. If you don't deal with it, it will take over acres of fields and forests, making it virtually impossible to enjoy that land. No picnics, no football games, no hide-and-seek – you dare not even walk through it without long pants on. If you skin comes in contact with it, you'll be miserable for days. Mowing it down won't help, because as long as its roots are left in the ground, it will always come back within a few months, stronger and more widespread than ever.

That's the spiritual target of this passage of Scripture:

> *Look after each other so that none of you fails to receive the grace of God. Watch out that no poisonous root of bitterness grows up to trouble you, corrupting many.*
>   **– Hebrews 12:15 (NLT)**

When we have been wounded in some way and feel helpless against the consequences, conditions are ideal for bitterness to grow. Our hatred for our attacker deepens, our frustration mounts, which makes us more angry and hate-filled – until finally nobody wants to be around us any more. The bitterness spreads, just like the poison oak The irony is that all this anger and poison does absolutely nothing to the guilty one – only to the one who was wounded. It makes him or her worse and worse.

Christian educator, counselor and behaviorist Dr. Bill Gothard says,

> In our counseling of troubled youth nowadays, we initially don't even bother about most of the other issues. The first thing we do now is to look for a root of bitterness in the person. In 90% of the cases, we find that's the primary reason the person is having psychological, emotional or spiritual problems.[2]

The only way to deal with it is to pull out its root – and that can only be done by forgiving the offender. When we remove that bitter root with God's help, the useless escalation of hatred and anger toward our offender stops, allowing us to move on to more constructive pursuits.

❋　❋　❋　❋　❋

? Spend a few minutes alone in prayer. Ask God to reveal to you whether or not you are harboring a "root of bitterness" in your heart toward those who hurt you and helped bring about your PTSD. If the answer is "yes," ask Him to let you know what you can do about it. Then keep your spiritual ears open. He may give you an immediate answer, or the solution may become apparent over the next few days or weeks. Once you have an action plan from God about this, write it down here:

_____

_____

_____

_____

❋　❋　❋　❋　❋

2. IT'S A GOD-LIKE CHARACTERISTIC

We are sons and daughters of a forgiving God – and His desire is that we grow up to be like Him.

> *He has not dealt with us according to our sins, nor rewarded us according to our iniquities. For as high as the heavens are above the earth, so great is His lovingkindness toward those who fear Him.*　　**– Psalm 103:10,11**

The main point here is that God doesn't treat us the way we deserve. He forgives. When you forgive, you're acting like God. The next time you decide to demand your rights, realize that you *really don't want* your rights. If you got your rights, you'd be in hell today! Instead, as God has done for us, He's asking us to do for others: not count their sins against them:

> *For God was in Christ, reconciling the world to Himself, no longer counting people's sins against them. And He gave us this wonderful message of reconciliation.*　　**– 2 Corinthians 5:19** (NLT)

❋　❋　❋　❋　❋

? The fact that you may feel deep anger toward someone who has caused you great pain is perfectly understandable. Why should they suffer no negative consequences when you have suffered so greatly? So when you consider forgiving that person, how hard do you think it will be? Put an X on the line:

Piece of cake. I could do it before breakfast	1	2	3	4	5	6	7	8	9	10	Absolutely, positively impossible

What is your level of confidence that God can perform a miracle in your heart and enable you to forgive your attacker(s)?

I'm absolutely confident that He can do this.	1	2	3	4	5	6	7	8	9	10	Absolutely, no way ever

Prayer Assignment. We weren't kidding when we said it may take a miracle for you to come to the point of being able to forgive the ones who've hurt you. This level of love and mercy is indeed "supernatural". If you placed your X's toward the "10" end of the two scales above, begin asking God for that miracle. You won't be able to generate it on your own – but He can build it into you, if you're open to it.

❄ ❄ ❄ ❄ ❄

3. IT'S A CHRIST-LIKE CHARACTERISTIC

The most monstrous, unjust wounding in history occurred when the sinless Son of God was crucified by brutal Roman soldiers at the behest of corrupt Jewish leaders. The ironic thing is that Jesus could have ended the procedure at any time by calling in His Quick Response Force of 10,000 angels – but He was willing to go through it for our sakes. During that six-hour period of agony on the cross while He was waiting to die, He made this incredible request of His heavenly father:

Father, forgive them; for they do not know what they are doing. **– Luke 23:34**

Rather than demand justice, He extended mercy to his killers.

A few months later, one of Jesus' disciples named Stephen was being stoned for being a Christ-follower (Acts 7). His final words as his body was being crushed by the stones was, *"Lord, do not hold this sin against them!"* He released his killers from their penalty before him and before God – just as Jesus did. It's interesting to note that one of those released was young Saul of Tarsus – the Christian Killer – who eventually was transformed into the Apostle Paul, one of the greatest Christians ever. This is the effect we have on the world around us when we act like Christ.

4. UNFORGIVENESS BLOCKS GOD'S BLESSINGS TO YOU

What did Jesus Christ say we should do when others have harmed us?

Forgive us our sins,
as we have forgiven those who sin against us. **– Matthew 6:12** (NLT)

He presupposes that we would forgive them. And why would we want to do this? Two verses later, Jesus shares a rather disturbing commentary on what He just said:

If you forgive those who sin against you, your heavenly Father will forgive you. But if you refuse to forgive others, your Father will not forgive your sins.
– Matthew 6:14,15 (NLT)

We humans are big on justice, aren't we? Especially when *we're* the ones who have suffered injustice. We generally think, "Lord, forgive me my debts… but as for those who owe debts to me – *whack 'em!*" We prefer grace, but everybody else should have judgment. That would definitely qualify as hypocrisy.

God wants us to apply the same standards to others that we expect from Him. He wants us to be like Him. When we are, it facilitates His blessings to us. When we aren't, it staunches the flow of his grace and mercy to us. Again – it doesn't affect our standing with Him or our heavenly destination. But as far as what God wants to do in and through us, we're going to be stuck here for awhile.

❄ ❄ ❄ ❄ ❄

? Do you feel you are being blocked from some of God's blessings right now If so, describe what you feel you're missing as best you can.

_____

_____

_____

Do you think it's possible they are being blocked because of unforgiveness in your heart?

_____

❀   ❀   ❀   ❀   ❀

5. IT ALLOWS GOD TO BRING PERFECT JUSTICE

Never take your own revenge, beloved, but leave room for the wrath of God, for it is written, "Vengeance is Mine, I will repay, says the Lord." — **Romans 12:19**

The Bible is full of laws. A great number of them have to do with penalties imposed when one person does something wrong to another person. They address murder, rape, assault, theft – all the usual issues. These are meant to be universal standards for all the kingdoms of earth.

When you're the victim of someone breaking those laws, God has given you a legal, moral, civic right to expect the appropriate punishment to be administered to the perpetrator. They owe you. You are in a position of superiority. You are due your pound of flesh.

But then Jesus Christ steps in and says, in effect, "That's all true. But in My kingdom, we do things differently. You have been sinned against, and you are entitled to justice. But how would you like it if I take care of it personally? If you'll step aside, give up your right to restitution and vengeance, and let Me handle it, I'll take care of you and your abuser _perfectly_. Vengeance is Mine, I will repay. But I'll do it in a way that will free you of your bitterness, bring your abuser to justice, and move _both_ of you closer to My righteousness. So what do you say?"

This is what happened when Stephen asked God to release his executioners from the penalty of their murderous sin. At that moment, heaven went into action for Saul of Tarsus and Jesus Christ dealt directly with the Christian Killer. (Extra Credit: Read about it in Acts 9:1-22.) For Saul, it involved punishment, condemnation, pain, guilt, torment and probably intense fear for his eternal future. But in the end, Stephen gets heaven (not a bad deal!) and an entire chapter-and-a-half in the Word of God (Acts 6&7), and Saul gets transformed into the greatest missionary for Christ in history: Paul. Stephen wins, Saul wins, and the Kingdom of God wins. That is an _exceptionally_ good outcome!

❀   ❀   ❀   ❀   ❀

? When the Apostle Paul finally died and entered heaven, how do you think Stephen greeted him – his murderer? Imagine their reunion and describe it as best you can.

_____

_____

_____

_____

❀   ❀   ❀   ❀   ❀

HOW DO I FORGIVE THOSE WHO HAVE WOUNDED ME?

1. ASK GOD TO GIVE YOU HIS SUPERNATURAL MINDSET FOR THIS

Satan wants you to add more fire to the fire. We often go along with that because of our desire for vengeance – whatever the cost. Here's our natural mindset, which Satan encourages:

- I'm hurt,
- He's hurt,
- Nobody wins,
- But at least the score's even.

But the Bible says that – rather than fighting fire with fire – we can overcome evil with good (Romans 12:21). By making the decision to forgive, you are *not* condoning their sin. You are *not* minimizing what happened to you. You're making a direct assault against your true enemy (Satan) who will use your bitterness and righteous indignation to destroy you.

Your mindset needs to become: "I know there is evil here, and I choose to break the cycle of pain and violence. Rather than to add to the evil, I will contain it, starve it out, and kill it – with good." God can give you that heart.

2. MAKE A LIST OF YOUR POINTS OF PAIN AND TRAUMA, AND WHO CAUSED EACH ONE

If you don't know their name, just describe them ("That dude that planted the IED that blew up my Humvee."). Make this list on a separate sheet of paper – not in this manual. Put *all* those points of pain down – not just the big ones. Don't say, "Oh, it doesn't matter. That wasn't really *that* big a deal." It may take you a while to accomplish this step, but that's okay. It's important.

3. MAKE AN ACT-OF-YOUR-WILL PRONOUNCEMENT OF FORGIVENESS FOR EACH PERSON

This is an act of obedience and may or may not involve your emotions. You might pray something like this:

> "Lord, as an act of obedience I choose to forgive _____. I don't feel like it, but I love You, and I know You love me, and I want to obey You. So I hereby release _____ from my judgment. Forgive me that I may have hindered Your work in me and in him/her by my unforgiveness. Now I step out of the way so that You can go into action for _____ and for me."

It's best if you pray this prayer out loud, rather than to just think it silently. Your spoken words have unique power.

4. STOP AT DIFFICULT PLACES AND TAKE TIME TO SEE WHAT THE LORD WANTS YOU TO DO

Like what? It's hard to say. That will depend on what's in your heart and in your past. God will work uniquely with each person, according to what they need. He may want you to go and talk to somebody, write a letter, go back to "the scene of the crime," deal with something in your heart ... Just keep your ears open and be willing to do as He directs. It will be for your *good*.

5. BEGIN TO ACT TOWARD YOUR ABUSER THE WAY JESUS SAID TO

> *But I say to you who hear, love your enemies, do good to those who hate you, bless those who curse you, pray for those who mistreat you... Love your enemies, and do good, and lend, expecting nothing in return; and your reward will be great, and you will be sons of the Most High; for He Himself is kind to ungrateful and evil men.*
>
> – Luke 6:27,28,35

When you come to the point that you can do what Jesus has directed in the above Scripture, you can know that you are really beginning to forgive someone. It's not an easy process The following graphic demonstrates that the path to forgiving is uphill, difficult and involves a series of choices – it's not a one-shot deal. To follow our natural reactive tendencies is easy: downhill all the way.

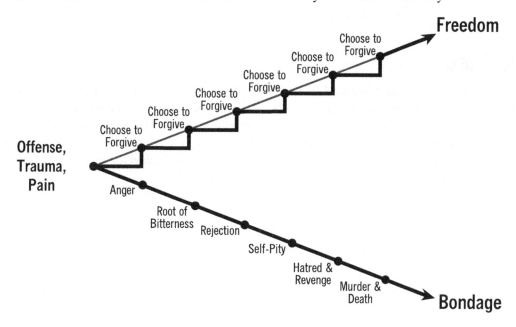

6. MAKE A MEMORIAL OF REMEMBRANCE

Memorial Project #2

This will be very similar to the Memorial Jar you made in Step 6A. Except this time, rather than enumerating and destroying *your* list of sins, you'll be destroying the list of sins of others against you.

When you feel you have worked through the list that you made in #2 above and have followed the directions in #3 about pronouncing forgiveness, it's time to offer up that list as a sacrifice to God.

Across the top of the list, write "Forgiven – Romans 12:21." That's the verse about overcoming evil with good.

Just like before, stuff the paper in a jar and burn it. As it burns, think about how you are releasing these people to God, asking Him to go into action for them as He sees fit. Also, thank Him for releasing *you* from the bondage of your unforgiveness.

When the jar is cool, put a piece of masking tape on the bottle and write "Romans 12:21" and the date on it. Screw the lid on with the ashes inside and set this Memorial Jar next to your first one. Whenever the anger starts to well up inside you again, and your thirst for vengeance starts to strengthen, take the jar out and remember the day you released your abusers – and yourself – from bondage through forgiveness.

If you find that difficult, pick up Jar #1, and remember what God did for you.

❋   ❋   ❋   ❋   ❋

Coming up… At the beginning of Step 6A, we told you about three separations that can occur when we sin: between us and God, between us and others, and between us and ourselves. We've examined those first two separations in this sixth Step. The third split has to do with how trauma can destroy a person's self-image. This important subject will be dealt with in Step 7: *Who Am I Now?*

❋   ❋   ❋   ❋   ❋

PRAYER SEED

Father, I have been deeply wronged and hurt. Everything within me cries out for justice and retribution. Your Word says I should be forgiving, but I find it difficult. In my own strength, I cannot do it. That's why I'm asking you to perform the miracles in my heart that will be necessary to accomplish this. Fill me with Your Spirit and supply in me that which I do not have right now. You were willing to forgive all of my offenses against You. Give me a heart to do the same for those who have sinned against me. Show me what it's like to be free of the bondage of unforgiveness. Amen.

❋   ❋   ❋

---

[1] From the International Forgiveness Institute's "About Forgiveness" page on their website: www.forgiveness-institute.org

[2] Shared during an informal talk by Dr. Gothard at Campus Crusade for Christ headquarters in Orlando, FL at a "Prayer and Fasting Summit" in 1995. Dr. Bill Gothard is the President of the Institute of Basic Life Principles in Oak Brook, IL. www.iblp.org.

STEP 7: WHO AM I NOW?

REBUILDING YOUR IDENTITY

During World War II a near-disastrous incident occurred off the coast of Newfoundland. A U.S. Navy destroyer was operating without running lights and under radio silence, because they'd received intelligence that a German sub had been prowling that area. They also knew there were other allied ships nearby, so they had to exercise caution navigating on that moonless night.

Around 0100 the ship's captain saw some small lights directly ahead. Due to the elevation of the lights, he knew it couldn't be the sub, so he directed his signalman to send the following flashing light message to alert the other vessel that they were on a collision course.

"Advise you to alter course ten degrees west."

Right away, they received this message back. "Negative. Advise you to alter course ten degrees east."

Now, very few commanding officers like to be countermanded, so he ordered his next message with a little pepper: "I am a U.S. Navy Commander. Alter your course ten degrees west."

"I am a Lieutenant (JG). Alter your course ten degrees east."

The captain was fit to be tied. The air turned blue in the wheelhouse and the captain ordered this final message be sent: "I am a U.S. Navy destroyer. Alter your course ten degrees west or suffer the consequences!"

In a few moments came this final response: "I am a lighthouse. Alter your course ten degrees east or suffer the consequences!"

❊   ❊   ❊   ❊   ❊

Perception and Self-Perception. We don't usually think very deeply about who or what we are, or how other people see us, but as the above story illustrates, our identity is extremely important – not something that either we or those around us should be confused about. It is crucial that both perception and self-perception is accurate. Not many things deter a destroyer, but going head-to-head with a lighthouse is a really bad idea.

COMBAT TRAUMA AND IDENTITY

When a person experiences severe trauma, their self-perception is often shaken to the core. While they used to see themselves as rational, self-sufficient, adaptive, strong and worthy, *that* destroyer was torpedoed. Those characteristics are replaced by feelings of fear, confusion, powerlessness and helplessness. And that's not all. As trauma and victimization authority Dr. Ronnie Janoff-Bulman writes:

> In addition, victims are apt to experience a sense of deviance. After all, they have been singled out for misfortune and this establishes them as different from other people. This self-perception of deviance no doubt serves to reinforce negative images of oneself as unworthy and weak.[1]

The effects of this negative transformation of your self-image don't remain in the psychological realm. They bleed into your behavior too – your plans, activities, priorities, reactions, values, hopes, dreams, ambition, social interaction … the list goes on and on. Pastor, educator, counselor and spiritual warfare expert Dr. Neil Anderson states:

> No person can consistently behave in a manner that is inconsistent with the way he sees himself.[2]

Can't be done. You can't hold one set of opinions about yourself and try to live according to a different set. You may succeed for a while, but the energy required to keep up that front is enormous. Eventually exhaustion sets in, the mask comes off and meltdown occurs. No matter how emphatically you command that lighthouse to move, it won't. And unless you alter *your* course, you'll end up wrecked on the shoals.

While trauma started your self-identity ball rolling downhill, there are three other factors that keep it rolling and spin it faster: Satan, the world around you and negative self-talk.

SELF-PERCEPTION ASSESSMENT

Dr. Steven Stosney,[3] an international authority on trauma and victimization, has developed a very useful template that will help assess your current self-perception – how positively or negatively you view yourself. Dr. Stosney's normal approach goes much deeper than we'll be able to apply in this manual, but some of the components will be very useful here. There are eight dynamics of self-perception listed below – the positive side and the negative side. Place an "X" somewhere on the line that indicates how you currently see yourself.

Regarded	Disregarded
Important	Unimportant
Forgiven	Accused/Guilty
Valued	Devalued
Accepted	Rejected
Powerful	Powerless
Lovable	Unlovable
Connected	Separated

Obviously, your adversaries want your "X's" as far to the right side as possible, which keeps you in a vulnerable position. If that's where they are at this point, it's because you have been fed compromised intelligence that has no credible independent verification – in other words **LIES!** Here's what the Son of God says about Satan:

> *He was a murderer from the beginning, not holding to the truth, for there is no truth in him.*
> *When he lies, he speaks his native language, for he is a liar and the father of lies.*
>
> **– John 8:44** (NIV)

At this moment, you are probably not on a physical battlefield, but you *are* in a war. And, as the great Chinese warrior Sun Tzu wrote, *"All warfare is based on deception."* Satan has been honing his covert tactics for thousands of years. He and his network of minions have been observing you since you were a kid, and they know just what to say and how to say it to deceive you to the max. Their objective is your destruction, which will diminish the Kingdom of God and grieve the great heart of the King.

Exposing your enemy's deception. In this Step, we're going to expose as many of Satan's lies as we can. Exposing deception means giving an advantage to the previously deceived. We want you to be able to say with the Apostle Paul, "We are not ignorant of his schemes." (2 Corinthians 2:11) This is most definitely "actionable intelligence."

These lies were spawned by Satan himself. He'll whisper them in your subconscious at your most vulnerable moments. You'll be reminded of incidents in your childhood that validate them. He'll contextualize them in your traumatic events. He'll reinforce them with messages bombarding you from the world system that surrounds you. He'll be sure you're listening when your friends mimic and verify them accidentally or on purpose. And before long, he'll have you telling *yourself* the lies. And we all know how closely we listen to our own opinions.

Following are **eight deceptive traps** Satan and the world have laid for you. Consider whether or not you've heard them before. Each lie will be followed by the countering **TRUTH** that God wants you to hear.

DECEPTION #1: DISREGARDED

Lies of the enemy:

- You are a nobody.
- No one cares about you. Why should they?
- No one wants to know you.
- You don't deserve the respect that others get.
- You are *such* a jerk.
- Who do you think you are, anyway?

Have you heard any of those comments before? Have you made them to yourself? Maybe those exact words weren't used, but after their world has been turned upside down, many combat trauma victims hear and swallow that devilish sentiment. "You've proven to be someone who should and must be disregarded." You hear that, you look at your situation, you look at how people respond to you, you consider your own "deviancy" and you resign yourself to the "truth" of those lies.

Spiritual IEDs. To be effective, every lie must have an element of truth. No good deception ever *looks* like a deception. It must appear plausible, rational and believable. The IEDs that are so hellishly effective at wounding and killing so many of our comrades look harmless: a tuft of grass beside the road, a bit of trash, a little rubble. That's why they work. And if we don't have some information to the contrary, we assume that the lies we perceive are the truth.

Well, God wants to give you *true* information that counters Satan's deceptions. Your trauma has changed you – that's the kernel of truth. But to say, "Because I've changed and I'm not functioning as I used to, I am worthy of disregard" is an absolute lie and needs to be opposed by God's truth.

Not only is His Word *true,* it is *living and active* according to Hebrews 4:12. That means that it's not just words that some ancient prophet scribbled on paper several centuries ago. It continues to live today. And as you read those words, and as the Holy Spirit energizes and breathes life into them, they become the words of God being spoken directly to *you,* right here in the twenty-first century.

The above facts hold true for all eight of the lie-countering truths that we'll be examining below …

YOUR TRUE IDENTITY: REGARDED

 After each verse, answer the questions which highlight who you *really* are.

[Jesus speaking:] *I no longer call you servants, because a servant does not know his master's business. Instead, I have called you friends, for everything that I learned from My Father I have made known to you.*   **– John 15:15** (NIV)

Jesus Christ, the Son of God, calls you His _____.

❀   ❀   ❀

So now Jesus and the ones He makes holy have the same Father. That is why Jesus is not ashamed to call them His brothers and sisters.   **– Hebrews 2:11** (NLT)

Jesus Christ is not ashamed to call you His _____.

❀   ❀   ❀

Even before He made the world, God loved us and chose us in Christ to be holy and without fault in His eyes.   **– Ephesians 1:4 (NLT)**

You were known, loved and chosen by God how long ago?

_____

❋   ❋   ❋

Now you are no longer a slave but God's own child. And since you are His child, God has made you His heir.   **– Galatians 4:7 (NLT)**

You are God's child and also His_____.

These Scriptures describe *you* as a friend, brother (or sister), child and heir of the King of the Universe! He has had plans for you even since before He created Adam and Eve. And you can be sure He's *really* excited that you finally showed up! You are *loved* and ***highly regarded!***

❋   ❋   ❋   ❋   ❋

DECEPTION #2: UNIMPORTANT

Lies of the enemy:

- Your input is unnecessary.
- You're a little fish in a big pond.
- Go sit on the sidelines.
- Don't call us, we'll call you.
- What have you *ever* accomplished?

YOUR TRUE IDENTITY: IMPORTANT

After each verse, answer the questions which demonstrate who you *really* are.

But as many as received Him, to them He gave the right to become children of God, even to those who believe in His name.   **– John 1:12**

Since you have received Christ, you have rightly been named as what?

_____

When you consider all of eternity and all the other animals and angels that God created, how important would you say *that* was?

_____

❋   ❋   ❋

You're here to be salt-seasoning that brings out the God-flavors of this earth.   **– Matthew 5:13 (MSG)**

God has made you His *what* on the earth?

_____

❋   ❋   ❋

You're here to be light, bringing out the God-colors in the world.   **– Matthew 5:14 (MSG)**

God has made you His *what* in the world?

For God so loved the world, that He gave His only begotten Son, that whoever believes in Him shall not perish, but have eternal life.   **– John 3:16**

What kind of life have you been given?

_____

How significant do you think it is to be an eternal being?

_____

_____

Not only do you hold important positions as an eternal child of God, His seasoning and His light, you have been trained and qualified for unique future leadership in Christ's Kingdom on earth. He was wounded, and all those who follow Him also receive wounds, as you have. Down through the ages, the men and women who were significantly used by God were wounded in some severe way. You've been through the refiner's fire. There are evil forces doing their best to propel our world into chaos. The Bible predicts that in the end times society will crumble and treacherous times will ensue – and those times may be very close. Who better to lead us through those traumatic times than someone like you? You've been to hell and back. It is hated but familiar territory for you. You're *important* now, but as you are more fully restored to health, you will prove to be *invaluable* then.

✳ ✳ ✳ ✳ ✳

DECEPTION #3: ACCUSED/GUILTY

Lies of the enemy:

- You really blew it.
- You're unforgivable.
- You need to be punished.
- You can't be trusted.
- Everyone knows what a hypocrite you are.

YOUR **TRUE** IDENTITY: **FORGIVEN**

? We've already spent an entire Step (6A) on this subject, but a little more input shouldn't hurt. After each verse, write what each says about who you *really* are.

Therefore there is now no condemnation for those who are in Christ Jesus.

     – Romans 8:1

Assuming you're a Christian, what will you *not* experience?

_____

✳ ✳ ✳

Therefore, having been justified by faith, we have peace with God through our Lord Jesus Christ.   **– Romans 5:1**

What happened to you by faith? (Hint: the word means "declared not guilty.")

_____

So you are no longer at war with God, now you have _____ with Him. The war is over. You and God are no longer enemies. Your war crimes are no longer being held against you.

✳ ✳ ✳

101

Their sins and lawless acts I will remember no more.

– Hebrews 10:17 (NIV)

What does God think about your sins and lawless acts? (watch it – trick question!)

❋   ❋   ❋   ❋   ❋

DECEPTION #4: DEVALUED

Lies of the enemy:

- We don't need you.
- You're not good enough.
- You don't have what it takes.
- You are absolutely worthless.
- You really *suck!*

YOUR TRUE IDENTITY: VALUED

 After each verse, observe why your true designation is "Valued By God":

> *The Lord appeared to us in the past, saying:*
> *"I have loved you with an everlasting love;*
> *I have drawn you with loving-kindness."*

– Jeremiah 31:3 (NIV)

Who loves ya, baby? _____ How long has this been going on?

How valuable do you think being loved eternally by God and wooed into an everlasting love relationship with Him makes you?

❋   ❋   ❋

Don't you realize that your body is the temple of the Holy Spirit, who lives in you and was given to you by God? You do not belong to yourself, for God bought you with a high price. So you must honor God with your body.

– 1 Corinthians 6:19, 20 (NLT)

What has your physical body become?

When Israel was strong, and before Christ came, the Temple in Jerusalem was the one place on earth where God was manifested and represented. It was the most magnificent and expensive building on the planet at the time for that reason. Since Christ's resurrection, *we* have become the Temple of God. Now *we* are where God is manifested and represented. Valuable or not valuable?

Additionally, this verse says we were bought with a high price. What was the price that God the Father paid to buy us?

❋   ❋   ❋

*For God knew His people in advance, and He chose them to become like His Son, so that
His Son would be the firstborn among many brothers and sisters. And having chosen them,
He called them to come to Him. And having called them, He gave them right standing with
Himself. And having given them right standing, He gave them His glory.*

– Romans 8:29,30 (NLT)

So, we were known by God, chosen by Him to become like Jesus Christ, called by God to come to
Him, given right standing with Him, and finally given *what*?

_____

Conquering generals are given glory by their countries. How valuable, then, is glory given by God?

_____

❋ ❋ ❋ ❋ ❋

DECEPTION #5: REJECTED

Lies of the enemy:

- You're a failure.
- You're such a loser.
- No one wants you.
- You're not qualified.
- Everyone else is better than you.

YOUR **TRUE** IDENTITY: **ACCEPTED**

After each verse, observe why your true designation is "Accepted By God":

To the praise of the glory of His grace, by which He made us accepted in the Beloved.

– Ephesians 1:6 (NKJV)

God's grace made you *what* in the Beloved (Christ)?

_____

❋ ❋ ❋

*As you come to Him, the living Stone – rejected by men but chosen by God and precious
to Him – you also, like living stones, are being built into a spiritual house to be a holy
priesthood, offering spiritual sacrifices acceptable to God through Jesus Christ.*

– 1 Peter 2:4,5 (NIV)

The "living Stone" is Jesus Christ, who was rejected by mankind (when He was crucified), but
always chosen and precious to the Father. In the same way, you were selected by the Master
Stonemason to be part of His spiritual construction, and you are therefore shown to be *what* to God
through Jesus Christ?

_____

❋ ❋ ❋

*Let us therefore come boldly to the throne of grace, that we may obtain mercy and find
grace to help in time of need.* **– Hebrews 4:16 (NKJV)**

How are we allowed to approach God's throne of grace?

_____

Would this indicate that we are *barely* acceptable or *totally* acceptable to God? *(Circle one.)*

Deception #6: Powerless

Lies of the enemy:

- You are weak.

- You are damaged goods.

- Can't you do *anything* right?

- How helpless can one person be?

- Someone's always got to take care of you.

Your TRUE Identity: POWERFUL

 After each verse, answer the questions which indicate your power as a son or daughter of the King.

For God has not given us a spirit of fear, but of power and of love and of a sound mind.
— **2 Timothy 1:7** (NKJV)

What kind of a "spirit" has God given us?

❋ ❋ ❋

You are from God, little children, and have overcome them; because greater is He who is in you than he who is in the world. — **1 John 4:4**

"He who is in the world" refers to Satan and his allies. Between us and them, which one is the more powerful?

❋ ❋ ❋

For everyone born of God overcomes the world. This is the victory that has overcome the world, even our faith. Who is it that overcomes the world? Only he who believes that Jesus is the Son of God. — **1 John 5:4,5** (NIV)

As a Christian, you are "born of God." "The world" referred to is the world system that is ruled over by Satan. When you and the world mix it up, who has the power to win?

If you are currently suffering from PTSD, you probably don't *feel* particularly "powerful." You may still be nursing physical injuries. You may feel powerless to accomplish basic goals, control your anger, sleep, conquer your depression. But your weakness is only temporary. When Jesus was taken into custody, flogged, tortured and crucified, He seemed *very* weak. But it was only temporary. In fact, He had massive *latent* power during that entire ordeal. The power was there, just not being used – and for good reasons. You have that same latent power, but the odds are good that it's not being used for *no* good reason!

Prayer Assignment: Begin asking God to help you release the latent power that He has placed within you. He wants to! Just ask Him!

❋ ❋ ❋ ❋ ❋

Deception #7: Unlovable

Lies of the enemy:

- Who would ever love you?

- You're so ugly and boring.

- You are beyond being loved, by God or by people.
- You really have no redeeming qualities.

Your TRUE Identity: LOVABLE

You are of infinite worth. God was so much in love with you that He was willing to sacrifice His Son to redeem you from your sins. Even if you were the only person on earth, He would have done it for you. Obviously, there is *something* about you that is *infinitely* lovable!

> *For I am convinced that neither death, nor life, nor angels, nor principalities, nor things present, nor things to come, nor powers, nor height, nor depth, nor any other created thing, will be able to separate us from the love of God, which is in Christ Jesus our Lord.*
> **– Romans 8:38,39**

 Make a list from the above verse of the things that God would fight through in order to get to you because of His love for you:

❀ ❀ ❀

Greater love has no one than this, that one lay down his life for his friends. **– John 15:13**

Jesus made this statement shortly before He was crucified. Who were the "friends" He was referring to, for whom He was about to lay down His life?

❀ ❀ ❀

> *But God showed his great love for us by sending Christ to die for us while we were still sinners.*
> **– Romans 5:8 (NLT)**

How much love would it take for you to be willing to die for someone else? Would you do it for your mother? For your daughter or son? How about for your best friend? You may have had an experience in battle where someone got in harm's way so that you could live. *That* was a supremely unselfish, loving act. But have you heard of a soldier who gave up his or her life for someone they didn't even know? It happens from time to time and it always amazes us. How could someone be *so* selfless? But would you be willing to die for someone who had betrayed you the night before, spit in your face, punched you in the stomach, stole your wallet, your car and your girlfriend or boyfriend? You would have to hold incredible love and forgiveness to die for *that* person. And yet, that's who we were, when Christ died on the cross for us. That's how much He loves us.

❀ ❀ ❀ ❀ ❀

Deception #8: Separated

Lies of the enemy:

- You are alone and you should stay that way.
- No one wants you on their team.
- You shouldn't bother other people so much.
- People wish you weren't here.
- You don't need anybody else anyway.

YOUR TRUE IDENTITY: CONNECTED

You are connected in two realms...

Connected to God:

[Jesus speaking:] *I am the vine, you are the branches; he who abides in Me and I in him, he bears much fruit, for apart from Me you can do nothing.* — **John 15:5**

 What picture of "connectedness" did Jesus use to show how attached we are to Him?

_____

❀ ❀ ❀

For you are all children of God through faith in Christ Jesus. — **Galatians 3:26** (NLT)

What are some deep, meaningful ways that children and parents are connected?

_____

_____

❀ ❀ ❀

I have been crucified with Christ; and it is no longer I who live, but Christ lives in me. — **Galatians 2:20**

This verse indicates that Christ lives *where?*

_____

❀ ❀ ❀

Connected to the Body of Christ – other Christians:

All of you together are Christ's body, and each of you is a part of it. — **1 Corinthians 12:27** (NLT)

 What are all Christians a part of?

_____

❀ ❀ ❀

What do you know about how connected various cells and organs of a body are?

_____

❀ ❀ ❀

You are no longer foreigners and aliens, but fellow citizens with God's people and members of God's household. — **Ephesians 2:19** (NIV)

This verse gives us two pictures of "connectedness" with other people. What are they?

_____

❀ ❀ ❀ ❀ ❀

As you work through the difficulties of your Combat Trauma, there will be times when you feel alone, rejected, unlovable, devalued and unimportant. That's when Satan will pile on and do all he can to affirm those thoughts. It's at that time that you need to recognize his tactics. He's using deception to move you closer to defeat. He is **lying**. How can you tell when Satan is lying? Whenever his mouth moves! Counter his lies with the truth.

Make this proclamation, out loud if possible, based on what you just learned from God's Word:

This Is Who I Am

REGARDED

I am a friend of the Almighty God of heaven and earth. (John 15:15)

Jesus is not ashamed to call me His brother (sister). (Hebrews 2:11)

I am chosen by God, holy and without fault in His eyes. (Ephesians 1:4)

I am an heir to the riches of the Creator of the universe. (Galatians 4:7)

IMPORTANT

I have been rightly called a child of God. (John 1:12)

God has made me His salt and light in the world. (Matthew 5:13,14)

I am an eternal being. (John 3:16)

FORGIVEN

I am no longer condemned. (Romans 8:1)

I have been justified before the righteous Judge. (Romans 5:1)

I am at peace with God. (Romans 5:1)

God no longer remembers my sins. (Hebrews 10:17)

VALUED

God loves me with an everlasting love. (Jeremiah 31:3)

I am God's temple, bought at a great price. (1 Corinthians 6:19,20)

God knows, chose, called, justified and glorified me. (Romans. 8:29,30)

ACCEPTED

I am accepted in Christ. (Ephesians 1:6 NKJV)

I am a chosen, costly, living stone in God's building. (1 Peter 2:4,5)

I have bold, unrestricted access to God's throne of grace. (Hebrews 4:16)

POWERFUL

God has given me the spirit of power, love and a sound mind. (2 Timothy 1:7)

God's Spirit in me is greater than any unholy spirits in the world. (1 John 4:4)

I am born of God and believe in Jesus – I'm a world-overcomer. (1 John 5:4,5)

LOVABLE

I am loved by God and *nothing* will keep us apart. (Romans 8:38,39)

I am loved supremely – enough for God to die for me. (John 15:13)

I am loved unconditionally, *even* when I sin. (Romans 5:8)

CONNECTED

I am intimately attached to Christ and bearing fruit. (John 15:5)

I am a member of God's eternal family. (Galatians 3:26)

Christ is as close to me as my heart and lungs. (Galatians 2:20)

I am part of Christ's body with millions of brothers and sisters. (1 Corinthians 12:27)

I am an eternal member of God's Kingdom and household. (Ephesians 2:19)

Follow-Up

Write today's date here: _____ One month from today, re-take the "Self-Perception Assessment" that you completed at the beginning of this Step. If you have been regularly thinking about and proclaiming the above truths concerning your true identity, you should notice that your "Xs" have traveled a considerable distance to the left!

❋ ❋ ❋ ❋ ❋

Prayer Seed

My Father, thank You that Your truth drives out lies like light rids a room of darkness. I wasn't aware of the lies and deceit that had been infiltrating my mind. But now I am. Sharpen my defenses. Help me to be aware every time my enemy tries to deceive me and help me to counter his attacks with Your truth. I am not a victim – I am a victor! I want to live like one! Enable me to incorporate Your truths about who I am into my daily thought life. Amen.

❋ ❋ ❋

---

[1] Quote by Dr. Ronnie Janoff-Bullman in "The Aftermath of Victimization: Rebuilding Shattered Assumptions, found in *Failure to Scream* by Dr. Robert Hicks, p. 28, 29.

[2] Quote from Dr. Neil T. Anderson in *Victory Over The Darkness*, p. 43.

[3] Opposed pairs of core values/core hurts are found in Dr. Steven Stosny's *Manual of the Core Value Workshop* [Copyright 1995, 2003 Steven Stosny] and in other publications of his. For a fuller explanation consult his website: www.compassionpower.com

STEP 8: HOW DO I FIGHT?

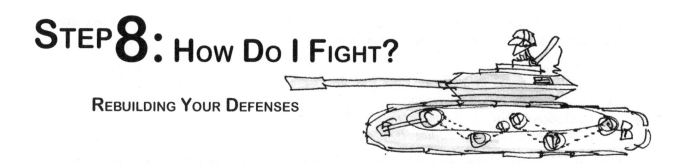

REBUILDING YOUR DEFENSES

> Know the enemy and know yourself.
> In a hundred battles you will never be in peril.
>
> – **Sun Tzu in *The Art of War*[1]**

He may or may not have known God, but this Chinese warrior of the sixth century B.C. knew warfare. After completing Step 7, you should have a much clearer concept of "yourself." In this Step, we will follow Sun Tzu's good advice and inform ourselves about "the enemy." The Apostle Paul expressed the same sentiment regarding our need for preparation in 2 Corinthians 2:11: *"We are not ignorant of his schemes."*

We must never lose site of the fact that – despite having been transported away from the physical battlefield – we are locked in a desperate war against a deadly enemy. It doesn't seem like it sometimes, because Satan is a master of deception. But the spiritual war our souls are engaged in is as real as the ones that use bullets and bombs – and just as consequential. As Arthur Mathews, English WWII vet and missionary wrote, "In Eden God decreed enmity between the serpent's seed and the seed of the woman. Because of this, the *law of strife* became the *law of life* for the human race."[2] Unfortunately, the Kingdom of God is taking heavy casualties because so many of her soldiers don't know their enemy, and aren't convinced there is even a war! We've engaged the enemy in much more than "a hundred battles," but won precious few victories. Peace in our souls is elusive, though we desire it desperately. Our top General during the Revolutionary War tells us how to win it:

> There is nothing so likely to produce peace as to be well-prepared to meet the enemy.
>
> – George Washington

❀   ❀   ❀   ❀   ❀

PREPARING TO MEET YOUR ENEMY

What do you already know about Satan? Do a little brainstorming and write down anything you can think of regarding his nature, his strategies, his likes, his dislikes, his motives, his destiny.

HIS ORIGIN

As we mentioned earlier in this manual, Satan started out as Lucifer, one of the most powerful angels in God's command. The prophet Ezekiel[3] describes him as having "the seal of perfection; full of wisdom; perfect in beauty; covered with bling – ruby, topaz, diamond, emerald…" well, you get the idea. He must have been an amazing being, because at some point he looked at himself, looked at the all-powerful

God of the universe, and thought, *I think I can take Him.* Pride was born in his heart and he made five pronouncements about the coup he intended to accomplish:

> *I will ascend to heaven;*
> *I will raise my throne above the stars of God;*
> *I will sit on the mount of assembly;*
> *I will ascend above the heights of the clouds;*
> *I will make myself like the Most High.*[4]

Revelation 12 indicates that one-third of the angels believed he could do it, and so they joined his rebellion. Why they made such a foolish choice, we're never told. But this left two-thirds still loyal to God, who triumphed. The rebels – including Satan – were banished from God's heaven, no longer free to roam the universe, confined to one planet: Earth.

His Objectives

Some time after this, God created man and woman and gave them authority over all the earth. Satan saw this as his grand opportunity to continue his rebellion. Four objectives formed in his mind:

1. Use deceit to steal some or all of their authority and use it against the Kingdom of God.
2. Afflict these objects of God's great affection and thereby afflict Him – and if possible, get them to blame their affliction on God.
3. Turn the humans against God – as he did one-third of the angels – and recruit them to his army.
4. Use them to stage a second coup attempt – which he feels certain will succeed this time.

Most of the book of Revelation contains prophesies about how that second attempt will play out. All the evil we've seen down through history, all the wars, all the pain, all the ungodly ways in which humans treat other humans is all part of Satan's staging of that final push to wrest control of earth from God's hands, and take His place. By the way, he won't succeed in this – we've read the last chapter of the book!

❋   ❋   ❋   ❋   ❋

His Tactics

Here is a little more detail about how Satan uses deceit to weaken and overcome us. Read each Bible passage below and in the space provided after each selection record what you observe about Satan's tactics. The first one is completed for you, so you'll get the idea what we're looking for.

Then Jesus was led up by the Spirit into the wilderness to be tempted by the devil.
– Matthew 4:1

Satan takes the initiative and intentionally tempts people to do wrong – especially when they

are isolated. He'll tempt anyone – even the Son of God! So we should all expect it.

But I am not surprised! Even Satan disguises himself as an angel of light. So it is no wonder that his servants also disguise themselves as servants of righteousness.
– 2 Corinthians 11:14,15 (NLT)

The Devil took him [Jesus] to the peak of a huge mountain. He gestured expansively, pointing out all the earth's kingdoms, how glorious they all were. Then he said, "They're Yours—lock, stock, and barrel. Just go down on your knees and worship me, and they're Yours."
– Matthew 4:8,9 (MSG)

_____

_____

_____

This is the meaning of the parable: The seed is God's word. The seeds that fell on the footpath represent those who hear the message, only to have the devil come and take it away from their hearts and prevent them from believing and being saved.
– Luke 8:11,12 (NLT)

_____

_____

_____

❋   ❋   ❋   ❋   ❋

BREAKING THE CODE

Satan's lies and temptations are very subtle – and they haven't changed much in thousands of years. They haven't needed to – they continue to work excellently. Examine the Genesis passage below in which the temptation of Adam and Eve are recorded. Draw a line from the underlined words of Satan on the left to what he's *really* saying on the right. This will help you recognize your enemy's voice…

And the Lord God commanded the man, "You are free to eat from any tree in the garden; but you must not eat from the tree of the knowledge of good and evil, for when you eat of it you will surely die."
– Genesis 2:16,17 (NIV)

Now the serpent [Satan] was more crafty than any of the wild animals the Lord God had made. He said to the woman, "<u>Did God really say, 'You must not eat from any tree in the garden'?</u>" ◉
The woman said to the serpent, "We may eat fruit from the trees in the garden, but God did say, 'You must not eat fruit from the tree that is in the middle of the garden, and you must not touch it, or you will die.'"
"<u>You will not surely die</u>," the serpent said to the ◉
woman. "<u>For God knows that when you eat of</u> ◉
<u>it your eyes will be opened, and you will be like</u> ◉
<u>God, knowing good and evil.</u>"
– Genesis 3:1-5 (NIV)

◉ "Do you mean that God – that restrictive old meanie – won't let you eat from *any* trees in the garden? I can't believe it!"

◉ "Don't you see what's going on here? God doesn't want you to experience new, mind-expanding things! He's *limiting* you!"

◉ "Oh, don't get excited. God tends to misrepresent the facts a lot. Let me straighten you out: you won't *really* die. He was just saying that to keep you under His control."

◉ "God isn't interested in associating with you – He wants to keep you ignorant and oppressed. He doesn't want you to be as smart as He is!"

ANATOMY OF A TEMPTATION

The framework of most of Satan's temptations contains these five elements. Can you see them implied in the interchange we just looked at?

Major Premise: Restrictions are bad.
Complementary Major Premise: Freedom is good.
Proposition: God's plans are restrictive.
Conclusion: God's restrictive plans are bad and *should not* be followed.
Corollary: My non-restrictive plans are good and *should* be followed.

Notice how logical and true the two Major Premises seem. How can people who appreciate their independence argue with them? No one likes to be restricted, and freedom *is* good. That's the kernel of truth. But we also know that some restrictions are good and some freedoms are bad. If we skate over that fact and accept the Proposition, we find ourselves nodding in agreement with the Conclusion and Corollary.

 Name a few restrictions that are good.

 Name a few freedoms that are bad.

SATAN'S PRIMARY TACTIC – DOORWAYS & FOOTHOLDS

DOORWAYS

Genesis 4:1-12 records the birth of Adam and Eve's first two sons, Cain and Abel. Unfortunately, it also records the first murder in history – inspired by The Murderer himself. Cain and Abel had made offerings to God, and for some reason Cain's was not acceptable. We're not sure why – perhaps it had to do with Cain's heart attitude as he presented it. At any rate, Cain became very angry and resentful. God could see what was in Cain's heart and confronted him about it, giving him some very valuable advice – which Cain didn't take.

In verse 7, God tells Cain,

> *You will be accepted if you do what is right. But if you refuse to do what is right, then watch out! Sin is crouching at the **door**, eager to control you. But you must subdue it and be its master.* (NLT)

What? Control? I thought Satan was offering me freedom! Anyone who has given in to the "freeing" temptations of Satan knows they eventually lead to bondage. It's interesting that in the last book of the Bible, Jesus also talks about standing at the door: *Here I am! I stand at the door and knock. If anyone hears my voice and opens the door, I will come in and eat with him, and he with Me* (Revelation 3:20). The door that is being spoken of at both ends of the Bible represents our **will**. Whatever we allow to come through that door will influence our choices, our life and our destiny – for good or for evil. And in both verses, *we* have control of the door. We decide who comes in, and who doesn't.

God describes sin (Satan) as crouching just outside the door of your will, trying to convince you hold it open for him – because he wants to master you, little by little. You've got two options. You can slam that door shut, sending a loud and clear message to both him and God that you're not interested in his propositions … or you can leave it open a crack. By doing that, you're saying, "Satan – I'm open to suggestions. How would you meet my needs?" He'll make his proposals. You'll listen. They will sound *very* good. As Eugene Peterson wrote, "Every temptation is disguised as a suggestion for improvement."[5] Improvement is good, right? So after a short period of deliberation, you'll swing the door open.

FOOTHOLDS

The principle is presented again in Ephesians 4:26,27 (NIV).

> *In your anger do not sin. Do not let the sun go down while you are still angry, and do not give the devil a **foothold**.*

Anger is not sin, as was mentioned in Step 7. But what we *do* when angry *can* be sin, or our anger can eventually *lead* us to sin if we don't deal with it in a timely manner. If we let negative attitudes – sinful or not – dwell in us un-addressed, we run the risk of giving the devil a "foothold."

When rock climbing, you need to find a series of footholds to make progress. One foothold will not conquer the pitch – each one enables you to make it to the next. This is a key point to remember about how Satan will try to influence your life. He won't blast in and take over all at once. He can't – such an obvious move would alert you. But if he can gain a little foothold – get you to agree to letting him have just a tiny bit of control in a small area, he's gotten just a little closer to conquering you in larger areas. God's advice to you: Don't give him even the first foothold! Once you've given it to him, it will be difficult to get it back!

One other important point: How does Satan get a foothold? **We give it to him**. He cannot seize it by force. He can't overrule our will. But he can deceive us into thinking that we will benefit by agreeing to his suggestions. So we give him that itty-bitty foothold in exchange for something we think will be of more value. We're always wrong.

EXPLOITING VULNERABILITIES

> To be certain to take what you attack is to attack a place the enemy does not protect.
> – Sun Tzu in *The Art of War*[6]

When it comes to targeting our open doors and footholds, Satan has stolen this stratagem from Sun Tzu's book – or vice versa. Each of us has areas of weakness, vulnerabilities and undefended places in our lives. Satan is aware of them, and *that's* where he waits. He won't waste time in your areas of strength – he's a skilled strategist patiently scoping out your soft spots and looking for an opportunity to strike.

 You will demonstrate *your* skill as a defensive strategist if you'll take the time to assess where your vulnerabilities are. Spend a few moments right now and ask the Lord to reveal to you where they might be. Where are your areas of chronic defeat? Which temptations are no match for your resolve? Where have you fallen before?

For a list of *potential* doorways, see Appendix B. You'll notice we emphasize "potential." Just because you have encountered one of these events, habits or experiences, it doesn't necessarily mean they have provided an open doorway or presented a foothold. But it's possible. If you have had experience with one of the items on the list, spend some time with God asking Him if there is an open door there that needs to be shut.

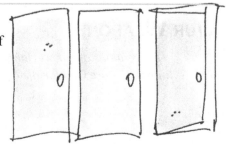

CLOSING DOORWAYS

"You must subdue it and be its master." (Genesis 4:7) Whenever you become aware of an open door in your life, there are three steps you need to take in order to shut it:

1. **Confess and repent of opening the door.**   If it was due to a willful choice on your part, this step is obvious. See Step 6A for a refresher on confession and repentance. But some doorways may have begun to be opened when you were in a passive state, and not disobeying God at all – like when you were under anesthesia or traumatized in a firefight. It may be that you later made a willful choice due to something that began then. It could be something like becoming psychologically addicted to pain meds after surgery (pain is no longer the problem, the desire to be "floating" all the time is), or an insatiable urge to kill developing sometime after the firefight. In those cases, you should confess the sin, but also intentionally close the original door.

2. **Take action to demonstrate repentance and purify your life.**

   - Release resentment and bitterness.
   - Seek forgiveness of anyone you offended or hurt.
   - Pay restitution if it's owed.
   - Renounce occultic involvement.
   - Destroy any offending objects (occultic amulets and games, pornography, books, satanic music, DVDs, drugs, alcohol, etc.).
   - Break off any harmful relationships.
   - Put yourself back under God's authority.

3. **Reappropriate the filling of the Holy Spirit** (Step 3A).

SUGGESTED PRAYER

Father, I confess that I have opened a door to my enemy. I have given him a foothold. I was vulnerable and deceived when I made the decision, but I'm still responsible for it. I confess to You that I [describe what you did to open the door]. I agree with You that it was sin, and I'm sorry for it. Please forgive me. On the basis of Your promise in Your Word, I accept our forgiveness of my sins. Thank You.

And now, Father, before You and before all the forces of darkness, I renounce my decision and renounce my opening of that door. I shut that door and take back that foothold. Satan, I remove your authority and ability to influence me in that area any longer. I bind you back from it in the name of Jesus Christ, who is my Lord, Savior and King.

Father, please strengthen that area of vulnerability. May it no longer be an undefended place. I commit to taking any further action You tell me to regarding this matter.

I relinquish the throne of my life to You once again. Please fill me, control me and empower me with Your Holy Spirit. Amen.

❀ ❀ ❀ ❀ ❀

OUR WEAPONS

The weapons of our warfare are not physical weapons of flesh and blood, but they are mighty before God for the overthrow and destruction of strongholds.

– 2 Corinthians 10:4 (AMP)

WEAPON #1: AUTHORITY

Being one of the most powerful beings God ever created, and honing his warfare skills for centuries, Satan is an adversary more powerful and deadly than anything we can imagine. If we were to go head-to-head with him in our own strength, he'd squash us like bugs.

But the Bible talks about the authority we have been given as servants and soldiers of Jesus Christ. The Greek word for it is:

EXOUSIA: "Right, power, authority, ruling power, a bearer of authority."[7]

It's more than *just* power – it's power *plus* authority. It's like in football. There are twenty-two men on the field with awesome power. They are strong, fast, and can inflict pain in a multitude of ways, but they aren't in authority. There are five or six other guys down there with striped shirts and whistles who have *exousia.* The players can put people *down,* but the refs can put people *out.*

Ephesians 1:19-23 has a lot to say about Jesus Christ's *exousia.*

> *That power is like the working of His* [the Father's] *mighty strength, which He exerted in Christ when He raised Him from the dead and seated Him at His right hand in the heavenly realms, far above all rule and authority* (exousia)*, power and dominion, and every title that can be given, not only in the present age but also in the one to come. And God placed all things under His feet and appointed Him to be head over everything for the church, which is His body, the fullness of Him who fills everything in every way.* (NIV)

 In the above passage, whose (plural) authority does Christ's authority exceed?

_____

Colossians 2:9,10 states that someone else besides Christ *also* is in possession of this same fullness and *exousia.* Circle who that is in the passage.

> *For in Christ all the fullness of the Deity lives in bodily form, and you have been given this fullness in Christ, who is the head over every power and authority* (exousia)*.* (NIV)

YOUR PLACE OF WARRING.

There is no authority in the universe higher than Jesus Christ's No king, no general, no president, no demon, no angel – not even Satan himself can stand before His exousia. And since we are now His children, God has equipped us to operate in that same authority as we deal with the forces of darkness. As the verse to the right says, we are positioned with Christ in the heavenly realms – a

> *God raised us up with Christ and seated us with Him in the heavenly realms in Christ Jesus.*
> – **Ephesians 2:6** (NIV)

position of immense power and authority over our spiritual adversaries. Christ – and we – have this authority because of Christ's willingness to die on the cross and rise again, thereby defeating Satan, sin and death once and for all.

> It is not for us to fight *for* victory, because "we are more than conquerors through Him that loved us" (Romans 8:37). Our fight is *from* victory: and from this vantage point, empowered with Christ's might, and completely enclosed in the whole armor of God, the powers of evil are compelled to back off as we resist them."
>
> – Arthur Matthews in *Born For Battle*[8]

We fight from victory and authority, seated with Christ in His heavenly command center. If we try to fight from any other vantage point, we will be defeated. Spiritual warfare expert Mark Bubeck writes in *Overcoming The Adversary:*[9]

> No believer who willfully walks in the sins of the flesh and world can hope to escape Satan's hurt and bondage. Can you imagine what would happen to a soldier who took a little stroll

into his enemy's territory during the heat of war? If not killed, he would soon be surrounded and taken captive. Yet there are believers who think they can carelessly engage in sin without being vulnerable to Satan.

WEAPON #2: OUR SPIRITUAL KEVLAR

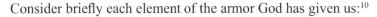

In football, basketball and war, we have learned that without a good defense, we have no offense. It doesn't matter how skillful we are with our offensive weapons, if we take one in the chest, we're done. That's why God invented armor.

He gave us spiritual armor for our spiritual battles as well. The Apostle Paul writes about it in **Ephesians 6:13-17 (NIV):**

> *Therefore put on the full armor of God, so that when the day of evil comes, you may be able to stand your ground, and after you have done everything, to stand. Stand firm then, with the **belt of truth** buckled around your waist, with the **breastplate of righteousness** in place, and with your **feet fitted with the readiness that comes from the gospel of peace**. In addition to all this, take up the **shield of faith**, with which you can extinguish all the flaming arrows of the evil one. Take the **helmet of salvation** and the **sword of the Spirit**, which is the word of God.*

Consider briefly each element of the armor God has given us:[10]

Belt of Truth.   Satan's chief tactic is deceit. Our only counter is truth. Any battle strategy is only as good as the intelligence that guides it. Jesus said that He is the truth (John 14:6), and He describes the Holy Spirit as "the Spirit of Truth" (John 14:17). As we strap on this Belt of Truth, it alerts us to the lies and deceitful tactics of the enemy and helps us fight with efficiency.

Breastplate of Righteousness.   The breastplate is like your flak jacket. Its main function is to protect the organs that are vital to your life. You can function without a hand or a leg, but if you lose a heart – no spares. King Solomon urges you to *"Guard your heart above all else, for it determines the course of your life"* (Proverbs 4:23 NLT). Our hearts are guarded by the righteousness of Jesus Christ that was given to us when we were saved. Righteousness is everything that Satan is not, so it repels him like WD-40 does water – only better!

Boots of the Gospel of Peace.   Boots protect your feet and give you traction and stability. Without them we tenderfeet would move too slowly and fearfully – an easy target in battle. You know that the Gospel brings peace to those who hear it. But don't forget that it also brings peace to you! Sometimes, when the world is so difficult to deal with, we become slow, unsteady and unstable.
It's easy to lose traction and stumble in that condition. Strap on those Gospel boots of peace, so that you can negotiate the rugged terrain before you. Jesus said in John 16:33, *"These things I have spoken to you, so that in Me you may have peace. In the world you have tribulation, but take courage; I have overcome the world."* Let His victories bring you peace and stability.

Shield of Faith.   The particular shield talked about here is a *thureos* – a very large shield. It could protect a soldier from *anything* that his adversary launched his way. Faith is our shield – or more accurately, the *object of our faith* is our shield. As we believe in and count on His power and authority to protect us, our shield will hold. If we shift our focus to our enemy and his strength, our faith can waiver. The Warrior-King David knew this well, as he wrote in Psalm 3:3, *"But You, O Lord, are a shield about me, my glory, and the One who lifts my head."*

Helmet of Salvation.   As the breastplate protects our torso's vital organs, the helmet protects our other vital organ and the command center of our lives: our brain. If the head is injured, the rest of the body will malfunction. Satan's *main* attacks won't target our feet or our houses or our jobs – though he may hit them as a diversion. His ultimate objectives have to do with our *minds*. If he can turn our wills to do his bidding, he's turned us completely. This is why, upon salvation, God gave us this helmet to protect our minds from Satan's influence.

Sword of the Spirit. This is a unique implement, because it can be both a defensive and an offensive weapon. The sword is the Word of God, and as such, it can serve us both defensively and offensively. When Jesus was attacked by Satan in the wilderness (Matthew 4:1-11), He parried every thrust of His adversary with a verse of Scripture, and eventually sent him on a hasty retreat. As the Apostle Paul affirms, *"For the word of God is living and active and sharper than any two-edged sword"* (Hebrews 4:12). More about this in the next section.

When you were in sector, you never went anywhere outside the wire without first putting on all your body armor, right? Very smart. In our international war on *Satan's* terror, there is no Green Zone. Every step we take is behind enemy lines. So it is also smart that we *intentionally* put on our *spiritual* armor each day before we venture out into the world. If you do, you will notice a much higher degree of effectiveness in your ability to cope and even to minister as you continue to recover from your Combat Trauma. You'll take a lot fewer hits, too.

Following is a suggested prayer you could pray each morning. This is not a magical prayer – the words aren't important. God looks at the heart, so to the degree these words reflect what your heart wants to express, God will hear them. Visualize each piece of armor as you put it on.

Dear Father, I stand before You this morning in order to receive the armor You have for me today. I receive from Your hand and wrap around my waist your belt of truth. May I receive, believe and speak only Your truth. I receive from Your hand and strap to my torso the breastplate of righteousness – the righteousness of Jesus Christ given to me the day I was saved. Guard my heart with it. I receive from Your hand and put on my feet the boots of the gospel of peace. May these boots give me stability and speed in my warring. And may Your peace fill my being and flow out to those around me.

I receive from Your hand and take in my [left/right] hand the shield of faith, with which I will deflect the missiles of my enemy, except for the ones You want to use for my purification and Your glory. I receive from Your hand the helmet of salvation, bought for me almost two-thousand years ago when Jesus Christ died on the cross for me, and rose again. Guard my mind with it. Finally, I receive from Your hand and take in my [right/left] hand the sword of the Spirit, which is Your Word. Give me skill to use it to defend myself and attack my enemy. So clothed in this armor, equipped with this sword and backed by Your authority, may I this day push back the kingdom of darkness and expand the Kingdom of Light. I pray this in the name of Jesus Christ, my Savior, Redeemer, God and King, Amen.

WEAPON #3: THE WORD OF GOD

HOW THINGS GET DONE IN THE KINGDOM OF GOD

In each of the following passages, something is being accomplished by God or by representatives of God. At the end write down what is common to each passage. What is it that is "making it happen?"

Then God said, "Let there be light"; and there was light.   **– Genesis 1:3**

Then Jesus said to him, "Go, Satan! For it is written, 'You shall worship the Lord your God and serve Him only.'"   **– Matthew 4:10**

Jesus said to the paralytic, "Get up, pick up your bed and go home." And he got up and went home.   **– Matthew 9:6**

Jesus said to the man, "Stretch out your hand!" He stretched it out, and it was restored to normal. **– Matthew 12:13**

Jesus rebuked him, saying, "Be quiet, and come out of him!" The unclean spirit cried out with a loud voice and came out. **– Mark 1:25,26**

Jesus rebuked the wind and said to the sea, "Hush, be still." And the wind died down and it became perfectly calm. **– Mark 4:39**

Jesus cried out with a loud voice, "Lazarus, come forth!" The man who had died came forth, bound with wrappings. **– John 11:43,44**

Peter said, "I do not possess silver and gold, but what I do have I give to you: In the name of Jesus Christ the Nazarene – walk!" With a leap he stood upright and began to walk. **– Acts 3:6-8**

Paul said to Elymas the magician, "You who are full of deceit and fraud... now, behold, the hand of the Lord is upon you, and you will be blind and not see the sun for a time." And immediately a mist and a darkness fell upon him. **– Acts 13:8-11**

Paul turned and said to the spirit, "I command you in the name of Jesus Christ to come out of her!" And it came out at that very moment. **– Acts 16:18**

 What does each passage have in common, in terms of what was done just before the supernatural event occurred?

Hopefully you were able to see that the way things are accomplished in the spiritual realm is not through muscle-power, electricity, computers, bulldozers or bombs. It gets done by *the spoken word.*

In the listing of your spiritual armor, the Sword of the Spirit is clearly equated with God's Word. When God wanted to create, He commanded matter into existence. When Jesus wanted to neutralize Satan, heal, calm a storm, raise the dead, control a demon, He spoke a word of commandment. When Jesus' disciples needed to heal or do spiritual warfare, they followed His example and spoke commands as representatives of their Master.

This is also how Jesus wants *you* to fight your enemy. You occupy the high ground, you have superior fire power, righteous authority and allies that are out of this world. You accomplish your offensives by *speaking* your commands to your enemy, just as Jesus did when He fought Satan in the wilderness in Matthew 4.

SPIRITUAL AMMO

Each time Jesus was attacked, He came back at His enemy with Scripture. Follow His example! Suppose your enemy is coming at you with a temptation to go to bed with someone other than your spouse. He or she is available and willing – what are you going to do? Grab some spiritual ammo, lock and load! Recall what God's Word says on this subject and use it against your tempter (Satan, not the one you're lusting after!), just as your arms instructor – Jesus Christ – showed you. Here's a suggested confrontational pattern:

"Father, Satan is tempting me to sin against You. He wants me to commit adultery. But I desire to master him. Please fill me with Your Holy Spirit. I take my position seated with Christ at Your right hand in the heavenly realms above all forces of darkness. With Your blessing and protection, and in Your authority, I ask You to help me resist my enemy, and thereby defeat him.

"Satan, I address you in the name and authority of the Lord Jesus Christ, King of kings and Lord of lords – who has bought me with His blood and made me a child of the Most High God. I am aware of your attempts to cause me to sin. In doing so, you have transgressed the commandment of God, for He has said in His Word, 'You shall not commit adultery.' You are trying to get me to commit this sin, so you are in the wrong. Therefore, in the authority given to me by God Himself, I command you to cease your activities directed at me, remove yourself from my area and go where Jesus Christ tells you to go.

"Thank you, Father, for this victory. Just as your angels ministered to Jesus after His fight with Satan, I ask that You would minister to me as well, and strengthen that vulnerable area in my life. Amen!"

In doing this, you are following a very clear pattern that God has set up in His word. You see it in James 4:7,8. Compare each component of the verse with each of the three paragraphs above.

First paragraph = ***Submit to God.***

Second paragraph = ***Resist the devil and he will flee from you.***

Third paragraph = ***Draw near to God and He will draw near to you.***

ADVANCE OR RETREAT?

Here's an important distinction that all God's spiritual warriors need to be aware of. You may have heard it said, "Resist temptation" and "Flee the devil." This is a good example of how Satan twists the truth in order to engineer our defeat, because God tells us to do the *exact opposite.*

When it comes to temptation, we are to *flee!* As Proverbs 4:14,15 says:

Do not enter the path of the wicked and do not proceed in the way of evil men. Avoid it, do not pass by it; turn away from it and pass on.

When it comes to eyeball-to-eyeball confrontation with the devil, we are to *resist!* Don't back down, don't run, *fight.* If we do, *he'll* run, as we just read in James 4:7: *Resist the devil and he will flee from you.*

Here's the fun part. It doesn't say we have to engage him and beat him to a pulp or try to pull off some overwhelming victory in order to make him retreat. All we have to do is resist. That's it! He'll see our *exousia*, recognize our training, and run for the hills!

Need some ammo? Check out your very own *Spiritual Warfare Ammo Bunker* found in Appendix C of this manual. There's plenty there! But if you come up against an attack of the enemy and don't see the exact cartridge you need in the bunker, do some searching of the Scriptures on your own and add it to your supplies.

Wouldn't you like to try out your new weaponry? Ask God to show you an area in which Satan has been attacking you lately. Select your "ammo" verse, and then engage the enemy! Use the prayer pattern suggested above. Then, sometime tomorrow come back to this manual and write down what happened.

Prayer Seed

Give me victory, Father! I've suffered so many defeats over the past months. I need to win some! Just as Uncle Sam taught my hands to war in the physical realm, I need you to teach me to fight in the spiritual realm. I know that, in my own strength I am useless against such a formidable enemy as Satan. But in Your authority, I am more than a conqueror! Help me to put on my spiritual armor every day. Give me the intelligence and discernment I need to counter the deceitful moves of my adversary. Equipped with your mighty weapons, may I secure victory for myself, my family, and for Your Kingdom. Amen.

❀   ❀   ❀

---

[1] From The Art of War by Sun Tzu, translated by Samuel B. Griffith (Oxford University Press, 1963), p. 84.

[2] Quote from R. Arthur Mathews in *Born For Battle*, p. 11

[3] Ezekiel 28:12-19. In this passage, the Spirit of God is speaking through the prophet Ezekiel against the King of Tyre – a very devilish king. In this pronouncement He was in essence saying, "King of Tyre, your characteristics are just like Satan's. Now let me tell you his history – and his destiny."

[4] Isaiah 14:13,14. Here God speaks to a different king (the King of Babylon – present day Iraq) using the same theme: "You're just like Satan – in these respects…"

[5] Quote from Eugene Peterson (translator of The Message) in *A Long Obedience In The Same Direction* (InterVarsity Press, 1980, 2000), p. 127.

[6] From *The Art of War,* p. 96.

[7] Colin Brown (Ed.), *The New Int'l Dictionary of New Testament Theology* (Regency, 1967, 1971), Vol. 2, p. 606.

[8] Quote from R. Arthur Mathews in *Born For Battle,* p. 27,28.

[9] Quote from Dr. Mark I. Bubeck in *Overcoming The Adversary,* p. 17.

[10] For an in-depth, inspiring, practical six-chapter treatment of our spiritual armor, see Dr. Mark I. Bubeck's *Overcoming The Adversary*, pages 64–120.

STEP9: HOW DO I GET ACROSS?

FINDING BRIDGE PEOPLE

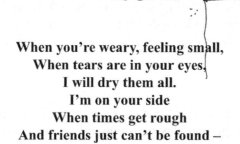

When you're weary, feeling small,
When tears are in your eyes,
I will dry them all.
I'm on your side
When times get rough
And friends just can't be found –
Like a bridge over troubled water
I will lay me down.

– Paul Simon[1]

THE NECESSITY OF BRIDGES

The day started slow but the squawk box shattered the stillness: "RPG ambush!" The adrenalin began to rush, even though the voice on the radio wasn't familiar to me. But then the radio squawked again, "KIA!" It was the fifth day since we took over command of this sector in Afghanistan and the reality of war was already too clear. The sergeant under fire relayed more vital information in the staccato cadence of a man fighting for his life – and the lives of his platoon members.

Somebody needed our help. The soldier who was killed wasn't even in my company, but the memory was fresh of the two great Americans we'd lost to RPGs just two days earlier. It made me mad. As I sprinted out of the TOC, it dawned on me that they were pinned down on bad ground, one of the worst parts of the sector to support, even *before* the socked-in weather severely limited our air support. They were only about five klicks north of us, but the storm we'd been getting the past twenty-four hours had turned the ditch north of us from a slight inconvenience to a roaring river. I knew there was a bridge west of us, but it would take at least forty-five minutes to take that detour. What would be left of them when we got there?

As I ran to my M1A1 Abrams tank I noticed an unfamiliar shadow moving off a flat bed that had come in during the night. It was a M60A1 AVLB (Armored Vehicle Launched Bridge) that was being unloaded. I learned later it belonged to a Wisconsin Reserve unit – their transport had busted an axle on its way to battalion. "Is that thing fueled and mission ready?" I shouted out as I ran. The vehicle's crew looked at me, startled, but one of them quickly responded, "It's ready, Sir! What do you need?" While I hadn't trained with them or built the trust needed to know that I could depend upon them, the situation called for placing trust where it had not yet been earned. "Mount up!"

We headed straight for the ditch. Moments later I was gawking as this monstrosity of metal on tracks started to look like one of my kid's Transformers unfolding itself. In minutes, the maelstrom of water was spanned by sixty-three feet of bridge able to support a tank. The AVLB disconnected and we rumbled across to engage the insurgents and bring our comrades home.

You should have seen the look on the face of that sergeant as my tank, the Bradley and two Humvees started providing cover enough to bring the engagement to an end! We quickly gathered both teams and retraced our tracks to where our bridge-builders were positioned to provide crossing cover. Then quietly, efficiently, the AVLB team hooked up and secured that beautiful folding bridge back onto its moving platform. It and they had brought us home, and those "Cheese-Head" Reserve engineers immediately became our best buddies.

❄ ❄ ❄ ❄ ❄

In the heat of battle, you can't be too fussy about where your help comes from. Normal people in abnormal circumstances need unique transfusions of support. While the M60A1 AVLB was the answer in this scenario, God's preserving and providing doesn't usually come in the form of a 750 HP diesel, 58 ton, 20-meter-spanning Transformer. It may not appear as you'd expect, but if He sent it, it will be just what you need.

BRIDGES TO HEALING

Throughout this manual we have stressed that God is your Healer (Exodus 15:26). But because we live in a fallen world with its various complexities, traps, weaknesses and land mines, your healing is no easy fix. It will take place when the environment surrounding your woundedness gives God maximum access to your soul. We've shared many practical measures you can take to facilitate that, but one of the most effective – and least used – has to do with people. You need to be in contact with people who are Spirit-filled, Spirit-directed, unselfish servants of God who want to provide direct help to others. When we get into trouble, God *expects* us to help each other out. There is safety and strength in numbers – even if it's only one or two others:

> *Two people are better off than one, for they can help each other succeed. If one person falls, the other can reach out and help. But someone who falls alone is in real trouble. Likewise, two people lying close together can keep each other warm. But how can one be warm alone? A person standing alone can be attacked and defeated, but two can stand back-to-back and conquer. Three are even better, for a triple-braided cord is not easily broken.*
>
> **– Ecclesiastes 4:9-12 (NLT)**

FRIENDS OF FAITH

When you get the chance, read **Mark 2:1-12**. This is the story of a paralyzed man and four of his "bridges." The word had gotten around that Jesus was at a certain house in Capernaum healing people. These four men immediately thought of their paralyzed friend. They knew there was no way he could get there, so they rushed to his house, put him on a stretcher, and carried him to Jesus. Unfortunately, they weren't the only ones who had heard about the Healer. The house was crammed full of people and surrounded by hundreds more. The four men cared about their incapacitated friend too much to give up and go home. They hoisted him up on top of the house, tore up the roof and lowered him through the hole down to Jesus! They would not be denied. Then Jesus – *seeing the faith of his friends* – healed the paralyzed man immediately.

There are faith-filled people who want to do that for *you* – if you'll let them. It goes against the macho GI image of a man or woman who is self-sufficient and in need of no one's help. But, if your pride isn't getting in the way, you know that you *do* need some help right now – just like that platoon north of the ditch-turned-river. There's no shame in needing and seeking help – every one of us does from time to time. The shame goes to the one who doesn't seek it, preferring to remain proud but forever paralyzed.

These "bridges" may be old friends, or you may not know who they are at this time. You might not even have met them yet. But they're nearby, motivated by their love for God and their love for you. In this Step we'll tell you what to look for…

The four men in the story did not heal their friend – Jesus did. But would the healing have taken place had the men not taken the initiative and altered their friend's environment so that it included Jesus? What does this fact make you think about your current situation and potential "roof demolishers" you have in your life?

_____

_____

❋ ❋ ❋ ❋ ❋

GOD INVENTED BRIDGES

There is an obvious principle of Bible interpretation that says, "If it's in the Bible, it's in God's will." As you read the following verses, would you say it is God's will that we should be "bridges" for each other?

Now we who are strong ought to bear the weaknesses of those without strength and not just please ourselves. **– Romans 15:1**

Bear one another's burdens, and thereby fulfill the law of Christ. **– Galatians 6:2**

Always be humble and gentle. Be patient with each other, making allowance for each other's faults because of your love. **– Ephesians 4:2 (NLT)**

Be kind and compassionate to one another, forgiving each other, just as in Christ God forgave you. **– Ephesians 4:32 (NIV)**

Confess your sins to one another, and pray for one another so that you may be healed. **– James 5:16**

❋ ❋ ❋ ❋ ❋

WHAT CAN WE EXPECT FROM A BRIDGE?

The "bridges" we're talking about in this Step are people who will help transport us to God, so that He can provide healing. In many ways, they are representatives of His, ambassadors, messengers and liaisons. The following Scriptures will give you some insight as to how a properly-functioning bridge can help you get closer to God. As you read through them, answer the questions asked after each verse.

A friend loves at all times, and a brother is born for adversity. **– Proverbs 17:17**

 There are probably a few people – perhaps you went through combat with them – to whom you could say, "For better or worse, I'm on your side. Even if you're wrong, I'm still on your side. I've got your back no matter what." You would consider it an honor to aid them, right? Write down their names:

_____

_____

There are people who feel the same way about you. If you were to list them now, that list would probably be the same as the one you just wrote. If any of your friends were in a jam, you'd come to their aid in a heartbeat, wouldn't you? And wouldn't you be upset with them if they concealed from you that they were having trouble, keeping you from putting yourself out for them?

The Point: *Expect* your "bridges" to be eager to help you out. They *want to!* Don't hesitate to call on them.

In everything I did, I showed you that by this kind of hard work we must help the weak, remembering the words the Lord Jesus himself said: "It is more blessed to give than to receive."

– Acts 20:35 (NIV)

 If you're an unselfish person, you would rather give than receive, right? How do you normally act when you have to be a receiver?

So, if you're reluctant to receive, that means you're reluctant to allow your friends to give – which means you are robbing them of a blessing! How can you *live* with yourself?!

The Point: Don't be a thief! Provide the opportunity for your friends to be blessed by allowing them to give to you.

❋   ❋   ❋

Understand this, my dear brothers and sisters: You must all be quick to listen, slow to speak, and slow to get angry.

– James 1:19 (NIV)

 From this, what would you say a "bridge" friend should be good at?

As was mentioned in previous Steps, one of the practices that will help you in your healing is to process your traumatic episodic memories in a safe environment. In other words, you need to *talk* about them. A good bridge will be a good listener. If they're constantly interrupting you in order to tell *their* story, or if they are freaked out by what you share and keep trying to change the subject, then they probably aren't the one to talk to at the deeper levels.

The Point: Expect a good bridge to be a good listener.

❋   ❋   ❋

As iron sharpens iron, so a friend sharpens a friend.

– Proverbs 27:17 (NIV)

 What does this verse say a bridge friend will do for you?

What do you think it means for one person to sharpen another?

Sharpening is an intentional process – a knife doesn't sharpen itself. So a good bridge will take the initiative, reaching out and proactively helping you improve your healing environment. By the way, sharpening is not always pleasant for the knife – sparks fly, it gets real hot, and some of its best cutting-edge material is ground off! In the same way, your bridge may not always stroke your ego just the way you'd like. You may have some nicks and burrs that need to be smoothed out. Be ready for it, and receive it in the same manner in which it's offered: in love.

The Point: Expect a bridge to be intentional, looking for ways to help you improve your healing environment – some of which might create a few sparks.

❋   ❋   ❋

An open rebuke is better than hidden love! Wounds from a sincere friend are better than many kisses from an enemy.   **– Proverbs 27:5,6** (NLT)

 If you had a cancerous tumor, would you prefer that your doctor use a scalpel in the appropriate area, or just say a lot of nice things to you?

_____

Sometimes it hurts to hear the truth, doesn't it? But truth is like medicine – it tastes bad but it's *good* for you! Sometimes we get mad at people when they tell us a distasteful truth. But a true bridge friend won't care. They are willing to risk their friendship with you, hurting you if necessary, in order to help you in your healing process. Think back to some of the most influential people in your life. Perhaps it was a parent, a coach, a friend, your DI, a doctor. Write a couple of their names here:

_____

No doubt you felt the love and respect they held for you (well, maybe not from the DI). But wasn't there another element in each case? Weren't they people who were willing to tell you some hard truths? Didn't they get a little tough on you from time to time? When you needed somebody to bust your chops, weren't they willing to volunteer for the honor?

The Point: A good bridge is willing to risk your friendship in order to open your eyes to a vital truth you may not know.

❈   ❈   ❈

But encourage one another day after day, as long as it is still called "Today," so that none of you will be hardened by the deceitfulness of sin.

– Hebrews 3:13

Yes, you need to know the hard truths. *But* ... you also need that input strongly balanced by a good dose of encouragement. You need to surround yourself with people who are positive and supportive – people who "day after day" catch you doing something right. No one has ever died from receiving too much encouragement, and you won't be the first.

 What is something that you need to hear? Write down a piece of encouragement that you have not been receiving lately.

_____

_____

Prayer Assignment: Bring this up with God. Let him know that you need for Him to bring others around you who will communicate those encouraging words.

Notice something else about that verse. It tells us two things about sin: It hardens us and it's deceitful. Sin has the same kind of effect on your conscience as your ill-fitting boot has on your foot. The rubbing hurts at first, but after a while callous forms and it doesn't bother you any more. Sin works the same way. It'll sting your conscience the first few times, but if you keep at it long enough the discomfort will fade. Then you'll figure it's OK, since you don't feel bad about it anymore. But that's when it's easiest for Satan to slip in his poison daggers.

However, if you've got good, positive, salt-and-light-sharing bridges around you, God's Spirit in them can throw a spotlight on your errors and sins and draw you back to the Father long after you've turned down the Spirit's volume knob in your life.

The Point: Expect massive doses of encouragement from your bridge friend, but also be open to their kind, corrective influence to keep your heart soft to God's conviction of sin in your life.

A FORMALIZED BRIDGE RELATIONSHIP

It's perfectly alright to carry on a "casual" relationship with people you have identified as bridge people in your life. They may not even know what an M60A1 AVLB is. They may have never even been in the military. But you can conduct CBAMs (Covert Bridge Acquisition Maneuvers) and they need never know. On the other hand, if you've become acquainted with someone who is spiritually mature, compassionate, resourceful and insightful, you may want to pursue a more formal bridge relationship with him or her.

If they aren't aware of the "bridge" concept, perhaps you could tell them about it or give them a copy of this manual. They may have been the one who gave *you* this manual, and in that case, they probably know a lot about how to be a bridge for you (assuming they've read it!).

One of the main things that causes any relationship to self-destruct is "uncommunicated expectations." One person has a set of expectations that the other knows nothing about, and when they aren't met, the pin gets pulled on the friendship grenade. So if you plan to formalize your relationship, it would be a good idea to ask him or her the following questions:

- ❑ Will you commit to listening to me with your ears, eyes and heart to try to grasp what I'm saying, even if I'm not doing a very good job of communicating?
- ❑ Will you simply accept and not judge me for what has happened downrange and how I am responding?
- ❑ Will you revise your civilian expectations and accept how I work at expressing my responses?
- ❑ Will you commit to walking with me through the emotions and thoughts this journey reveals?
- ❑ Will you encourage me by reminding me that I am a normal person who has experienced abnormal events?
- ❑ Will you acknowledge that it is normal for a grieving person to express the full array of emotions including anger, helplessness, and frustration?
- ❑ Will you commit to not withdrawing from me because of what I've opened up and shared with you, no matter how painful?
- ❑ Will you understand that at times, all I want is for you to sit with me and wait?
- ❑ Will you commit to listening, even if I am sharing the same experience over again?

Having agreed to these terms, I now pronounce you Combat Trauma Survivor and Bridge. You may now… shake hands.

[?] Make a list of people that you would like to start a "formal" bridge relationship with. Then start praying that God will bring it about.

_____

_____

_____

❋   ❋   ❋   ❋   ❋

GROUP BRIDGES

Those with extensive experience in research and therapy for Combat Trauma and PTSD survivors almost unanimously sing the praises of group settings in helping them work through the difficulties of their past horrific experiences. There are many reasons for this:

- In a group, you are actively countering a Combat Trauma survivor's normal tendency to self-isolate.

- You are forging deep friendships with men and women who truly understand what you have experienced, because they have too.

- The depth of your shared experiences opens up communication and support lines that few non-CT survivors could ever understand or appreciate.

- As group members get to know each other at deeper levels, they take a more active roll in "watching each other's back."

- They won't be judgmental, alarmed or abandon you during any "kookin' out" episodes you experience. They'll be far more motivated than most to stick with you through them.

- You have the option of benefiting from the experiences and insights of several people who are in the same boat you are.

- You are multiplying bridge people in your life – and you are being a bridge to each of them as well, which enhances your own healing environment.

- During periods when you're taking your "two steps back," you can be encouraged and harvest some hope by hearing of another group member's "three steps forward."

- The give-and-take of a group situation is sometimes less threatening than a one-to-one, eyeball-to-eyeball session with someone you don't know very well.

- You're multiplying your prayer power; see Matthew 18:19,20.

Some helpful tips.   Here are a few principles to keep in mind as you begin to participate in group sessions. Most of these are taken from support group expert Jody Hayes' book, *Smart Love*[2]

- Once you're in the right group, you may feel safe, but you may also feel shy. This brings us to another paradox of recovery: The more you reveal yourself, the safer you will feel. The more vulnerable you make yourself, the quicker you can recover.

- Share your experiences. Your problems will become clearer when you give words to them. You will discover how much harder it is to fool yourself when you actually hear yourself saying something that you know is either a partial truth or a full lie. At the same time, when you are describing signs of progress or small victories, you will find their effect amplified when you applaud yourself in the presence of others.

- Acknowledge how you feel at the moment, whatever those feelings are. Remember, you are not speaking to please others or to be graded on your recovery. You are speaking to help yourself.

- Embrace your feelings and accept them, even if you feel momentarily miserable. By honestly describing your feelings, you will get a clearer understanding of the experience you are going through. Moreover, there is a significant chance that your painful feelings will diminish. A side benefit is that you will almost always help someone else who is not yet brave enough to speak.

- When speaking, it is important to avoid long, detailed descriptions of your experiences, going into great, gory detail. This will only feed your problem, not release you from it. In addition, it may frustrate and trigger other group members. Keep the focus on how you feel, how events affected you and what you are doing about it.

- When sharing in the group, avoid comparing yourself with others. Each person is at a different place in their healing. Keep your focus on yourself and on how God is working in *your* life.

Have you considered joining a group of Combat Trauma survivors? What are your thoughts about it?

WHEN IS IT TIME TO CALL IN THE PROS?

You may have done an excellent job of connecting with a number of bridge people, but still experience struggles that seem more than you can bear. Your level of trauma may be such that you need to see a professional counselor or therapist. Following is a checklist that therapist and writer J. Elizabeth Oppenheim[3] devised to help a person determine if they should seek professional help.

If any of these first 4 warning signs are evident, GET HELP NOW!

- ❑ You are thinking that suicide or death is a plausible, acceptable way to stop your pain.
- ❑ Your concentration is so poor that you are accidentally hurting yourself or others.
- ❑ You are out of control in some way that is endangering your health or the health of others.
- ❑ You have no plans for the future, no hope of your life getting better.

If you don't have a counselor, doctor, pastor or friend you can call, and if you are planning to hurt yourself or someone else right now, call 911, go to an Emergency Room or call a Suicide Prevention Hotline and ask for help. We're serious! *Right now!* Put down the manual and *GO!*

For the next nine signs, if you notice that three or four of them are present, ask friends, your doctor or your pastor for a referral to a counselor or other professional, or go to a nearby Vet Center or VA Hospital and ask for a counselor. If you have no other leads, look in the Yellow Pages under Counselors, Therapists or Psychologists and keep looking until you find someone who really helps you.

- ❑ You are unable to work.
- ❑ You cannot keep food down or are eating uncontrollably.
- ❑ You are not sleeping or are sleeping all the time.
- ❑ You have lost interest in everything you used to enjoy; nothing can make you smile.
- ❑ It is too much effort to get dressed, shave, put on make-up, etc.
- ❑ You cannot clean your house to basic sanitation levels or you compulsively clean it late into the night.
- ❑ You are barely functioning but you have other people depending on you to take care of them (children, elders, disabled).
- ❑ You have no one you can talk to honestly about what you're going through – or you've worn out all your friends who would listen.
- ❑ You have a health problem that flares up when you're under stress.

You're not committing to a lifetime of therapy – just hooking up with a well-qualified bridge for a while. This place is only temporary. Get all the support you can as you move through this phase of life.

Professional therapists can be extremely helpful – or not. Those who come from a strictly clinical/psychological frame of reference can be helpful with coping mechanisms, talking about your past, dealing with triggers, getting you in touch with your pain and your emotions, among other things. But unless they are aware of the spiritual dimensions of trauma, and understand God as the great Healer, they won't be a true bridge for you. Their input will be helpful, but you need more.

By the same token, you may encounter a Biblical counselor or Christian therapist who really walks closely with God, but isn't well-versed in the physical and psychological aspects of PTSD. They may be a less-than-optimal bridge as well.

Following is a list of questions you could ask a potential counselor to get an idea of how effective a bridge they will be:

1. What is your approach to understanding people's problems and helping them grow, change and become whole again through counseling?

2. What education and experience have you had that has most influenced your approach to counseling individuals struggling with Combat Trauma or PTSD?

3. Are you a Christian? How does your faith influence your perspective and practice of counseling?

4. Is it your custom to bring Biblical truth into your counseling practice?

5. Do you pray with those you counsel? Do you invite those you counsel to pray as part of their counseling journey?

6. Do you go to a church? If so, where, and how long have you been a member?

7. What are your educational credentials for offering to counsel CT/PTSD survivors? How has your preparation influenced you?

8. Have you experienced severe loss, crisis or trauma in your own life? How has this affected how you counsel CT/PTSD survivors?

❈ ❈ ❈ ❈ ❈

Walking with a friend in the dark
is better than walking alone in the light.

– Helen Keller

❈ ❈ ❈ ❈ ❈

LOCATING A CHRISTIAN COUNSELOR

If you aren't sure where to look for a Christian counselor in your area, here are two places to inquire. They are in contact with two nationwide networks of counselors who could be of help:

- **American Association of Christian Counselors** has constructed a Christian Care Network that you can access online. Go to www.aacc.net. At their home page, you will see several tabs across the top – click on the "Divisions" tab. There will be a drop-down menu – click on "Christian Care Network." Follow the instructions to see if someone in their network has a practice near you.

- **Focus On The Family** also maintains a nationwide network of Christian counselors. You can visit their web site at www.focusonthefamily.com or simply call their headquarters in Colorado Springs at (719) 531-3400 and ask for the Counseling Department.

A FEW OTHER HELPFUL LINKS

- Alcoholics Anonymous – www.alcoholics-anonymous.org. (212) 870-3400

- Al-Anon – www.al-anon.org. (888) 425-2666

- Narcotics Anonymous – www.na.org. (818) 773-9999

❈ ❈ ❈ ❈ ❈

PRAYER SEED

Thank You, Father, that it is Your desire to make me like Your Son Jesus Christ. Thank you also that you have equipped members of Your Body to help me in that process, and have surrounded me with them. Open my eyes so that I might be aware of them, and give me discernment to know who I can count on to be "bridges" in my life. I know that You are my Healer, as You have said in your Word, but I need a bridge to get closer to You. Also, help me to be a bridge to other people, too. Amen.

❋ ❋ ❋ ❋ ❋

Think where man's glory most begins and ends,
And say, "My glory was I had such friends."

– William Yeats

❋ ❋ ❋

---

[1] From *Bridge Over Troubled Water* by Paul Simon, 1969. Sung by Paul Simon and Art Garfunkle on the album "Bridge Over Troubled Water."

[2] *Smart Love* by Jody Hayes, p. 22,23.

[3] From a currently unpublished manual by therapist and writer J. Elizabeth Oppenheim, MA: *A Crash Course In Crisis Management: Useful Life Skills for People Who Don't Want Them.* Also available from her: *Survival Rations: Encouragement for Troops at the Crossroads* (devotional). You can contact her at elizabeth@oppenheimgroup.com

STEP 10: HOW DO I GET BACK TO "NORMAL"?

DEFINING YOUR MISSION

May the God of all grace, who called us to His eternal glory by Christ Jesus, after you have suffered a while, perfect, establish, strengthen, and settle you. — 1 Peter 5:10 (NKJV)

The test of success is not what you do when you're on top. Success is how high you bounce when you hit bottom. — General George S. Patton, Jr.

At this point in your recovery, General Patton's words shed light on three very important truths you must hang on to:

1. You have hit bottom.
2. Your impact is now propelling you upward to "success."
3. The incredible force of *your* impact predicts a lofty zenith.

More than most people who currently occupy the "top" positions of peace and comfort in our land, you are intimately acquainted with what the bottom looks like. And you've gained this familiarity not because you sought it or expected it, but because you were taken there forcibly by the trauma resulting from your unselfish commitment to protect the freedoms of our country.

But as Ralph Waldo Emerson wrote, "He has seen but half the universe who has never been shown the house of Pain."[1] It's an education that you probably would rather have done without, but you have gained much knowledge and wisdom having seen that dark half of the universe.

And it won't be for nothing. As God promised in the Scripture above, *after you have suffered a while,* you will experience a perfecting, an establishing, a strengthening and a settling which the rest of the world knows nothing about. You have been placed in an environment that has the potential of bouncing you to heights of satisfaction, strength, influence and leadership that were out of reach prior to your wounding. You have gained precious credentials that uniquely qualify you to hold positions that few can occupy. And whether it feels like it or not right now, God is *well-pleased* with you.

> *I will bring that group through the fire and make them pure.*
> *I will refine them like silver and purify them like gold.*
> *They will call on My name, and I will answer them.*
> *I will say, 'These are My people,' and they will say, 'The Lord is our God.'*
> **– Zechariah 13:9** (NLT)

But it won't be *normal,* as the title to this Step implies. At least, not the normal you remember. When you hear the word "normal" your mind probably snaps back to how things were prior to your deployment. How desperately you would love to return to *that* normal! But if we were to sell you the illusion that you *could* go back there, it would be a cruel and heartless deception. You have been changed, and your world has been changed. The pre-deployment "normal" no longer exists.

What God now has in mind is a **"new normal"** for you. And it's going to be *better* than the old normal in many, many ways. We're not saying necessarily that your *current* condition is better, nor are we saying that "new normal" will be all puppies and butterflies. But we *are* saying that you are on your way to level of existence that will be better than ever. Just as Jesus' "normal" was burned away by the trauma of his crucifixion so that He could inherit the "new normal" of the resurrection, so your old normal is being transformed into a glorious *new* normal. As Elisabeth Elliot wrote, "There is a necessary link between suffering and glory."[2] Jesus said,

> *I tell you the truth, unless a kernel of wheat is planted in the soil and dies, it remains alone. But its death will produce many new kernels—a plentiful harvest of new lives.*
>
> **– John 12:24 (NLT)**

 Would it be too shocking to say you died over there on the battlefield? In many respects you did. Spend a few moments thinking about that concept. In what ways did you die while you were deployed? Feel free to use extra paper – or extra notebooks – if you need more room…

Jesus' promise in the above Scripture is that, because of those deaths, abundant new life is going to be produced – in you and because of you. You have suffered many losses, as did Jesus. And just as Jesus' biggest loss became the doorway to His greatest gain, so your sacrifices will crack open the door of your PTSD and give you entrance to a world of light and life that you never could have experienced otherwise.

 Name one outrageous, over-the-top thing that you hope you will find in that "new normal" world:

AFTER YOU HAVE SUFFERED AWHILE…

This metamorphosis we've been speaking of doesn't happen quickly or all at once. We don't get to experience "microwave maturity." God likes crockpots – He likes what the *process* produces. He likes quality, and quality can't be rushed. He takes a thousand years to make a decent redwood tree; a squash He can do in a month.

And it doesn't happen if we sit passively and wait for Him to "zap" us. God has required that we partner with Him in the process. He's expecting us to be intentional about creating that environment that gives Him maximum access to our hearts and souls. Our transformation will occur as we respond positively to His overtures and obey His instructions. There is no easy way. The only way to resurrection is through the cross and the tomb. As you look around, it's easy to see you're on the right road, isn't it?

✺ ✺ ✺ ✺ ✺

BECOMING INTENTIONAL ABOUT THE NEW NORMAL

In this Step, we want to help you to make a plan – "define your mission." Just as every mission in a war is comprised of many interrelated and coordinated movements, so your mission to "new normal" will also have several components that need to be thought through:

- **What Needs To Change?** – Vocation? Location? Companions?
- **Facing Your Fears** – Dealing with triggers
- **Setting Personal Goals** – Regarding your family, exercise, finances, etc.
- **Serving Others** – How giving becomes receiving

If you don't set about actually making objective plans in these four areas, you will continue to "float" at your current level of confusion and stagnation. As Benjamin Franklin once said, "The Constitution only gives people the right to *pursue* happiness. You have to catch it yourself." So let's go catch some!

WHAT NEEDS TO CHANGE?

VOCATION?

If you're still on active duty, you may feel like you are already in the right vocation for the long term. God may have given you a Warrior's heart and a commitment to serve as part of our country's "exoderm." In that case, a career in the military is a good fit for you. Or it may be that after your significant contribution to our nation's defense, you visualize yourself contributing in other ways, such as through education, business, police/fire, Christian ministry, etc.

Whatever the case, ask yourself a simple question: *How much do I like my job?* What would you give it on a scale of 1 to 10, with 10 being perfect? Put your answer here:

If you answered anything less than a 7, then you should probably begin thinking and praying about God *eventually* leading you in a different direction.

However, we want to emphasize "eventually" very strongly. If you are still dealing with severe symptoms of PTSD, you do *not* need the extra stress of trying to learn a new job right now. You shouldn't make *any* major changes to your present routines until you feel good-and-ready – even eager – to do so, with confirmation from your spouse and/or bridge people. A good rule of thumb is: for every month you spent downrange, you should give yourself at least that many months before you make any major decisions - *minimum*. Give your decision-making skills a chance to calm down and become a bit more objective and less emotional.

On the other hand, *do* make as many smaller, daily decisions as possible (like what you want to eat, what movie you want to go to, etc.). This helps you re-establish feelings of control over your life.

This may not be the time for major change – but it is a *great* time for dreams. It's a period where you should be asking God what *He* would suggest for your future. He has something in mind for which you would be perfectly suited. He created you and wired you in a certain way. He wants to communicate to you what would fulfill you – if you'll be willing to listen and take action.

> *"For I know the plans that I have for you,"* declares the Lord, *"plans for welfare and not for calamity to give you a future and a hope."*   **– Jeremiah 29:11**

There's a big difference between a "job" and a "career." When you got your first job, it's likely that your only criteria was: "Will they actually pay me *money*?" You landed the burger-flipping job, and quickly realized it wasn't something you wanted to do for the rest of your life. But you didn't quit because you needed the money. Based on that experience, though, you began to ponder what kinds of jobs you would *prefer*. Once you started to gravitate toward one general vocation, you took steps to break into it. That may even be the reason you joined the military.

The "happily-ever-after" story ends with you finding your ideal vocation which becomes a life-long *career,* and is more like a "calling" because of how satisfying it is. Unfortunately, expectations are sometimes torpedoed along the way to perfection. When that happens, people are often so far down the road they can't figure out how to do a U-turn, so they choose to continue on, abandoning their dreams and considering their disenchantment to be acceptable.

This is a time for new beginnings for you – time to define your "new normal." And if your current job doesn't fit your dream, it's time to imagine what would.

Prayer Assignment: Start making it a part of your daily prayer time to ask God to give you a vision for what you should do with the rest of your life. And while you're at it, ask Him to show you how to bring that vision into the realm of reality. As scientist and writer Douglas H. Everett wrote: "There are some people who live in a dream world, and there are some who face reality; and then there are those who turn one into the other." God can help you turn your dreams into reality, if you'll look to Him for direction. He wants you in the right spot just as intensely as you do!

 Dream Career. Do you already have a dream? If you could do *anything* career-wise, what would it be? What would you like to see yourself doing ten years from now?

Frederick Buechner a WWII combat veteran, minister and writer counsels us:

> The voice we should listen to most as we choose a vocation is the voice that we might think we should listen to least, and that is the voice of our own *gladness*. What can we do that makes us gladdest, what can we do that leaves us with the strongest sense of sailing true north and of peace, which is much of what gladness is? … I believe that if it is a thing that makes us truly glad, then it is a *good* thing and it is *our* thing and it is the calling voice that we were made to answer with our lives.[3]

Check the bibliography for this chapter in the back of this manual for some good books that will help you think through what would be a fulfilling career choice.

❁ ❁ ❁ ❁ ❁

LOCATION?

Obviously, if you are still on active duty, you don't have a lot of control over your location. "Military readiness" never takes a time out. We know how rough it can be when you've returned from a difficult deployment to have to saddle up again after only a short period of down time. The intense preparation, integration of new people into your unit, getting equipment back in shape, late hours and probable training deployments require yet more time away from home. This post-deployment tempo has both good and bad aspects to it, but it's a reality of military life – as you well know.

But if you are now separated from the military and are in control of where you live, there are some important things to consider. As we tried to demonstrate in Step 9, "bridge people" are one of the most vital elements of your healing environment. If you are married and your spouse is struggling with secondary trauma issues because of your woundedness, he or she also needs a good contingent of bridge people. In most cases, if you left "home" for war, and then returned "home," those bridge people for both of you are probably right there in your area. The relationships are already established and strong, and no additional energy is needed to find and build new ones. Moving to a new location would mean trying to get established in a place where you don't know anybody, and would therefore be without that key "bridge" element. You might think, "Well, I'll just make new friends," but don't forget that you are probably in a strong self-isolating mode right now. With your other stresses wearing you down, it's likely you'll be hiding in the back room when the Welcome Wagon® shows up.

A move is stressful for anyone, any time. And as mentioned before, you don't need additional stress in your world right now. Again – if at all possible – we recommend that you delay any decision regarding a major move using the same criteria we mentioned for a major vocational change: a minimum of one month of contemplation for each month you were downrange.

If you're still active duty and get assigned to a new location, it is imperative that you begin looking for new bridge people for your life immediately. Asking God to help you (and your family, if applicable) assemble a new support network needs to become a part of your daily prayer time.

You may be perfectly content to stay right where you are the rest of your life. Great! If you can match your dream vocation with your current location, that's a good recipe for contentment. But if you're not happy with your location, or if your dream vocation might mean that you need to live elsewhere, there will come a time when you'll feel strong and stable enough to make the move.

But let your vocation dictate your location. You may find this very difficult to believe, but there are people living in *Hawaii* who have grown tired of it and are thinking about a move to Arizona! True! Your location can provide a wonderful context for life, but it's *only a context*. What you exchange your time for day-in and day-out forms a much larger portion of your life, and if that isn't satisfying, even Hawaii seems like a prison. But if your career and calling make you wake up every morning saying, "I can't wait to get to work!" it doesn't really matter where you live. Writer Tad Williams gives us a good perspective:

> Never make your home in a *place*. Make a home for yourself inside your own head. You'll find what you need to furnish it – memory, friends you can trust, love of learning, and other such things. That way it will go with you wherever you journey.

And as the Apostle Paul put it:

> *I have learned in whatever state I am, to be content.*   – **Philippians 4:11** (NKJV)

The ideal, of course, would be to combine your dream vocation with your dream location. Do you feel called to be a dolphin trainer? Then you probably also love warm, sunny locales. Professional snowboarder? You'd better love places that get snowbound from time to time. Launching manned rockets? Is Houston or Cape Kennedy okay with you?

Then again, your dream *vocation* may involve frequent shifts of *location*. Some people start to feel stagnant after they've been in the same spot for more than a few months. Some of you specifically joined the military to "see the world," and that mobile lifestyle suits you just fine. If you're still active duty, you are definitely in the right place. Your vocation will certainly dictate your location! If you're not active duty any more, you can still pursue a career that will keep you flitting around the world to your heart's content. Take your home with you, as Tad Williams recommended above.

You may not be able to name a particular city, state or country, but you can probably identify certain characteristics of your ideal location. If it could match up with your vocation, what would be five characteristics of your ideal location?

1. _____
2. _____
3. _____
4. _____
5. _____

Prayer Assignment: In your prayer times, begin asking God if He would combine your dream vocation with your ideal location. It may seem like too much to ask, but our God *loves* to delight His children – especially those who have had to endure the hardships you have. Jesus said so Himself:

> *Until now you have asked nothing in My name. Ask, and you will receive, that your joy may be full.*   – **John 16:24** (NKJV)

As amazing and extravagant as it may seem, sometimes the main criteria God has for answering your prayer with a *Yes!* is simply, "Will it bring My child joy?"

COMPANIONS?

Battle-blasted or not, *everyone* needs good friends. But *especially* the battle-blasted. So many people don't appreciate the wealth represented by a loyal, compassionate friend until they are in desperate need of one. Have you got at least a couple of friends like this:

"A friend is someone who sees through you and still enjoys the view."   – Wilma Askinas

"A real friend is one who walks in when the rest of the world walks out." – Walter Winchell

"A friend knows the song of my heart and sings it to me when my memory fails."- Unknown

"A friend is a person with whom you dare to be yourself."   – C. Raymond Beran

"A friend is a single soul living in two bodies."   – Aristotle

So if you *do* have some friends like this, it is *not* time for a change concerning them! If, in addition, you have shared battle experience with them, you are wealthy indeed. They can understand and relate to you at levels that no one else can. Cultivate those friendships like you were growing money trees!

But not all of your companions are necessarily *good* friends – even among your battle-buddies. It's natural that you would feel a strong bond with anyone you went through combat with. Your shared experiences have connected you at deep levels, and friendships forged on the anvil of crisis are strong indeed. But you may need to do some hard thinking about whether of not some of these companions are a liability to your healing. Think about each "marginal" companion of yours and assess their effect on you. Consider each of the following statements:

- ❑ When you're with them, do they make you feel "up" or do they drag you down emotionally?
- ❑ Will they let you talk about your traumatic experiences, or do they avoid or change the subject?
- ❑ Do you tend to drink too much alcohol when you're with them?
- ❑ Are they encouraging you – either directly or indirectly – to use illegal drugs?
- ❑ Do they influence you to re-take the throne of your life and engage in behavior that you know grieves the Holy Spirit?
- ❑ Are they frequently finding reasons for you to skip church and other Christian functions?
- ❑ Are they antagonistic or critical about your relationship with God?
- ❑ Are they trying to pull you away from other friends that are a positive influence on you?
- ❑ Do they engage in a lot of negative, critical talk, seldom having anything good to say about anyone or anything?
- ❑ Do they stifle your creativity, enthusiasm, hope and faith, or show disdain for your dreams in the name of "Be realistic!"?

If more than two or three of the negative statements above apply to your friend, this person may not be the best companion for you. This doesn't mean you can't be available to support him or her as needed, but for the sake of your own recovery, you should limit your "hang time" with them. You may be thinking unselfishly, "But I can be a good influence on *them*." And you might be. But if you are still struggling with strong PTSD symptoms, the reverse is more likely. As the Apostle Paul warns us:

Do not be misled: "Bad company corrupts good character."

– 1 Corinthians 15:33 (NIV)

So choose your company carefully – but do choose! We all need those bridge people from time to time. To try to make it through your current battle without them will prove very difficult. As anthropologist and writer Zora Neale Hurston observed:

It seems to me that trying to live without friends is like milking a bear to get cream for your morning coffee. It is a whole lot of trouble, and then not worth much after you get it.

Taking stock: In Step 9 you made a short list of people that you would begin praying about beginning a formal "bridge relationship" with. Continue praying about that and cultivating those good friendships! But are there some other people that might fall into the category of "bad company" who – at least for the present – you need to spend less time with? Ask God who they might be, and if anyone comes to your mind, write their names down here (if you worry about confidentiality, you could skip writing them down here if you'd prefer):

_____

_____

※   ※   ※   ※   ※

FACING YOUR FEARS

In Step 2, we discussed the physiological and psychological basis of PTSD. What you experienced while downrange was so traumatic that your brain took special note of it, and anytime you approach a person, place, thing or experience that is similar to your original trauma, your right brain whips out its "photo album" and puts on an intense presentation (sights, sounds, smells, tastes) attempting to alert you of the mortal danger that could be waiting there. Your logical left brain gets muted, and the calming influence of your hippocampus gets pinched off. You're off on a "re-experiencing" jaunt which, if your right brain would only *listen,* your left brain could explain why you didn't need to take that detour today.

In Step 4, we introduced the concept of inviting Jesus Christ into the episodic memories of your trauma, visualizing Him experiencing it with you. Hopefully, you've been able to continue engaging in this spiritual exercise, giving Him more and more access to your places of pain and darkness and thereby bringing about some direct healing.

In this Step we want to encourage you – with Jesus' help – to take action concerning the things that trigger your re-experiencing episodes. By now, you are probably well-aware of what your triggers are. In the space following, write down any people, places, things or experiences that trigger your re-experiencing episodes, and what the typical effect is (use additional paper if needed):

TRIGGER	EFFECT

You may have heard the old joke about the guy who said, "Doc, every time I do *this,* it hurts." And the doctor says, "Well, then, don't *do* that. That'll be fifty bucks." That advice keeps the pain away, but it doesn't fix the problem. In the same way, your brain – with every good intention – is giving you advice about how to avoid the pain associated with your trauma: "Don't *go* there!" But it's unrealistic advice. The suicide bomber had a brown, bushy beard, so now every time you see a man with a brown, bushy beard, your brain advises you, "RUN!"

This can't go on for the rest of your life. For one thing, it's rather annoying to the men with brown, bushy beards you encounter. But mainly because it's very disruptive to your "new normal." It's a reaction based on non-reality, it's no longer needed, and it hampers your day-to-day life. The original event was fearfully and explosively real, but all the re-experiencing isn't.

You have a lot in your arsenal to counter this with. With the introduction of God's Word, prayer, the Christian community and the positive mindset of your Spiritual Battlemind, you've created an environment where the Holy Spirit can transform and heal your wounded soul directly. You have bridge people in your life who will walk with you through the dark forests. You have the Spirit of Jesus sharing your traumatic experiences in the past and accompanying you in the present. You have the assurances from God that you have nothing to fear. And you have the testimony of reality that He's telling you the truth – there will probably not be a sniper on the interstate overpass today.

How can you face these fears? First of all, meditate on God's Word where He tells you the facts regarding your anxieties. Allow His healing words to sink deep into your soul and renew you. Memorize them.

> *The Lord is my light and my salvation; whom shall I fear?*
> *The Lord is the defense of my life; whom shall I dread?*
> — **Psalm 27:1**

> *God met me more than halfway, He freed me from my anxious fears.*
> — **Psalm 34:4** (MSG)

> *When I am afraid, I will put my trust in You. In God, whose word I praise,*
> *In God I have put my trust; I shall not be afraid.*
> *What can mere man do to me?*
> — **Psalm 56:3,4**

"When I am *afraid*"? Who wrote this wimpy, limp-wristed drivel? Who's this fraidy-cat who cowers behind the skirts of religion? The guy who killed the 9'8" giant, forcibly circumcised 200 grown men, killed a lion and a bear and was respected and feared by some of the baddest dudes that ever walked the planet, that's who. And he wasn't hiding behind anything, by the way. Even King David struggled with various anxieties and fears. May you never get over the fact that this valiant, conquering general and king was *afraid* sometimes. But he dealt with his fears pro-actively. He faced them head-on fully aware that God Almighty had his back and both flanks. And that gave him confidence to step forward.

For more insight into King David's struggles with PTSD, the focus of his hope, the foundation of his healing and his attitude toward his God Who rescued him from every enemy, see Appendix D: *Prayer Life of a PTSD Victor: King David* (pages 165-170). It could be an excellent pattern for your own prayer life.

BATTLEPLAN

Look over the list of triggers you just wrote. Spend some time in prayer, and ask the Lord to suggest just one of them that you and He could work on. Make it the easiest one. Write it down here:

_____

Like any difficult project, start slow and easy, and build on your successes. Every time you encounter that particular trigger, your trauma-rattled brain switches on its alarm, and you begin to re-experience and probably react with fear. What action could you take that would defy that alarm and face that fear ***just a little bit*** in a safe environment?

We realize it's not easy to anticipate or control a trigger. And the variety of triggers is extensive. For you, it could be the sound of a helicopter or a siren, the smell of a decaying animal or of gasoline, a sudden loud noise, a difficult anniversary, etc. You never know when they're going to pop up. But in the same way an athlete will create artificial scenarios and repeatedly hone his or her reactions in order to be ready for the "real thing," you can proactively devise situations that will help you confront your triggers – with Christ at your side – in a safe, controllable environment.

Example: Let's say your trigger has to do with the smell of gasoline. Because of this, you are unable to go to a gas station to fill up the tank and your husband must always do it. Perhaps you could get him to prepare a small jug of gasoline for you and bring it home. Once a day, you take a few minutes to put on your spiritual armor, seek the filling of the Holy Spirit, ask God and your husband to stand with you by your side, and then walk to where the jug is and open it up. Your goal: five seconds before you put the lid back on and leave the room. You will find that you can do it! And the next time, perhaps your goal will be seven seconds. Then ten.

After a period of time that only you and God can determine, you and your husband will take a trip to the gas station. Maybe the first time you won't even get gas – perhaps you'll just drive through it once and go home. The next time you still won't get gas – you'll just park there and sit for thirty seconds. Then for a minute. Eventually, you could sit in the car while your husband pumps the gas. Then you stand next to him. Eventually, you do it yourself. These victorious steps – accompanied by your husband (or some other bridge person) and Jesus while filled with His Spirit provide those more-powerful episodes that can eclipse the episodic memories of your original trauma and retrain your mind.

Now it's your turn to be creative and come up with a plan. Based on the trigger you chose and following the pattern above, what steps can you take – just a little bit at a time – to defy your anxieties with Jesus at your side? Ask God to help you think it through and give you some creative ideas. Write them down here:

_____

_____

_____

_____

Eventually, you will find that this trigger is no longer debilitating. You might still feel a little anxious when you encounter it, but it won't control your life any more. Though a trigger isn't the same thing as sin, God's advice to Cain in Genesis 4 could be applied here: "It wants to master you, but you must master it." By confronting it intentionally like this, little by little, you and the Lord *will* show it who's boss!

❋   ❋   ❋   ❋   ❋

SETTING PERSONAL GOALS

Planning is bringing the future into the present so that you can do something about it now.
– Alan Lakein, time management expert

This section could have begun with the old and absolutely true adage: "If you fail to plan, plan to fail." But Lakein's observation should help us to recognize the positive side of planning: it is *future oriented*. Your present is *stuck*, and continuing to focus on it isn't going to get you unstuck. Like with a Humvee sunk past its axles in a mud bog, a cable needs to be stretched out and secured to something solid and stable and the winch turned on. In Christ, your future is secure. Spirit-directed planning is your cable-and-winch that will pull you out of your current quagmire.

Besides, as baseball legend and Yankee philosopher Yogi Berra warns us: "You got to be careful if you don't know where you're going, because you might not get there." Your future awaits – and you *do* want to get there!

SETTING GOALS: HOW TO

Setting goals involves getting a clear idea of what you want to ultimately accomplish (like "graduate from college") and then writing out the steps that will help you attain it. How to actually *write* those goals in a way that will make them achievable takes a little work, but it will be worth it.

A good criterion for writing any goal uses the acronym SMART. Here's what each letter means:

Specific – There must be some detail and precision to it, and some sense of time. To say, "I would like to learn martial arts" is not very specific. But to say, "I want to become a black belt in *tae kwon do* within three years of today" is very specific.

Measurable – It must contain some objective element that will let you know when you've achieved it or are achieving it. To say, "I would like to be a better father" is a worthy goal, but how would you know when you *became* a better father? Instead, link your desire to measurable action. "I will read my son a bedtime story every night I'm home for the next month," or "I will read three books about parenting within the next year and discuss it with my wife," would both be measurable. Can you put it on a checklist? Then it's probably measurable.

Attainable – It must be a goal for which you can devise a plan to attain it. If you can't work out the steps that would be involved in getting you to your destination, it's not attainable. Enthusiasm, faith and courage are advantages when setting out on any journey, but if you leave with no roadmap, they won't help much.

Realistic – Given your present resources, is it reasonable to believe the goal could be achieved? If you're only 5'6" and your name isn't Spud Webb, it probably isn't realistic to think you have a career ahead of you in professional basketball.

Tangible – It must have substance and objectivity rather than be merely a vague desire. "I would like to be happy" is a nice sentiment, but not tangible. What specifically would *make* you happy? That would more likely be a *goal*. Can you put it on your calendar? That's a good test of tangibility.

SETTING GOALS: LAYERING THEM ACCORDING TO PRIORITIES

As you begin to write out goals, realize that there are only so many hours in a day, and that you probably won't have unlimited time to pursue *all* your goals at all times. So it will be necessary for you to layer and prioritize them.

A very simple way of doing this – relative to each major desire that God brings into your mind – is to set them according to three time frames:

- **Long-range** – Major pursuits that may take five to twenty years to achieve.
- **Medium-range** – Specific goals that can be achieved in one to five years.
- **Short-range** – Specific goals that can be achieved within a day to a year.

> You must have long-range goals to keep you from being frustrated by short-range failures.
> – Charles C. Noble

A collection of Short-range goals will add up to one Medium-range goal. The achieving of a series of Medium-range goals will bring about the accomplishment of a Long-range goal.

Next, prioritize them according to how passionately you desire each Long-range goal. Decide which goals belong on your "A" list, which on your "B" list, and which go on your "C" list. Based on this prioritizing, it will be much easier for you to decide which specific activities relative to each goal need to be transferred to your "To do list" and your calendar. If you're like most of us, if it doesn't get on the calendar, *it does not exist!* So calendarize your goals whenever possible!

SETTING GOALS: DREAMING IN THE IMPORTANT AREAS

I have had dreams and I have had nightmares,
but I have conquered my nightmares because of my dreams.
– Dr. Jonas Salk (developer of the Polio vaccine)

How thoroughly have your nightmares eradicated your dreams? Nightmares happen when you're asleep and passive, but the dreams we're talking about here spring into being when we are awake and intentional. *Those* dreams, fed by God's Spirit, are what have the power to conquer our nightmares.

"Major on the majors" is a popular credo. If we aren't succeeding in the major areas of our lives, no amount of success in the minor areas will gratify us. And minor dreams won't displace major nightmares.

For this reason, we'd like you to spend a little time thinking about those major areas. We're supplying you with a list of eight areas here, but it is not necessarily complete. There may be other issues unique to your life that need to be addressed. Please write them out on additional sheets of paper.

In each of the following areas, ask God to give you some vision regarding where you need to be headed. What do you think would be *good* for you? What would be good for your family? What are some of your long-range desires in each area? At this point, you don't need to work out layering or prioritizing them. Just write down whatever the Lord brings to your mind.

1. Goals regarding my relationship with my spouse (or parents, if single):

2. Goals regarding my relationship with my kids (or siblings, if single):

3. Goals regarding my vocation:

4. Goals regarding my location:

5. Goals regarding my finances:

6. Goals regarding diet and exercise:

7. Goals regarding my medical issues:

8. Goals regarding my excesses (alcohol, drugs, food, sex, etc.):

Now, if you're serious about this, here's what we want you to do. In a separate notebook, or on separate sheets of paper, write out each of the goals you wrote at the top of a page – one goal per page. Those constitute your "Long-range Goals." Break each down into two to five "Medium-range Goals" that would combine to help you reach the long-range goal at the top of the page. Then, beneath each medium-range goal, write out two to five "Short-range Goals" that would help you accomplish each medium-range goal. If those goals are "SMART" enough, transfer them to your calendar.

By doing this, you are indeed "bringing the future into the present" so that you can truly bring about your "new normal" and the rest of your life. Nothing can be done about what happened to you in the past, but *everything* can be done about what happens to you in the future!

> *Delight yourself in the Lord; and He will give you the desires of your heart.*
> *Commit your way to the Lord, trust also in Him, and He will do it.*
> **– Psalm 37:4,5**

SERVING OTHERS

> *Whoever wants to be great must become a servant. Whoever wants to be first among you must be your slave. That is what the Son of Man has done: He came to serve, not to be served—and then to give away His life in exchange for many who are held hostage.*
> **– Mark 10:44,45 (MSG)**

Having been in our armed forces, you know a little something about "service." During your entire active duty period, you have been serving. It was while you were serving that you – like Jesus – "gave away your life in exchange" for peace and security for your loved ones and fellow-citizens back home. Some of our service men and women gave the ultimate sacrifice and they no longer walk among us. But you – and many others – sacrificed profoundly and died in that "kernel of wheat" sense we studied earlier (John 12:24). Yes, you know a lot about service.

And though it was service that got you into your present traumatized condition, it is service that will help pull you out as well.

One of the facts that virtually every expert on PTSD affirms has to do with the healing power of helping others who are hurting. There's something about giving of ourselves to those who are hurting that empowers us, takes our focus off ourselves and invigorates us. As Ralph Waldo Emerson wrote: "It is one of the most beautiful compensations of life that no man can sincerely try to help another without helping himself." Or as J.M. Barrie wrote, "Those who bring sunshine into the lives of others cannot keep it from themselves."

? What talents, gifts or abilities do you have that you think might be of use to others who are hurting? There are talents that are common to us all, such as the ability to listen, to sit with someone, to offer some simple manual labor, to buy a cup of coffee, to provide a ride, to tell your story to others who need to hear it. Or even to simply be available to others. Some have called "availability" the most important of all the abilities when it comes to serving others. But what *unique* talents do you own that you could press into the service of others?

_____

_____

_____

Spend some time in prayer, and then spend some time with one of your bridge friends, and talk with him or her about how you might employ your availability and talents to help others who are hurting. Perhaps you might also talk with your pastor, or people at your Veterans center how you might be of service to them. After you've done this, make a plan. Write down three ways that you would like to serve others – either right away, or sometime in the future when you are more healed and able to do so.

1. _____

2. _____

3. _____

❋   ❋   ❋   ❋   ❋

WHY SERVE: YOUR UNIQUE QUALIFICATIONS AND BENEFITS

You probably remember the story in John 11 of when Jesus raised Lazarus from the dead. Jesus delayed coming to Bethany on purpose until Lazarus had been dead for four days. He wanted to make sure that everyone was keenly aware of the fact that this man was *really* dead, and that what was about to take place was not a resuscitation, but a genuine resurrection. When Jesus gave the command, "Lazarus, come out!" the dead man got up and walked. Lazarus had been bound in the traditional grave clothes of that day – like fifty Ace Bandages from head to toe. He walked, but not very well.

The next command Jesus gave was interesting and relates to you. He said, "Take off his grave clothes and let him go." Don't you think that a Person who just raised somebody from the dead would have the wherewithal to unwrap those grave clothes Himself? Why did he instruct others to do it? Because by partnering with Jesus in this miracle, their faith would be made stronger. By walking up to this astonishing, dreadful figure and touching him, unwrapping the bandages and setting him loose, actually saving his life a second time (because the grave clothes even tightly covered his nose and mouth), they were being honored by Jesus, included, and experienced something that would motivate them for the rest of their lives.

You are among the resurrected ones. You died and now new life is being generated in you and through you. You've struggled with your own grave clothes, and this has made you profoundly qualified to unwrap those smelly bandages that bind others. Jesus honors *you* by asking you to now help Him to help others with their grave clothes.

Think, also, of the wisdom of Solomon found in the book of Ecclesiastes 4:1,3. It was the first Scripture reference you came to when you opened up this book:

> *To everything there is a season, a time for every purpose under heaven:*
> *A time to kill, And a time to heal;*
> *A time to break down, And a time to build up.*

There was a season in your life when it was your job, calling and duty to kill and break down. These things were done for an honorable purpose, and they were carried out with unselfishness and courage and at great expense to you and your loved ones. But now a new season has come – a new normal. It's a season for healing and for building up. A time for you to heal, and a time for you to help in the healing of others. This, too, is for an honorable purpose, and will also require unselfishness and courage. It will also cost you something, for anytime we give, by definition, it costs us. But the benefits you receive will far exceed any disability pay or pension you might ever receive from the sacrifices you made in your first season. God lists a few of them for you in Isaiah 58:10-12 (NKJV):

> *If you extend your soul to the hungry*
> *And satisfy the afflicted soul,*
>> *Then your light shall dawn in the darkness,*
>> *And your darkness shall be as the noonday.*
>> *The Lord will guide you continually,*
>> *And satisfy your soul in drought,*
>> *And strengthen your bones;*
>> *You shall be like a watered garden,*
>> *And like a spring of water, whose waters do not fail.*
>> *Those from among you shall build the old waste places;*
>> *You shall raise up the foundations of many generations;*
>> *And you shall be called the Repairer of the Breach,*
>> *The Restorer of Streets to Dwell In.*

❋   ❋   ❋   ❋   ❋

Thank you – again – for your service … past, present and future.

❋   ❋   ❋   ❋   ❋

PRAYER SEED

Father, it saddens me that I cannot return to "normal." But, with Your help, I know that I can make the journey to "new normal." Help me see the steps I need to take. Help me recognize the bridge people You have sent to help me walk through the difficult times. Keep my eyes on You, not on the storm that surrounds me. Give me frequent visions of where You are taking me, and how I can get there. Help me face my fears with You alongside me. Give me the same courage that You gave King David as he faced his fears. I need You to let me know for sure that You are right there with me. Bring me to the place where I can minister to the needs of others. Use me in ways that are either common or unique – as long as it will serve those who are hurting, build up Your Kingdom and add to the process of my own healing as well.

You have shown me the house of Pain, O Lord. Now lead me to Your house of stability, peace and triumph. May I be one of the ones called "Repairer of the Breach, Restorer of the Streets to Dwell In." By the authority of the Holy Spirit, with the companionship of Your Son Jesus Christ, and in the sovereignty of Your will, I know it can be accomplished. I ask all these things in the name of my Lord and Savior Jesus Christ, Amen.

❋   ❋   ❋

---

[1] Quote by Ralph Waldo Emerson in his essay "The Tragic," found in *Unspeakable* by Os Guinness, p. 44.
[2] Quote by Elisabeth Elliot in *A Path Through Suffering*, p. 14.
[3] Spoken by Frederick Buechner in a graduation address, quoted in *Windows of the Soul* by Ken Gire (Grand Rapids: Zondervan, 1996) p. 71.

EPILOGUE

In a certain region of northern Italy, many of the villages produce beautiful vases, each piece fetching a very good price due to the skill that has been passed down from generation to generation.

But there is one particular village that produces vases that command ten times the price of any of their neighbor's goods. They are so valuable because of the crafting technique the artisans of this village use. They make the vases just as all the other villages in the region do, but then they smash them on the ground, shattering them into dozens of pieces.

Then, with the greatest of care and skill, the artisan laboriously reassembles the vase, using glue that has been mixed with gold. When finished, every golden vein contributes a magnificent element to the vase, adding immensely to its beauty and value.

This process is very similar to what you are experiencing currently. Combat has shattered your life in many ways, but the eternal Artisan is in the process of rebuilding you. Every re-glued crack, every scarred-over wound will contribute to your beauty and value in ways you probably cannot fathom yet.

This may be why even the resurrected Christ retained His scars, even in His glorified body. For all of eternity, what they symbolize will be *beautiful* to each of us who were saved by them, to all the angels who observed His ultimate sacrifice of love, and to the Father Who observed the deadly obedience of His only Son.

Your scars – the seen and the unseen – will also be gloriously beautiful.

You have been in some dark places since your traumatic experiences downrange. You are probably still fighting your way out of that darkness into your new normal. God's desire is to *help* you. The sentiment of what God said to His servant King Cyrus can be a promise to you as well:

> *I will go before you and will level the mountains;*
> *I will break down gates of bronze and cut through bars of iron.*
> *I will give you the treasures of darkness,*
> > *riches stored in secret places,*
> > > *so that you may know that I am the Lord,*
> > > > *the God of Israel, who summons you by name.*

– Isaiah 45:2,3 (NIV)

He knows your name. He has called you. He'll see to it that neither mountains, gates of bronze, bars of iron or the blackest darkness will keep you from where He wants you to go. And there are treasures hidden in that darkness that He wants to give you. As you receive them, you'll know for sure that the God of Israel is the One who has been with you in that dark cave of trauma. Those who have not entered the darkness will never touch them. But He's holding them out to you.

May God give you the sight to see them, accept them and use them for your healing and for the glory of the Kingdom of God.

And may the golden veins of your restored soul be evident to all, for all eternity.

❊　❊　❊

ADDITIONAL READING

STEP 1: WHERE WAS GOD?

As Silver Refined: Learning to Embrace Life's Disappointments by Kay Arthur [Waterbrook Press, 1997]. Tackles the questions that arise when life doesn't turn out as planned. Arthur demonstrates that Christ uses our disappointments, failures and despair as tools to burn away the dross to refine us like silver to be reflections of His goodness.

The Hiding Place by Corrie Ten Boom [Chosen Books (Baker), 1970]. The story of a young woman whose family was sent to a Nazi concentration camp. They all died, but she survived due to a clerical error. It's gripping tale of how faith triumphs over evil.

Hope for the Troubled Heart by Billy Graham [Billy Graham Evangelistic Association,1991]. Filled with an abundance of stories of real-life people and timeless wisdom from the Bible to show how to cope when your heart is breaking. Whether experiencing the loss of a loved one, memories of childhood abuse, personal failure or a terminal medical illness, Graham teaches us the nature of pain and how to cope with it to avoid bitterness and depression and how to comfort others who are hurting.

PAIN: The Gift Nobody Wants by Dr. Paul Brand and Philip Yancey [HarperCollins, 1993]. This is a personal saga of Paul Brand, a world-renowned hand surgeon and leprosy specialist whose pioneering work amongst leprosy patients has earned him numerous awards. He comes to the conclusion that pain is a necessary part of life. Dr. Brand provocatively questions our societal inability to accept or deal with pain, and provides strategies to treat, live with, and heal pain.

The Problem of Pain by C.S. Lewis [HarperCollins, 1940]. Makes the point that we always consider pain to be a "problem" because our finite, human minds selfishly believe that pain-free lives would prove that God loves us. By asking for this, we actually want God to love us *less*, not more than he does. "Love, in its own nature, demands the perfecting of the beloved; the mere 'kindness' which tolerates anything except suffering in its object is in that respect at the opposite pole from Love."

Unspeakable: Facing Up to the Challenge of Evil by Os Guinness [HarperSanFrancisco, 2005]. A Christian perspective of why there is evil and suffering in a world ruled by an omnipotent, benevolent God. An historical examination of man's inhumanity to man and how eastern religions, secular humanists and Bible-followers attempt to account for it.

When God Doesn't Make Sense by Dr. James C. Dobson [Living Books, 2001] .Examines the question of why God allows terrorist attacks, sickness, sorrow, death, etc. Very encouraging to someone who has been left disillusioned by life's afflictions and trauma. Sensitive answers to the "why" questions.

Where is God When it Hurts? by Philip Yancey [HarperCollins, 1977]. Deals realistically with the challenging and painful questions that come after crises of pain and suffering. Drawing from powerful scriptural examples as well as the life experiences of others, Yancey tackles the tough questions of the faith like, "Why is there so much pain in the world?" And "Is there a message behind the suffering?"

"Trauma and PTSD: A Clinical Overview," in *Caring for People God's Way* by Tim Clinton et al [Thomas Nelson, 2005].

STEP 2: WHAT HAPPENED TO ME?

Down Range: To Iraq and Back by Bridget C. Cantrell, Ph.D and Chuck Dean [WordSmith Publishing, 2005]. Cantrell is an expert in Traumatic Stress and specializes in counseling war veterans. Dean is a Vietnam war veteran and has served as the National Chaplain for the Society of the 173rd Airborne Brigade. This book provides a great resource on PTSD in general and dedicates a lot of space to reintegration issues. It's written not only for the veteran, but for his or her family as well.

Failure To Scream by Robert Hicks [Thomas Nelson, 1993]. Hicks is an Air Force Reserve specialist on traumatic stress issues, military chaplain, counselor and instructor at military schools and conferences. The book examines the hazards of internalizing posttraumatic pain and gives sound, encouraging insight into how to gain freedom from your past hurts and experience lasting healing. Strong biblical basis for his approach and the points he makes.

I Can't Get Over It – A Handbook for Trauma Survivors by Aphrodite Matsakis, Ph.D. [New Harbinger Publications, 1996]. Matsakis is a private psychotherapist and the clinical coordinator for the Vietnam Veterans' Outreach Center in Silver Springs, MD. This is a very practical, extensive resource which explains the nature of PTSD and describes the healing process with a number of practical concepts, approaches, and suggestions. Great section on identifying triggers that set off flashbacks, anxiety attacks, etc. Also a great section that will help a person determine whether he or she has PTSD through the extensive use of assessment questionnaires.

The New Guide To Crisis & Trauma Counseling – A Practical Guide for Ministers, Counselors and Lay Counselors by Dr. H. Norman Wright [Regal, 2003]. Wright is a certified trauma specialist who has had a very successful counseling and teaching ministry for decades. Author of over 70 books on counseling and other Christian subjects. This book is a must-read treasure-trove of practical, biblically-based concepts for any counselor, covering subjects of loss, grief, trauma, crisis intervention, PTSD, death, suicide, family and children's issues, etc.

Searching For Memory: The Brain, The Mind and The Past by Dr. Daniel L. Schacter [Basic Books, 1996]. Schacter, a Harvard psychology professor, has produced a full, rich picture of how human memory works, an elegant, captivating tour de force that interweaves the latest research in cognitive psychology and neuroscience with case materials and examples from everyday life.

Tear Soup: A Recipe for Healing After Loss by Pat Schwiebert & Chuck DeKlyen [Grief Watch, Portland, OR, www.griefwatch.com]. This is a DVD version of a classic book, suitable for all age groups. It's a story of a woman who has suffered a great loss in her life, and so she must cook up her own unique batch of "tear soup" to help her process her grief, find comfort and ultimately fill the void in her life created by her loss. Not combat-related, but the principles here will be useful to anyone. Affirms the bereaved, educates the unbereaved.Great for grieving kids, too.

War and the Soul by Edward Tick, PhD [Quest Books, 2005]. Tick is a clinical psychotherapist and the Director of Sanctuary: A Center for Mentoring the Soul. This book focuses on PTSD as a disorder of the identity. Tick feels that war's violence can cause our very soul to flee and be lost for life. It's a book that's sometimes mystical, sometimes very practical and always insightful.

Winning Life's Toughest Battles: Roots of Human Resilience by Dr. Julius Segal [Ivy Books, 1987]. Using his studies of people in adverse situations (including P.O.W.'s, concentration camp survivors, and hostages) as well as personal experiences, Segal has created a short but powerful guide for anyone facing the crises of everyday life. Five strategies: communication, taking control, finding a purpose, shedding guilt, and showing compassion are each given separate chapters and then combined in an epilogue that neatly summarizes the essence of the work.

STEP 3: WHERE'S THE HOSPITAL?

Connecting With God by Chris Adsit [Disciplemakers International, 2001]. National Director of Branches Of Valor International, Adsit has been making disciples and training disciplemakers since the early 1970's, and he is the author of the manual you now hold in your hands. *CWG* examines twelve foundational areas in which every Christian needs to be functional. It goes into much more depth on most of the subjects in this Step. As the title suggests, the study's goal is to help the growing Christian deepen his or her various connections with God.

STEP 4: HOW DID I CHANGE?

Healing the Wounds of Trauma: How the Church Can Help, by Margaret Hill, Harriet Hill, Richard Bagge, Pat Miersma [Paulines Publications of Africa, 2004, 2007]. Written by four members of Wycliffe International who have conducted extensive workshops on trauma counseling for church leaders in African countries experiencing war and genocide. Excellent chapters on how to help people communicate and process their grief.

On Killing: The Psychological Cost of Learning to Kill in War and Society by Lt. Col. David A. Grossman [Back Bay Books/ Little, Brown & Co., 1995]. Grossman is a former army Ranger and paratrooper, taught psychology at West Point and is currently the Professor of Military Science at Arkansas State University. This is a scholarly, landmark book studying the techniques the military uses to overcome the powerful reluctance to kill, how killing affects the soldier, and the societal implications of escalating violence.

STEP 5: HOW CAN I STAND IT?

100 Ways to Defeat Depression by Frank B. Minirth; States V. Skipper; and Paul D. Meier [Baker Book House, 1979]. This short read takes scriptures from the Bible, and uses the wisdom of three excellent Christian counselors to offer pertinent tips to a person suffering with depression. Organized well, this book allows you to focus quickly on specific problems and symptoms of depression.

Affliction by Edith Schaeffer [Fleming H. Revell, 1978]. Attempts to answer the age-old question that comes with affliction – why? This books helps to identity the sources of affliction – "our own failures; the sins of others; the nature of physical existence; the wiles of Satan," and helps you to discover the source of your affliction which may be important when dealing with it. This book doesn't attempt to give an easy answer to suffering; rather, she recognizes that affliction does not come from God – but He uses it to help us grow in our faith and to teach us how to comfort others.

Crisis Counseling: What To Do and Say During the First 72 hours by H. Norman Wright [Regal Books, 1993]. Wright is one of America's best known Christian marriage and family counselors. This is a classic written for the professional counselor, the teacher, pastor, youth worker, or concerned friend who seek the tools "to provide honest, practical and biblically based assistance to anyone who is in crisis." Wright combines biblical advice with his practical experience gleaned from years of counseling, teaching, and writing counseling materials.

Experiencing Grief by H. Norman Wright [Broadman and Holman, 2004]. Filled with numerous constructive suggestions for those experiencing the loss of a loved one.

God Works The Night Shift: Acts of Love Your Father Performs Even While You're Asleep by Pastor Ron Mehl [Multnomah, 1994]. Gold Medallion Winner. Pastor Ron died in 2003 after a 23-year-long battle with leukemia – so he is well-acquainted with the night shift. In this book he demonstrates that, despite the way things sometimes appear, God is continually at work in our lives. He reminds us that God often does His best work in the darkness.

A Grief Observed by C.S. Lewis [HarperSanFrancisco, 2001, 1961]. This is a journal that C.S. Lewis kept in the months following his beloved wife Joy's death from cancer. Though Lewis is one of the most learned, influential and inspirational Christians of the past hundred years, even he could not escape the dark agony of trauma. In his step-son's words, "It is a stark recounting of one man's studied attempts to come to grips with and in the end defeat the emotional paralysis of the most shattering grief of his life."

The Grief Recovery Workbook: Helping You Weather the Storms of Death, Divorce, and Overwhelming Disappointments by Chaplain Ray and Cathy Giunta [Integrity Publishers, 2002]. This is an excellent self-guided workbook, useful for the hurting individual, small group leader, or any person caring for wounded souls. Chaplain Ray uses his experience in professional crisis care to explore the recovery process which involves: "learning to live without the fear of abandonment; enjoying fond memories without painful feelings of loss, guilt, and remorse; acknowledging and talking about your feelings to others," and many more.

If You Want to Walk on Water, You've Got to Get Out of the Boat by John Ortberg [Zondervan, 2001]. This is an inspiring book which reflects on the Biblical story in Matthew 14, where Peter walks on water. Challenging you to face your fears of failure, to discover the unique calling that God has on your life, and to experience the exhilaration of living life through the power of God. This books helps you to recognize the obstacles in your life which are preventing you from experiencing the power of God that allows the believer to do the unimaginable.

On Death and Dying by Elisabeth Kubler-Ross [Simon and Schuster, 1997]. Kubler-Ross was a Swiss physician who was outraged at how other physicians of her day would shun those who had received a diagnosis of terminal illness. She spent the next several decades staying close to the dying and studying how they reacted and coped with end-of-life crisis. This book is a landmark classic on the stages of grief.

A Path Through Suffering: Discovering the Relationship Between God's Mercy and Our Pain by Elisabeth Elliot [Servant Publications, 1990]. In this book, Elliot shows through Scripture that "there is a necessary link between suffering and glory." Through a journey that is sometimes filled with pain, suffering, loss and grief, Elliot tenderly asks challenging questions to explore the sovereign nature of a God who cares for us, even in our finite understanding of life's challenging circumstances.

Shattered Dreams: God's Unexpected Pathway to Joy by Larry Crabb [WaterBrook, 2001]. Graphically retelling the biblical story of Naomi and Ruth, Crabb shows us how God sometimes strips us of our dreams and happiness, in order to bestow dreams that are even more wonderful for His children.

Turn My Mourning Into Dancing: Finding Hope in Hard Times by Henri Nouwen [W Publishing/Thomas Nelson, 2001]. Gathers Nouwen's deep experiences as a pastor, a teacher and a thinker to gently point the way towards a grounded way of life – even during the darkest trials.

The Way of the Wound: A Spirituality of Trauma and Transformation by Dr. Robert Grant [self-published, 1999]. Grant conducts workshops in the U.S. and internationally for professionals who encounter trauma. He addresses not only the psychological side of their crisis, but also the spiritual needs of trauma victims. The book takes the reader through four phases of experience and recovery, with a strong spiritual message throughout. Contact him at 1121 Juanita Ave.; Burlingame, CA 94010.

STEP 6: HOW DO I MOVE ON?

Exploring Forgiveness by Robert Enright and Joanna North [University of Wisconsin Press, 1998]. World-renowned authorities in the study of forgiveness, Enright and North have compiled a collection of twelve essays ranging from a first-person account of the mother of a murdered child to an assessment of the United States' post-war reconciliations with Germany and Vietnam. This book explores forgiveness in interpersonal relationships, family relationships, the individual and society relationship, and international relations through the eyes of philosophers and educators as well as a psychologist, police chief-turned-minister, law professor, sociologist, psychiatrist, social worker, and theologian.

Forgive and Forget by Lewis Smeeds [HarperOne, 1996]. Dr. Smeeds is one of the pioneers in the area of forgiveness research. For anyone who has been wounded by another and struggled to understand and move beyond feelings of hurt and anger, this classic book on forgiveness shows how to heal our pain and find room in our hearts to forgive. Included in the book: The four stages of forgiving; forgiving people who are hard to forgive; how people forgive; why forgive? Dr. Smeeds comes from a Christian perspective, but the principles are universally applicable.

Forgiveness By Charles Stanley [Thomas Nelson, 1987]. Charles Stanley's book clearly explains what forgiveness is, why you need it, and what happens when we will not forgive. Stanley's direct approach to the topic makes it easy to read and evaluate on a personal level.

The New Freedom of Forgiveness by David Augsburger [Moody Press, 2000]. In this provocative book, Augsburger uses the example of Jesus in the Bible as the *only* model of forgiveness. Augsburger writes that forgiveness should not be motivated by a self-centered desire for personal peace, rather, we ought to forgive and strive for reconstructing the broken relationship with the offender as a normal course of action.

Trust After Trauma: A Guide to Relationships for Survivors and Those Who Love Them by Dr. Aphrodite Matsakis [New Harbinger Publications, 1998]. Dr. Matsakis is a private psychotherapist and the clinical coordinator for the Vietnam Veterans' Outreach Center in Silver Springs, MD specializing in PTSD. This book provides a great deal of practical information so that trauma survivors understand their emotions, and behavior. It also offers insight for loved ones and partners of trauma survivors. Great sections on dealing with feelings of guilt, and on stabilizing relationships with non-traumatized partners.

Step 7: Who Am I Now?

Christlife: Identifying Your True and Deepest Identity by Ruth Myers [Multnomah, 2005]. Written very personally, especially engaging to women. Draws from her years of experiences as a Christian leader with the Navigators, and her own journey through life. The focus is on understanding who you really are in Christ and discarding false impressions, leading to self acceptance and joy.

Discovering Your Identity in Christ by Charles Stanley [Thomas Nelson, 1999]. Part of the "In Touch Bible Study Series." It gives a very biblically based treatment of what God's word says about you. Shows how God uses life's challenges and experiences to unlock your potential and confirm that you truly are a "masterpiece in the making."

Free At Last: Experiencing True Freedom Through Your Identity in Christ by Dr. Tony Evans [Moody Publishers, 2001]. A very engaging, conversational, yet deep work by one of the best Christian communicators in the United States. It covers topics such as clarifying your identity, recognizing the "battle within," and "reprogramming your mind." The main objective of this book is to break the bondages in your life by knowing the truth about who you are in Christ.

Manual of the Core Value Workshop by Dr. Steven Stosny [copyright 1995, 2003; Steven Stosny]. Stosny is the founder of Compassion Power and author of *Treating Attachment Abuse: A Compassionate Approach*. His techniques for emotional regulation are practiced all over the world. Check his website at www.compassionpower.com.

Roll Away Your Stone by Dutch Sheets [Bethany, 2007]. A very inspirational and motivational book by one of the most effective Christian leaders of our day. Full of insights about how we can recognize the bondages our enemy has introduced in our lives and who we truly are in Christ. "An action plan for conquering the lies that keep you defeated."

Victory Over the Darkness: Realizing the Power of Your Identity in Christ by Neil T. Anderson [Regal Books, 1990]. Teaches how realizing who you are in Christ can help free you from burdens from your past, and how to become the spiritual man or woman you want to be. This book teaches the necessities to knowing how to help yourself grow deeper in your relationship with the Lord.

Step 8: How Do I Fight?

The Adversary: The Christian Versus Demon Activity by Mark I. Bubeck [Moody Press, 1975]. In this book, Bubeck seeks "to alert Christians to the battle they are engaged in and to give them specific, effective guidelines in dealing with the devil and demonic powers." This book addresses the key elements of spiritual warfare the Christian must be aware of with topics like: warfare with the flesh, with the world, fear, aggressive prayers, tools for warfare, and many others.

The Bondage Breaker by Neil T. Anderson [Harvest House, 1990]. Daring to face the tough issues of bondage, Anderson explains how and why the believer needs to be aware of the traps of the enemy, while providing Scripture from the Bible to help you to find the freedom and victory that God has for every one of his children. The book confronts sin head-on, but does so in a way that inspires and facilitates change.

Breaking Strongholds: How Spiritual Warfare Sets Captives Free by Tom White [Servant Publications, 1993]. This book will open your eyes to the realities of spiritual strongholds which may be affecting you, your family or church. White will help you to understand spiritual warfare, and help arm you with the weapons to defend yourself against the attacks of the enemy.

Overcoming The Adversary: Warfare Against Demon Activity by Mark I. Bubeck [Moody Press, 1984]. The focus of this powerful book is to help prepare the believer for battle. Bubeck spends a great deal of time digging into the Scriptures teaching you how to wear the full armor of God in warfare. Very grounded in Scripture, this book teaches and examines the strategies and weapons that God provides for victory in the life of the believer.

The Spiritual Warrior's Prayer Guide by Quin Sherrer and Ruthanne Garlock [Servant Publications, 1992]. Sherrer and Garlock advocate that using the Word of God is the strongest spiritual weapon that God has given each believer. In this book, they teach how to declare God's promises over your life to help you gain spiritual victory. Organized topically, this book allows for easy access to a myriad of Scriptures to claim and apply to your life.

The Weapons of Your Warfare: Equipping Yourself to Defeat the Enemy by Larry Lea [Creation House, 1989]. Lea boldly writes that spiritual warfare is not an option for the believer, but a requirement. He challenges you to become aware of the tactics of the enemy so you can exercise your God-given authority to overcome the dark influences that the enemy uses against us. This book will provoke you to become an unyielding warrior against the influence of the enemy in your life.

A Woman's Guide To Spiritual Warfare by Quin Sherrer and Ruthanne Garlock [Servant Publications, 1991]. This book will open every women's eyes to the spiritual battles and attacks that the enemy uses to threaten and overwhelm women in particular. It will help you to recognize and break the effects of generational curses, show how to incorporate and strengthen spiritual disciplines and how to use the strength of the Lord to fight for your marriage and children.

STEP 9: HOW DO I GET ACROSS?

Hope for the Home Front by Marshéle Carter Waddell [One Hope Ministry, 2003]. The most important "bridge" a wounded warrior must have is his or her spouse. Marshéle is the wife of Navy SEAL Mark Waddell, who served his country through nine deployments in every hot spot in the world over the past two decades. The price he paid was PTSD, and the price Marshéle paid is secondary trauma. This book honestly describes the struggles associated with being married to a PTSD sufferer and the triumphs God brings to their relationship. The book "ministers to those who are entrenched at home in the battle for their marriage, their children, their faith, and their sanity, which are all caught in the crossfire."

Hope for the Home Front Bible Study: God's Timeless Encouragement for Today's Military Wife by Marshéle Carter Waddell [One Hope Ministry, 2004]. Practical, 10-week, in-depth, interactive Bible study for individual or small group application. Goes deeper into many of the same subjects as her book, and facilitates a great deal of biblical input along the way. It is a call to arms for every woman who wants not only to survive but to live in victory on life's battlegrounds. www.hopeforthehomefront.com.

Learning How to Trust…Again by Dr. Ed Delph and Alan & Pauly Heller [Destiny Image, 2007]. Because of your PTSD your spouse may have broken trust with you, or vice versa. This book will give you a very practical roadmap for re-establishing that trust. Perhaps you have difficulty trusting anyone because of your trauma. This book's principles will help with that too.

Smart Love by Jody Hayes [Jeremy P. Tarcher/Putnam, 1989]. Though the book is written as a codependency recovery workbook for women in addictive over-dependant relationships, the principles enumerated in the book regarding group therapy are classic, practical and helpful in a wide variety of applications.

Two Hearts Praying as One by Dennis & Barbara Rainey, [Multinomah Publishers, 2002]. The toughest part of your healing journey may come as you invite your spouse into the journey with you. Joining your hearts before God is the single most transforming, intimate experience in your marriage following your life downrange. This ten-minutes-a-day 30-day adventure provides a bridge in your marriage to understand each other, reduce conflict, and knit your hearts back together again.

STEP 10: HOW DO I GET BACK TO "NORMAL"?

Buyers, Renters, & Freeloaders: Turning Revolving-Door Romance into Lasting Love by Willard Harley [Revell, 2002]. Especially for singles. If you've come to the point where you've tired of revolving-door romance and want to create one romantic relationship that remains passionate and fulfilling for the rest of your life, then this book might be a bridge for you. What makes a dating experience exciting one day and boring the next is quite predictable once you understand the principles to lasting love.

Courage After Fire by Keith Armstrong, L.C.S.W., Suzanne Best, Ph.D., Paula Domenici, Ph.D. [Ulysses Press, 2006]. This book is specifically for the returning veteran and his or her family. It gives them a clear idea of the challenges that lie ahead for them, and provides a toolbox of useful insights and coping exercises that can assist in saving a marriage or put a vet's life back on track.

Defending The Military Marriage by Lt. Col. Jim and Beatrice Fishback [FamilyLife Publishing, 2004]. In this excellent small group Bible study, the Fishbacks (European Directors of Cru Military) discuss how to maintain a strong, Christ-centered, supportive marriage while one or both spouses are in the military. This *Homebuilders Couples Series* study covers items such as communicating, basic training, sexual accountability and love.

Defending The Military Family by Lt. Col. Jim and Beatrice Fishback [FamilyLife Publishing, 2005]. A small group Bible study by the Fishbacks (mentioned above) that focuses on how to build a strong, Christ-centered family in the midst of the stresses, moves and separation generated by a military career.

How To Get Control of Your Time and Your Life by Alan Lakein [Signet, 1974, 1989]. Lakein is one of the most sought-after experts on time management. This book is a classic containing practical suggestions for setting goals, achieving them and organizing your life. It has sold over 3 million copies since it first came out, and continues to be inspirational to anyone wanting to live life more efficiently.

I Don't Know What I Want, But I Know It's Not This: A Step-by-Step Guide to Finding Gratifying Work by Julie Jansen [Penguin, 2003]. Jansen is a strong proponent of "one size does NOT fit all." Contains many creative exercises to help you get in touch with what you really love to do, and why you find certain jobs unsatisfying. A very practical and inspirational guide.

Loving Your Military Man by Beatrice Fishback [FamilyLife Publishing, 2007]. Bea and her husband Jim are the European directors for Cru Military. When Jim was an army officer, he and Bea had to learn how to maintain a strong Christian marriage in the midst of the pressure, loneliness and separations of military life. This ten-part Bible study based on Philippians 4:8 does an excellent job of encouraging military wives in how to triumph over these difficulties, support their husbands and become the women God intends them to be.

Marriage Makeover: Minor Touchups to Major Renovations by George Kenworthy [FamilyLife Publishing, 2005]. Think back to Step Two: PTSD is a *normal* reaction to *abnormal* events. Your marriage has been exposed to those *abnormal* events, too. Whether your time downrange has dinged your marriage or has pressed you to your limits, there is hope. This book provides numerous "makeover" principles that will provide health and healing to your marriage.

The Rich Single Life by Andrew Farmer [Sovereign Grace Ministries, 1998] (Pursuit of Godliness Series). Some people think that singleness is something to grieve over, but is that true? This book is going to help you for two reasons: 1) it's soaked in Scripture; and 2) it doesn't encourage you to find your identity in singleness. When we focus on our destination (getting married, having kids, owning a home, etc.) as the source of our contentment, it never arrives, because we're always looking for it somewhere off in the future. As you begin to understand your singleness you can discover the pathway to much more.

What Color Is Your Parachute 2007: *A Practical Manual for Job-Hunters and Career-Changers* by Richard Nelson Boles [Ten Speed Press, 2006]. This has been the best-selling job hunting book in the world for the past 20+ years (it's obviously been revised from time to time). The book offers up-to-date, practical techniques to help job seekers find meaningful work and mission.

Wounded Soldier, Healing Warrior by Allen Clark [Zenith Press, 2007]. As the subtitle explains, this is an autobiography of "A Vietnam Veteran Who Lost His Legs but Found His Soul." Clark shares his odyssey from being a cocky teenager not very interested in God, to a West Point cadet, to being a covert operative in Vietnam, to a double amputee. During his crisis, his faith in God became to focal point of his life. He has served as an Assistant Secretary in the Department of Veterans Affairs, and currently heads up Combat Faith Ministry. Check their website at www.combatfaith.com.

APPENDIX A

WOULD YOU LIKE TO KNOW GOD PERSONALLY?

Yes, you can know God personally, as presumptuous as that may sound. God is so eager to establish a personal, loving relationship with you that He has already made all the arrangements. He is patiently waiting for you to respond to His invitation. You can receive forgiveness of your sin and assurance of eternal life through faith in His only Son, Jesus Christ.

The major barrier that prevents us from knowing God personally is ignorance of who God is and what He has done for us. Read on and discover for yourself how you can begin a life-changing relationship with God.

✳ ✳ ✳ ✳ ✳

The following four principles will help you discover how to know God and experience the abundant life He promised.

1 GOD LOVES YOU AND CREATED YOU TO KNOW HIM PERSONALLY.

God's Love

> God so loved the world, that He gave His only begotten Son, that whoever believes in Him should not perish, but have eternal life.
>
> – **John 3:16**

God's Plan

> Now this is eternal life: that they may know You, the only true God, and Jesus Christ, whom You have sent.
>
> – **John 17:3** (NIV)

What prevents us from knowing God personally?

2 MAN IS SINFUL AND SEPARATED FROM GOD, SO WE CANNOT KNOW HIM PERSONALLY OR EXPERIENCE HIS LOVE.

Man is Sinful

> All have sinned and fall short of the glory of God.
> – **Romans 3:23**

Man was created to have fellowship with God; but, because of his own stubborn self-will, he chose to go his own independent way and fellowship with God was broken. This self-will, characterized by an attitude of active rebellion or passive indifference, is an evidence of what the Bible calls sin.

Man is Separated

> *But your iniquities have made a separation between you and your God, and your sins have hidden His face from you so that He does not hear.*   **– Isaiah 59:2**

> *The wages of sin is death.* [spiritual separation from God]
>   **– Romans 6:23***a*

This diagram illustrates that God is holy and man is sinful. A great gulf separates the two. The arrows illustrate that man is continually trying to reach God and establish a personal relationship with Him through his own efforts, such as living a good life, philosophy, or religion – but he inevitably fails.

The third principle explains the only way to bridge this gulf...

3

JESUS CHRIST IS GOD'S ONLY PROVISION FOR MAN'S SIN. THROUGH HIM ALONE WE CAN KNOW GOD PERSONALLY AND EXPERIENCE GOD'S LOVE.

He Died in Our Place

> *God demonstrates His own love toward us, in that while we were yet sinners, Christ died for us.*
>   **– Romans 5:8**

He Rose From the Dead

> *Christ died for our sins…He was buried…He was raised on the third day according to the Scriptures… He appeared to Peter, then to the twelve. After that He appeared to more than five hundred…*   **– 1 Corinthians 15:3-6**

He is the Only Way to God

> *Jesus said to him, "I am the way, and the truth, and the life; no one comes to the Father, but through Me."*
>   **– John 14:6**

This diagram illustrates that God has bridged the gulf that separates us from Him by sending His Son, Jesus Christ, to die on the cross in our place to pay the penalty for our sins.

It is not enough just to know these three truths…

WE MUST INDIVIDUALLY <u>RECEIVE</u> JESUS CHRIST AS SAVIOR AND LORD; THEN WE CAN KNOW GOD PERSONALLY AND EXPERIENCE HIS LOVE.

WE MUST RECEIVE CHRIST

> *As many as received Him, to them He gave the right to become children of God, even to those who believe in His name.*
> **– John 1:12**

WE RECEIVE CHRIST THROUGH FAITH

> *By grace you have been saved through faith; and that not of yourselves, it is the gift of God; not as a result of works, that no one should boast.*
> **– Ephesians 2:8-9**

When We Receive Christ, We Experience A New Birth

> Read
> **John 3:1-8**
> in your Bible.

WE RECEIVE CHRIST BY PERSONAL INVITATION

> [Christ speaking] *Behold, I stand at the door and knock; if anyone hears My voice and opens the door, I will come in to him.*
> **– Revelation 3:20**

Receiving Christ involves turning to God from self (repentance) and trusting Christ to come into our lives to forgive us of our sins and to make us what He wants us to be. Just to agree intellectually that Jesus Christ is the Son of God and that He died on the cross for our sins is not enough. Nor is it enough to have an emotional experience. We receive Jesus Christ by faith, as an act of our will.

These two circles represent two kinds of lives:

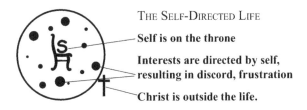

THE SELF-DIRECTED LIFE

Self is on the throne

Interests are directed by self, resulting in discord, frustration

Christ is outside the life.

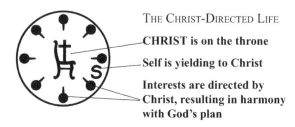

THE CHRIST-DIRECTED LIFE

CHRIST is on the throne

Self is yielding to Christ

Interests are directed by Christ, resulting in harmony with God's plan

Which circle best represents your life?

Which circle would you like to have represent your life?

THE FOLLOWING EXPLAINS HOW YOU CAN RECEIVE CHRIST:

YOU CAN RECEIVE CHRIST RIGHT NOW BY FAITH THROUGH PRAYER
(Prayer is simply talking with God)

God knows your heart and is not so concerned with your words as He is with the attitude of your heart. The following is a suggested prayer:

> *"Lord Jesus, I want to know You personally. Thank you for dying on the cross for my sins. I open the door of my life and receive You as my Savior and Lord. Thank You for forgiving me of my sins and giving me eternal life. Take control of the throne of my life. Make me the kind of person You want me to be."*

Does this prayer express the desire of your heart?

If it does, pray this prayer right now, and Christ will come into your life, as He promised.

HOW TO KNOW THAT CHRIST IS IN YOUR LIFE

Did you receive Christ into your life? According to His promise in Revelation 3:20, where is Christ right now in relation to you? Christ said that He would come into your life and be your friend so that you can know Him personally. Would He mislead you? On what authority do you know that God has answered your prayer? (The trustworthiness of God Himself and His Word.)

> *The witness is this, that God has given us eternal life, and this life is in His Son. He who has the Son has the life; he who does not have the Son of God does not have the life. These things I have written to you who believe in the name of the Son of God, in order that you may know that you have eternal life.* **— 1 John 5:11-13**

The Bible Promises Eternal Life to All Who Receive Christ

Thank God often that Christ is in your life and that He will never leave you (Hebrews 13:5). You can know on the basis of His promise that Christ lives in you and that you have eternal life from the very moment you invite Him into your life. He will not deceive you.

An important reminder…

DO NOT DEPEND ON FEELINGS

The promise of God's Word, the Bible – not our feelings – is our authority. The Christian lives by faith (trust) in the trustworthiness of God Himself and His Word. This train diagram illustrates the relationship among **fact** (God and His Word), **faith** (our trust in God and His Word), and **feeling** (the result of our faith and obedience) (John 14:21).

The train will run with or without the caboose. However, it would be useless to attempt to pull the train by the caboose. In the same way, we as Christians do not depend on feelings or emotions, but we place our faith (trust) in the trustworthiness of God and the promises of His Word.

NOW THAT YOU HAVE ENTERED INTO A PERSONAL RELATIONSHIP WITH CHRIST...

The moment you received Christ by faith, as an act of your will, many things happened, including the following:

1. Christ came into your life (Revelation 3:20 and Colossians 1:27).
2. Your sins were forgiven (Colossians 1:14).
3. You became a child of God (John 1:12).
4. You received eternal life (John 5:24).
5. You began the great adventure for which God created you (John 10:10; 2 Corinthians 5:17 and 1 Thessalonians 5:18).

SUGGESTIONS FOR CHRISTIAN GROWTH

Spiritual growth results from trusting Jesus Christ. A life of faith will enable you to trust God increasingly with every detail of your life, and to practice the following:

G – Go to God in prayer daily (John 15:7).
R – Read God's Word daily (Acts 17:11). Begin with the Gospel of John.
O – Obey God moment by moment (John 14:21).
W – Witness for Christ by your life and words (Matthew 4:19; John 15:8).
T – Trust God for every detail of your life (1 Peter 5:7).
H – Holy Spirit – Allow Him to control and empower your daily life and witness (Galatians 5:16,17; Acts 1:8).

> *The righteous man shall live by faith.*
> **– Galatians 3:11**

If you would like to learn more about your new relationship with God, contact Military Ministry at (800) 444-6006 and ask for the "Rapid Response Center," or go online to www.looktojesus.com.

FELLOWSHIP IN A GOOD CHURCH

God's Word admonishes us not to forsake "the assembling of ourselves together..." (Hebrews 10:25). Several logs burn brightly together; but put one aside on the cold hearth and the fire goes out. So it is with your relationship with other Christians. If you do not belong to church, do not wait to be invited. Take the initiative; call the pastor of a nearby church where Christ is honored and His Word is preached. Start this week, and make plans to attend regularly.[1]

---

[1] This is a version of the Four Spiritual Laws, written by Bill Bright. Copyright 1965, 1988, Campus Crusade for Christ, Inc.

APPENDIX B

DOORWAYS AND FOOTHOLDS

Please keep in mind that this list represents *possible* doorways. Just because you have experienced one of the occurrences listed below, it doesn't mean that you have opened a doorway or provided a foothold for the enemy. But you *may* have. That's something you and the Lord will have to discern together.

But if any of you lacks wisdom, let him ask of God, who gives to all generously and without reproach, and it will be given to him.   **– James 1:5**

1. Indulgence in occultic music, literature, art, dancing, etc.

2. Possession of (known or unknown) and/or use of occultic records, tapes, books, pictures, charms, books, souvenirs, tools, games (*Ouija Board*tm, *Dungeons & Dragons*®, etc.).

3. Holding on to grudges or bitterness against God and others.

4. Destructively negative self-image.

5. Anorexia; bulimia.

6. Attempted suicide; thoughts of suicide.

7. Rebellion against authority.

8. Dating relationships or close friendships with demonized people.

9. Sexual immorality with demonized people.

10. Habitually participating in sexual immorality with anyone.

11. Sexual involvement with a prostitute – even once.

12. Parents, relatives or other close authority figures who have accepted satanic influence; i.e., witch, warlock or satanist.

13. Ancestors or dead relatives who accepted satanic influence.

14. Seeking or giving consent to occultic power or revelation (spirit guides, going to a psychic, medium or fortune teller, having an astrological chart made, etc.).

15. Fascination with occultic power, occultic revelation, or psychic phenomena in general (taking e.s.p. tests or psychic aptitude tests).

16. Involvement in psychic phenomenon, such as astral projection, levitation, spells, magic, fortunetelling, séances, channeling, or being present when these phenomena occurred.

17. Involvement in or attending occultic rituals, festivals, masses, sacrifices, etc.

18. Involvement in martial arts rituals (no problem with martial arts, it's a matter of how deeply you may have participated in their rituals).

19. Being exposed to therapies that might induce a passive state which – if not monitored properly and administered by trained professionals – could be spiritually harmful, such as biofeedback, hypnosis, self-hypnosis, subliminal tapes, acupuncture, etc. (Most of these procedures are harmless and often beneficial, but there is the *potential* for satanic influence, so ask God for discernment.)

20. Deliberate rejection of what is known and understood to be true.

21. Participation in false religions or cults.

22. Abuse of drugs and/or alcohol.

23. Abuse of herbs.

24. Escapism through thrill-seeking, science fiction, soap operas, or some other addicting hobby or activity (again, these activities can be harmless, but if they have led to an addiction, it's a vulnerability).

25. Hedonism; an absorbing pursuit of entertainment and/or body pleasure.

26. Fascination with violence, especially violence devoid of justice, such as sadism or masochism.

27. Torture - either as a victim or a perpetrator.

28. Prolonged or persistent jealousy.

29. Pornography.

30. Fascination with UFO phenomena; attempts to contact extraterrestrial beings.

31. Prolonged sleeplessness (this could simply be a symptom of PTSD, but still you should ask the Lord if there is possibly a doorway here).

32. Chanting or other cultic/occultic forms of worship.

33. Blaspheming the Holy Spirit; i.e. repeatedly and consistently rejecting the work of the Holy Spirit as He reveals truth and convicts of sin.

34. Vivid, recurrent, disturbing dreams as a child.

35. Victim or perpetrator of rape or incest.

36. Victim or perpetrator of violent sexual, physical or emotional assault.

37. Victim or perpetrator of child abuse.

38. Institutionalization (jail, psych ward, etc.).

39. Shock or trauma. (Yes, your combat experiences *could* have created open doors, but not necessarily. Ask God about it.)

40. General anesthesia. (In this totally passive state, open doors are *possible,* but not probable. Ask God.)

41. Very prolonged, unshakable grief.

42. Involvement at high levels with Masons, Eastern Star, Rainbow, etc.

43. Obsession with occultic novels (such as *Harry Potter* and *Goose Bumps*).

For direction regarding how to close open doorways, see Step 8, page 114.

❋　❋　❋

Appendix C

Spiritual Warfare Ammo Bunker
[From Step 8]

Use these Scriptures when involved in spiritual warfare. They are your *"sword of the Spirit, which is the Word of God"* (Ephesians 6:17). Remember how Jesus used these weapons against Satan when He was tempted in the wilderness (Matthew 4:1-11): *"It is written …"*

Anger

Proverbs 16:32 – He who is slow to anger is better than the mighty, and he who rules his spirit, than he who captures a city.

James 1:20 – For man's anger does not bring about the righteous life that God desires.

Deceit/Lying

Leviticus 19:11,12 – Do not steal. Do not lie. Do not deceive one another. Do not swear falsely by my name and so profane the name of your God. I am the Lord.

Proverbs 12:22 –-The Lord detests lying lips, but he delights in men who are truthful.

Disobedience to God

John 14:21 – Whoever has My commands and obeys them, he is the one who loves Me; and he who loves Me will be loved by My Father, and I too will love him and show Myself to him.

1 Samuel 15:22b – To obey is better than sacrifice, and to heed is better than the fat of rams.

Disrespect for Authority

Ephesians 5:21 – Submit to one another out of reverence for Christ.

1 Peter 2:13 – Submit yourselves for the Lord's sake to every authority instituted among men; whether to the king, as the supreme authority, or to governors, who are sent by him to punish those who do wrong and to commend those who do right.

Drugs and Alcohol

Proverbs 20:21 – Wine is a mocker and beer a brawler; whoever is led astray by them is not wise.

Ephesians 5:18 – Do not get drunk on wine, which leads to debauchery. Instead, be filled with the Spirit.

Envy

Galatians 5:26 – Let us not become conceited, provoking and envying each other.

Proverbs 14:30 – A heart at peace gives life to the body, but envy rots the bones.

Fearfulness

Isaiah 41:10 – Do not fear, for I am with you; do not be dismayed, for I am your God. I will strengthen you and help you; I will uphold you with my righteous right hand.

2 Timothy 1:7 – For God did not give us a spirit of timidity, but a spirit of power, of love and of self-discipline.

Greed/Coveting

Exodus 20:17 – You shall not covet...

Matthew 16:26 – What good will it be for a man if he gains the whole world, yet forfeits his soul?

Hatred

Leviticus 19:17 – Do not hate your brother in your heart...

1 John 4:20 – If anyone says, "I love God," yet hates his brother, he is a liar. For anyone who does not love his brother, whom he has seen, cannot love God, whom he has not seen.

Idolatry

Exodus 20:4 – You shall not make for yourself an idol in the form of anything in heaven above or on the earth beneath or in the waters below.

1 John 5:21 – Dear children, keep yourselves from idols.

Jealousy

Proverbs 27:4 – Anger is cruel and fury overwhelming, but who can stand before jealousy?

Romans 13:13 – Let us behave decently, as in the daytime...not in dissension and jealousy.

Lack of Faith

Romans 1:17 – ... the righteous will live by faith.

Hebrews 11:6 – And without faith it is impossible to please God, because anyone who comes to Him must believe that He exists and that He rewards those who earnestly seek Him.

Laziness

Proverbs 6:9-11 – How long will you lie there, you sluggard? When will you get up from your sleep? A little sleep, a little slumber, a little folding of the hands to rest - and poverty will come on you like a bandit and scarcity like an armed man.

Colossians 3:23 – Whatever you do, work at it with all your heart, as working for the Lord, not for men.

Lust

2 Timothy 2:22 – Flee the evil desires of youth, and pursue righteousness, faith, love and peace, along with those who call on the Lord out of a pure heart.

1 Peter 2:11 – Dear friends, I urge you, as aliens and strangers in the world, to abstain from sinful desires, which war against your soul.

Malice

1 Peter 2:1 – Therefore, rid yourselves of all malice and all deceit...

1 Peter 2:16 – ... not using your liberty for a cloak of maliciousness, but as the servants of God.

Materialism

Hebrews 13:5 – Keep your lives free from the love of money and be content with what you have, because God has said, "Never will I leave you; never will I forsake you."

Luke 12:15 – Then He said to them, "Watch out! Be on your guard against all kinds of greed; a man's life does not consist in the abundance of his possessions."

PRIDE

1 Peter 5:5,6 – ... Clothe yourselves with humility toward one another, because, "God opposes the proud but gives grace to the humble." Humble yourselves, therefore, under God's mighty hand, that He may lift you up in due time.

Proverbs 29:23 – A man's pride brings him low, but a man of lowly spirit gains honor.

PROFANITY

Ephesians 4:29 – Do not let any unwholesome talk come out of your mouths, but only what is helpful for building others up according to their needs, that it may benefit those who listen.

Ephesians 5:3,4 – But among you there must not be even a hint of ... obscenity, foolish talk or coarse joking, which are out of place, but rather thanksgiving.

REBELLION

Proverbs 17:11 – An evil man is bent only on rebellion…

Romans 13:2 – He who rebels against the authority is rebelling against what God has instituted, and those who do so will bring judgment on themselves.

REVENGE

Leviticus 19:18 – Do not seek revenge or bear a grudge against one of your people, but love your neighbor as yourself. I am the Lord.

Proverbs 25:21,22 – If your enemy is hungry, give him food to eat; if he is thirsty, give him water to drink. In doing this, you will heap burning coals on his head, and the Lord will reward you.

Matthew 6:14,15 – For if you forgive men when they sin against you, your heavenly Father will also forgive you. But if you do not forgive men their sins, your Father will not forgive your sins.

SELF-CENTERED

Proverbs 12:15 – The way of a fool seems right to him, but a wise man listens to advice.

Philippians 2:3,4 – Do nothing out of selfish ambition or vain conceit, but in humility consider others better than yourselves. Each of you should look not only to your own interests, but also to the interests of others.

SLANDER/GOSSIPING

Proverbs 10:18 – He who conceals his hatred has lying lips, and whoever spreads slander is a fool.

Ephesians 4:29 – Do not let any unwholesome talk come out of your mouths, but only what is helpful for building others up according to their needs, that it may benefit those who listen.

SULLENNESS

Psalm 118:24 – This is the day the Lord has made; let us rejoice and be glad in it!

Philippians 4:4 – Rejoice in the Lord always. I will say it again: Rejoice!

THEFT

Exodus 20:15 – You shall not steal.

1 Peter 4:15 – If you suffer, it should not be as a murderer or thief or any other kind of criminal…

UNFORGIVING SPIRIT

Matthew 18:21,22 – "... Lord, how many times shall I forgive my brother?" ... Jesus answered, "I tell you, not seven times, but seventy times seven."

Matthew 6:14,15 – For if you forgive men when they sin against you, your heavenly Father will also forgive you. But if you do not forgive men their sins, your Father will not forgive your sins.

WRATH/RAGE

Psalm 37:8 – Refrain from anger and turn from wrath; do not fret – it leads only to evil.

Proverbs 12:16 – A fool's wrath is quickly and openly known, but a prudent man ignores an insult.

❋ ❋ ❋

Appendix D
Prayer Life of a PTSD Victor: King David
[From Step 10]

We've made reference in several places in this manual to King David. Not only was he a man of great courage, a brilliant military leader, and the most powerful king the nation of Israel ever had, he was also "a man after God's own heart." (Acts 13:22) But David was one other thing that surprises a lot of people – though it shouldn't. David also was a PTSD sufferer. How could one think otherwise when you read passages like this which David wrote:

> **Psalm 31:9-13** Be gracious to me, O Lord, for I am in distress; my eye is wasted away from grief, my soul and my body also. For my life is spent with sorrow, and my years with sighing; my strength has failed because of my iniquity, and my body has wasted away. Because of all my adversaries, I have become a reproach, especially to my neighbors, and an object of dread to my acquaintances; those who see me in the street flee from me. I am forgotten as a dead man, out of mind, I am like a broken vessel. For I have heard the slander of many, terror is on every side; While they took counsel together against me, they schemed to take away my life.

David wrote over seventy-five desolate, anguish-filled passages like this in the Psalms. So why would we want to offer King David to you as an example of a PTSD victor when he writes such despairing words? Because David recognized that God was his Healer, his only hope of escape from his distress. When you read many of David's Psalms, you are reading the writings of a man in process. He fought with depression, guilt, fear, anger, despair – probably many of the same emotions you fight with. But in practically every one of his Psalms, you will see him lifting his eyes and his hopes to God. Here's what he wrote in the very next section in the Psalm we just shared:

> **Psalm 31:14-22** But as for me, I trust in You, O Lord, I say, "You are my God." My times are in Your hand; deliver me from the hand of my enemies and from those who persecute me. Make your face to shine upon Your servant; save me in your lovingkindness … How great is Your goodness, which You have stored up for those who fear You, which You have wrought for those who take refuge in You, before the sons of men! You hid them in the secret place of Your presence from the conspiracies of man; You keep them secretly in a shelter from the strife of tongues. Blessed be the Lord, for He has made marvelous His lovingkindness to me in a besieged city. As for me, I said in my alarm, "I am cut off from before Your eyes"; Nevertheless You heard the voice of my supplications when I cried to you.

David's "normal" was the youngest son of a rural shepherd, peacefully tending his father's sheep in the hills around Bethlehem. You couldn't ask for a more idyllic life. But God had other plans for the boy. Looking at death in the face of a giant, having his country's king attempt to murder him twice, running for his life, being pursued by thousands of soldiers because the king had put a bounty on his head, seeking refuge in a hostile country with an enemy king, fighting battles without number, being betrayed by his own son, punished by God Himself for an adulterous affair and murder – these things shattered David's life over and over, and he had to find his "new normal."

And he did. God sustained him throughout his many years of trauma, crisis and despair, and finally brought him to a place of peace. His life was not without turmoil and disappointment, even in his latter years. He was reaping what he sowed in many ways. But he had come to a place where he could live triumphantly above the storms that had so completely engulfed his life in his earlier days.

Following are a number of David's prayers. We hope that you will identify with this man who, despite his courage, skills and accomplishments, was only a man. He was a man who recognized his need for a Savior, and his need for God's help. He's a good man for us to imitate as we grow through our dark days.

PRAYERS OF A WOUNDED WARRIOR

Note David's honesty as he pours out his heart to God. He doesn't hold back – and you don't need to either. You won't hurt God's feelings; He already knows what's in your heart, and He wants you to communicate it to Him, no holds barred. Try making David's words your words. Pray David's prayers as if they're coming from your heart. They probably are in many ways. David – and the Spirit of God – are just helping you to find the words to say. When David talks about his "adversaries," he could be talking about his literal adversaries, or he could be talking about his spiritual ones. There are forces of darkness that are "rising up against you." As David did, ask God for His help in defeating them.

Psalm 3:1-6   O Lord, how my adversaries have increased! Many are rising up against me. Many are saying of my soul, "There is no deliverance for him in God." But You, O Lord, are a shield about me, my glory, and the One who lifts my head. I was crying to the Lord with my voice, and He answered me from His holy mountain. I lay down and slept; I awoke, for the Lord sustains me. I will not be afraid of ten thousands of people who have set themselves against me round about.

Psalm 5:1-3   Give ear to my words, O Lord, consider my groaning. Heed the sound of my cry for help, my King and my God, for to You I pray. In the morning, O Lord, You will hear my voice; in the morning I will order my prayer to You and eagerly watch.

Psalm 16:1   Preserve me, O God, for I take refuge in You. I said to the Lord, "You are my Lord; I have no good besides You."

Psalm 22:1-5   My God, my God, why have You forsaken me? Far from my deliverance are the words of my groaning. O my God, I cry by day, but You do not answer; and by night, but I have no rest. Yet You are holy, O You who are enthroned upon the praises of Israel. In You our fathers trusted; they trusted and You delivered them. To You they cried out and were delivered; in You they trusted and were not disappointed.

Psalm 25:15-20   My eyes are continually toward the Lord, for He will pluck my feet out of the net. Turn to me and be gracious to me, for I am lonely and afflicted. The troubles of my heart are enlarged; bring me out of my distresses. Look upon my affliction and my trouble, and forgive all my sins. Look upon my enemies, for they are many, and they hate me with a violent hatred. Guard my soul and deliver me; do not let me be ashamed, for I take refuge in You.

Psalm 32:7   You are my hiding place; You preserve me from trouble; You surround me with songs of deliverance.

Psalm 38:21,22   Do not forsake me, O Lord; O my God, do not be far from me! Make haste to help me, O Lord, my salvation!

Psalm 40:17   Since I am afflicted and needy, let the Lord be mindful of me. You are my help and deliverer; do not delay, O my God.

Psalm 42:1-3,5,8   As the deer pants for the water brooks, so my soul pants for You. My tears have been my food day and night, while they say to me, "Where is your God?" Why are you in despair, O my soul? And why have you become disturbed within me? Hope in God, for I shall again praise Him for the help of His presence. The Lord will command His lovingkindness in the daytime; and His song will be with me in the night, a prayer to the God of my life.

Psalm 51:15-17   O Lord, open my lips, that my mouth may declare Your praise. For You do not delight in sacrifice, otherwise I would give it; You are not pleased with burnt offering. The sacrifices of God are a broken spirit; a broken and a contrite heart, O God, You will not despise.

Psalm 56:8-13   You have taken account of my wanderings; put my tears in Your bottle. Are they not in Your book? Then my enemies will turn back in the day when I call; this I know, that God is for me. In God, whose word I praise, in the Lord, whose word I praise, in God I have put my trust, I shall not be afraid. What can man do to me? Your vows are binding upon me, O God; I will render thank offerings to You. For You have delivered my soul from death, indeed, my feet from stumbling, so that I may walk before God in the light of the living.

Psalm 69:1-3,13-17 Save me, O God, for the waters have threatened my life. I have sunk in deep mire and there is no foothold, I have come into deep waters, and a flood overflows me. I'm weary with my crying; my throat is parched; my eyes fail while I wait for my God. But as for me, my prayer is to You, O Lord, at an acceptable time. O God, in the greatness of Your lovingkindness, answer me with Your saving truth. Deliver me from the mire and don't let me sink; may I be delivered from my foes and from the deep waters. May the flood of water not overflow me, nor the deep swallow me up, nor the pit shut its mouth on me. Answer me, O Lord, for Your lovingkindness is good; according to the greatness of Your compassion, turn to me, and do not hide Your face from Your servant, for I am in distress; answer my quickly.

Psalm 71:1-3 In You O Lord, I have taken refuge; let me never be ashamed. In Your righteousness, deliver me and rescue me; incline Your ear to me and save me. Be to me a rock of habitation to which I may continually come; You have given commandment to save me, for You are my rock and my fortress.

Psalm 86:1-7 Incline Your ear and answer me, for I am afflicted and needy. Preserve my soul, for I am a godly man; You are my God, save Your servant who trusts in You. Be gracious to me, for to You I cry all day long. Make glad the soul of Your servant, for to You I life up my soul. For You, O Lord, are good and ready to forgive, and abundant in lovingkindness to all who call on You. Give ear, O Lord, to my prayer; and give heed to the voice of my supplications! In the day of trouble I shall call upon You, for You will answer me.

There are many additional passages that you can find on your own in the Psalms that reflect David's mix of honest expression of his despair balanced by his faith in God as his Healer and Deliverer. Find them, and underline them or highlight them in your Bible.

PROMISES TO A WOUNDED WARRIOR

The next set of passages expresses David's confidence in God's ability to deliver, strengthen, heal him and to cause him to triumph. Read these verses over when your faith is flagging. Meditate on them. Pray them back to God, proclaiming your confidence in them just as David did.

Psalm 4:3 Know that the Lord has set apart the godly man for Himself; the Lord hears when I call to Him.

Psalm 4:8 In peace I will both lie down and sleep, for You alone, O Lord, make me to dwell in safety.

Psalm 9:9,10 The Lord will be a stronghold for the oppressed, a stronghold in times of trouble; and those who know Your name will put their trust in You, for You, O Lord, have not forsaken those who seek You.

Psalm 10:17,18 O Lord, You have heard the desire of the humble; You will strengthen their heart, You will incline Your ear to vindicate the orphan and the oppressed, so that man who is of the earth will no longer cause terror.

Psalm 12:5 "Because of the devastation of the afflicted, because of the groaning of the needy, now I will arise," says the Lord; "I will set him in the safety for which he longs."

Psalm 16:11 You will make known to me the path of life; in Your presence is fullness of joy; in Your right hand there are pleasures forever.

Psalm 23:1-6 The Lord is my shepherd, I shall not want. He makes me lie down in green pastures; He leads me beside quiet waters. He restores my soul; He guides me in the paths of righteousness for His name's sake. Even though I walk through the valley of the shadow of death, I fear no evil, for You are with me; Your rod and Your staff, they comfort me. You prepare a table before me in the presence of my enemies; You have anointed my head with oil; my cup overflows. Surely goodness and lovingkindness will follow me all the days of my life, and I will dwell in the house of the Lord forever.

Psalm 30:4,5 Sing praise to the Lord, you His godly ones, and give thanks to His holy name. For His anger is but for a moment, His favor is for a lifetime; weeping may last for the night, but a shout of joy comes in the morning.

Psalm 34:7   The angel of the Lord encamps around those who fear Him, and rescues them.

Psalm 34:15-19   The eyes of the Lord are toward the righteous and His ears are open to their cry. The face of the Lord is against evildoers, to cut off the memory of them from the earth. The righteous cry, and the Lord hears and delivers them out of all their troubles. The Lord is near to the brokenhearted and saves those who are crushed in spirit. Many are the afflictions of the righteous, but the Lord delivers him out of them all.

Psalm 37:23,24   The steps of a man are established by the Lord, and He delights in his way. When he falls, he will not be hurled headlong, because the Lord is the One who holds his hand.

Psalm 46:10-11   "Cease striving and know that I am God, I will be exalted among the nations, I will be exalted in the earth." The Lord of hosts is with us; the God of Jacob is our stronghold.

Psalm 50:15   Call upon Me in the day of trouble; I shall rescue you, and you will honor Me.

Psalm 55:22   Cast your burden upon the Lord and He will sustain you; He will never allow the righteous to be shaken.

Psalm 91:1-16   He who dwells in the shelter of the Most High will abide in the shadow of the Almighty. I will say to the Lord, "My refuge and my fortress, my God, in whom I trust!" For it is He who delivers you from the snare of the trapper and from the deadly pestilence. He will cover you with His pinions, and under His wings you may seek refuge; His faithfulness is a shield and bulwark. You will not be afraid of the terror by night, or of the arrow that flies by day; of the pestilence that stalks in darkness, or of the destruction that lays waste at noon. A thousand may fall at your side and ten thousand at your right hand, but it shall not approach you. You will only look on with your eyes and see the recompense of the wicked. For you have made the Lord, my refuge, even the Most High, your dwelling place. No evil will befall you, nor will any plague come near your tent. For He will give His angels charge concerning you, to guard you in all your ways. They will bear you up in their hands, that you do not strike your foot against a stone. You will tread upon the lion and cobra, the young lion and the serpent you will trample down. "Because he has loved Me, therefore I will deliver Him; I will set him securely on high, because he has known My name. He will call upon Me, and I will answer him; I will be with him in trouble; I will rescue him and honor him. With a long life I will satisfy him and let him see My salvation."

Psalm 92:12-15   The righteous man will flourish like the palm tree, he will grow like a cedar in Lebanon. Planted in the house of the Lord, they will flourish in the courts of our God. They will still yield fruit in old age; they shall be full of sap and very green, to declare that the Lord is upright; He is my rock, and there is no unrighteousness in Him.

Psalm 121:1-8   I will lift up my eyes to the mountains; from where shall my help come? My help comes from the Lord, who made heaven and earth. He will not allow your foot to slip; He who keeps you will not slumber. Behold, He who keeps Israel will neither slumber nor sleep. The Lord is your keeper; the Lord is your shade on your right hand. The sun will not smite you by day, nor the moon by night. The Lord will protect you from all evil; He will keep your soul. The Lord will guard your going out and your coming in from this time forth and forever.

Psalm 139:7-10   Where can I go from Your Spirit? Or where can I flee from Your presence? If I ascend to heaven, You are there; if I make my bed in Sheol, behold, You are there. If I take the wings of the dawn, if I dwell in the remotest part of the sea, even there Your hand will lead me, and Your right hand will lay hold of me.

Psalm 146:7*b*-9   The Lord sets the prisoners free. The Lord opens the eyes of the blind; the Lord raises up those who are bowed down; the Lord loves the righteous; the Lord protects the strangers; He supports the fatherless and the widow, but He thwarts the way of the wicked.

Psalm 147:3   He heals the brokenhearted and binds up their wounds.

PRAISES FROM A WOUNDED WARRIOR

We know that God came through for David because of how saturated the Psalms are with his praise and thanksgiving to God. Read through David's expressions of praise and make them yours. You may not feel too much like praising God at the moment, but try praising Him "by faith." The Bible says that God is enthroned upon the praises of his people (Psalm 22:3). As you intentionally make the attempt, you will sense His presence.

Psalm 13:5,6   I have trusted in Your lovingkindness; my heart shall rejoice in Your salvation. I will sing to the Lord, because He has dealt bountifully with me.

Psalm 16:5,6   The Lord is the portion of my inheritance and my cup; You support my lot. The lines have fallen to me in pleasant places; indeed, my heritage is beautiful to me.

Psalm 18:1-3   I love You, O Lord my strength. The Lord is my rock and my fortress and my deliverer, my God, my rock, in whom I take refuge; my shield and the horn of my salvation, my stronghold. I call upon the Lord, who is worthy to be praised, and I am saved from my enemies.

Psalm 18:16-19   He sent from on high, He took me; He drew me out of many waters. He delivered me from my strong enemy, and from those who hated me, for they were too mighty for me. They confronted me in the day of my calamity, but the Lord was my stay. He brought me forth also into a broad place; He rescued me, because He delighted in me.

Psalm 18:46-49   The Lord lives, and blessed by my Rock; and exalted be the God of my salvation, the God who executes vengeance for me, and subdues peoples under me. He delivers me from my enemies; surely You lift me above those who rise up against me; You rescue me from the violent man. Therefore I will give thanks to You among the nations, O Lord, and I will sing praises to Your name.

Psalm 28:6-8   Blessed be the Lord, because He has heard the voice of my supplication. The Lord is my strength and my shield; my heart trusts in Him, and I am helped; Therefore my heart exults, and with my song I shall thank Him. The Lord is their strength, and He is a saving defense to His anointed.

Psalm 29:1,2   Ascribe to the Lord, O sons of the mighty, ascribe to the Lord glory and strength. Ascribe to the Lord the glory due to His name; worship the Lord in holy array.

Psalm 30:1-3   I will extol You, O Lord, for You have lifted me up, and have not let my enemies rejoice over me. O Lord my God, I cried to You for help, and You healed me. O Lord, You have brought up my soul from Sheol; You have kept me alive, that I would not go down to the pit.

Psalm 30:11-13   You have turned for me my mourning into dancing; You have loosed my sackcloth and girded me with gladness, that my soul may sing praise to You and not be silent. O Lord my God, I will give thanks to You forever.

Psalm 31:7,8   I will rejoice and be glad in Your lovingkindness, because You have seen my affliction; You have known the troubles of my soul, and You have not given me over into the hand of the enemy; You have set my feet in a large place.

Psalm 34:4-6   I sought the Lord, and He answered me, and delivered me from all my fears. They looked to Him and were radiant, and their faces will never be ashamed. This poor man cried, and the Lord heard him and saved him out of all his troubles.

Psalm 36:5-9   Your lovingkindness, O Lord, extends to the heavens, Your faithfulness reaches to the skies. Your righteousness is like the mountains of God; Your judgments are like a great deep. O Lord, You preserve man and beast. How precious is Your lovingkindness, O God! And the children of men take refuge in the shadow of Your wings. They drink their fill of the abundance of Your house; and You give them drink of the river of Your delights. For with You is the fountain of life; in Your light we see light.

Psalm 40:1-3   I waited patiently for the Lord; and He inclined to me and heard my cry. He brought me up out of the pit of destruction, out of the miry clay, and He set my feet upon a rock making my footsteps firm. He put a new song in my mouth, a song of praise to our God; many will see and fear and will trust in the Lord.

Psalm 57:7-11 My heart is steadfast, O God, my heart is steadfast; I will sing, yes, I will sing praises! Awake, my glory! Awake, harp and lyre! I will awaken the dawn. I will give thanks to You, O Lord, among the peoples; I will sing praises to You among the nations. For Your lovingkindness is great to the heavens and Your truth to the clouds. Be exalted above the heavens, O God; let Your glory be above all the earth.

Psalm 59:16,17 But as for me, I shall sing of Your strength; yes, I shall joyfully sing of Your lovingkindness in the morning, for You have been my stronghold, and a refuge in the day of my distress. O my strength, I will sing praises to You; for God is my stronghold, the God who shows me lovingkindness.

Psalm 63:6-8 When I remember You on my bed, I meditate on You in the night watches, for You have been my help, and in the shadow of Your wings I sing for joy. My soul clings to You; Your right hand upholds me.

Psalm 68:19,20 Blessed be the Lord, who daily bears our burden, the God who is our salvation. God is to us a God of deliverances, and to God the Lord belong escapes from death.

Psalm 71:14-16 But as for me, I will hope continually, and will praise You yet more and more. My mouth shall tell of Your righteousness and of Your salvation all day long; for I do not know the sum of them. I will come with the mighty deeds of the Lord God; I will make mention of Your righteousness, Yours alone.

Psalm 84:5a How blessed is the man whose strength is in You.

Psalm 86:10,12,13 You are great and do wondrous deeds; You alone are God. I will give thanks to You, O Lord my God, with all my heart, and will glorify Your name forever. For Your lovingkindness toward me is great, and You have delivered my soul from the depths of Sheol.

Psalm 94:17-19 If the Lord had not been my help, my soul would soon have dwelt in the abode of silence. If I should say, "My foot has slipped," Your lovingkindness will hold me up. When my anxious thoughts multiply within me, Your consolations delight my soul.

Psalm 94:22 The Lord has been my stronghold, and my God the rock of my refuge.

Psalm 100:1-5 Shout joyfully to the Lord, all the earth. Serve the Lord with gladness; come before Him with joyful singing. Know that the Lord Himself is God; it is He who made us, and not we ourselves; we are His people and the sheep of His pasture. Enter His gates with thanksgiving and His courts with praise. Give thanks to Him, and bless His name. For the Lord is good; His lovingkindness is everlasting and His faithfulness to all generations.

❋　❋　❋

The reality of war is that everyone gets wounded. Some wounds heal rapidly, but some last for a lifetime.Some wounds can be seen. Some wounds are invisible inside the heart, soul, and spirit of the warrior. These unseen wounds are often the most difficult to heal – they must heal from the inside out.

The Faith and Hope Gap

Posttraumatic Stress Disorder (PTSD) is on the extreme end of the spectrum of trauma-related symptoms and conditions. PTSD was not an official psychological diagnosis until the early 1980s, but it has existed over the history of warfare, being referred to as "Soldiers Heart," "Battle Fatigue" or "Shell Shock" in former conflicts. Today, PTSD along with Traumatic Brain Injury (TBI) is called by many the "signature injury" of the wars in Afghanistan and Iraq.

Government agencies are working hard to help wounded warriors from past battlefields of WWII, Korea, Vietnam and wounded warriors from current conflicts in the Persian Gulf and around the world. In particular, the Armed Forces and the Department of Veterans Affairs, as well as numerous civilian organizations, are working tirelessly to help with the mental wounds of war.

A Department of Defense Mental Health Task Force report found that 49 percent of National Guard members, 38 percent of active duty Soldiers, and 31 percent of Marines are experiencing mental health issues after serving in Iraq and Afghanistan. The Task Force recognized that programs within DoD are not adequately reflecting the increasing demand. The treatment shortfall is partly caused by a lack of resources, but the fear of stigma to military and civilian careers is also a significant hurdle blocking requests for treatment.

In response to the need for more PTSD care, Veterans Affairs is seeking to add 40,000 new mental health hospital beds costing roughly 3 billion dollars, and also on significantly increasing the numbers of available mental health professionals.

The Services are likewise scrambling to reach the capacity needed to handle the PTSD challenge. In spring 2007, the Army surveyed over 100 combat-tested company commanders who indicated that "dealing with combat stress/ PTSD among soldiers" is a major area in which they and others need deeper understanding. The Army, seeking to better train its leaders, recently conducted "chain teaching" for all echelons of command regarding PTSD. All the Services are working PTSD issues and related family issues hard and fast.

The reality, however, is that the Department of Veterans Affairs and the Department of Defense simply don't have the capacity or the means to address the magnitude of this national challenge, particularly for the many National Guard, Reserve, and former troops and families who often suffer invisibly because they are not eligible for the same programs as active duty military.

The reality, also, is that wounds of the heart, soul and spirit are not addressed adequately by government services. Despite the valiant efforts of chaplains and many organizations and the commitment of billions of dollars, there remains a serious gap – the faith and hope gap.

For Christians, addressing this gap starts with the premise that God is the true healer and that Jesus Christ is the avenue to experience true recovery from the ravages of combat trauma, particularly those visited on the mind and emotions. For many of our veterans and returning warriors, this will be a long road – but there is hope. In my own life and in the lives of many wounded warriors, I have observed the peace, the calm and the healing that God can bring to war-ravaged souls.

Whether it's the veteran who has lived in the lonely isolation of combat memories for decades, or young warriors just returning from their first combat horrors, the power of God, the power of God's written word, and the community of God's people around our nation can become powerful resources in this healing process. And this healing can certainly extend to military families and many others impacted by these mental, emotional and spiritual wounds of war.

As an example from the Bible, David was honored as a "man after God's own heart" and as a "mighty man of God." Yet, David's Psalms indicate he was also a serious PTSD sufferer. For instance, consider his following lament:

> "My heart is in anguish within me, and the terrors of death have fallen upon me. Fear and trembling come upon me, and horror has overwhelmed me."
> —Psalms 55:4,5 (NASB)

And we read about David's trust in God for his ultimate healing:

> "He will redeem my soul in peace from the battle which is against me."
> —Psalms 55:18 (NASB)

Faith is absolutely a critical factor in resilient recovery from combat trauma, every bit as relevant today as in David's age.

Cru Military is a caring community passionate about connecting the global military community to Jesus Christ. Daily, we receive reports from Iraq, Afghanistan and other corners of the earth that testify to the importance, the eternal importance, of "faith in the foxhole." We hear constantly from troops, chaplains and commanders about the power of prayer before dangerous missions, about the value of the Bible to their sense of hope and comfort, and about the healing that comes from faith. They believe wholeheartedly, with David, that God is their "Rock, Fortress, and Deliverer (Psalm 18:18 NASB)."

Whether in peace or in war, American troops (Soldiers, Sailors, Airmen, Marines, and Coast Guardsmen) seek faith to anchor their souls. And families on the home front need the same anchor as they wait in fear and uncertainty. This anchor is available through faith in Jesus Christ.

Cru Military

At Cru Military (CruMilitary.org), our privilege and responsibility is to assist chaplains and commanders with caring for the spiritual well-being of troops and their families. We do this at our armed forces initial entry training sites (boot camps) and operational locations,

on ROTC and academy campuses and on the Internet, with military family seminars and small groups and by publishing and distributing spiritual resources direct and through chaplains, to troops and families. In addition, we seek to help every troop, every leader and every family member hear, receive and draw hope from the life-changing message of Jesus. Only in this way will these ones who selflessly serve us at home and abroad be truly ready, spiritually ready, to face the challenges which will certainly come their way.

In our present time of war and the aftermath of war, Cru Military is working diligently to provide spiritual solutions relevant and sensitive to the needs of combat trauma and PTSD sufferers. We seek to accelerate the spiritual healing of many thousands of veterans and returning warriors. Hence, we have established the "Bridges to Healing Ministry" to mobilize, equip and support Christians in churches across America creating a "corps of compassion" that will help heal and restore PTSD sufferers, families and caregivers. We have seen churches and communities across the country capture this vision.

We published the *Combat Trauma Healing Manual* in 2007 to offer PTSD sufferers a roadmap to for spiritual healing. By combining the latest insights from the medical and psychological communities with the timeless principles of God's Word, this book outlines a step-by-step program that will help PTSD sufferers …

- understand their trauma – spiritually, psychologically and physiologically
- adopt therapeutic spiritual disciplines to bring them closer to God
- process their loss and grief
- experience the freeing influence of giving and receiving forgiveness
- rebuild their identity based on what God says about them
- strengthen themselves spiritually against future attacks
- connect with those who will support them in many ways
- define plans to fully reintegrate into society as a strengthened man or woman of God, to include becoming an asset to other trauma sufferers

Also, in the fall of 2008, Cru Military published *When War Comes Home*, a companion to the *Combat Trauma Healing Manual*, for military wives.

In 2015, we published a series of books for children who have parents with Combat Trauma. The books, written by Sherry Barron and illustrated by Nick Adducci, are directed to children in K-3rd Grade (*My Hero's Home!!*), 4th-6th Grades (*Helping My Hero!!*), and teens (*My Hero Hurts!!*).

Cru Military's partnership with the American Association of Christian Counselors (AACC) is particularly relevant to reversing the PTSD epidemic in our land. The 50,000-plus Christian counselors within the AACC community will have a far-reaching impact in the lives of many military men, women and families. In October 2008, AACC and Cru Military delivered a jointly-produced, 30-hour video series and certification program, *Care and Counsel for Combat Trauma*, to help prepare professional, pastoral and lay counselors for serving military members and families. Together, Cru Military and the AACC will join forces to deploy tens of thousands of Christians from thousands of churches in the fight to build bridges between PTSD suffering and God's love and healing power.

When War Comes Home:

Christ-centered Healing for Wives of Combat Veterans

by Chris Adsit, Rahnella Adsit and Marshéle Carter Waddell

Published by the Military Ministry Press

When War Comes Home: Christ-centered Healing for Wives of Combat Veterans offers spiritual comfort and practical, Christ-centered solutions for wives of combat veterans struggling with the hidden wounds of war ranging from reintegration challenges to potentially devastating Posttraumatic Stress Disorder (PTSD). These are solutions for the "Secondary Trauma" she is experiencing when his trauma symptoms impact the family and even begin to show up in her. Insights from the medical and counseling community are wrapped in biblical principles and combined with the shared experiences of wives who are veterans of their own husbands' PTSD struggles. The book guides wives to:

- understand what happened to her husband – spiritually, psychologically and physiologically
- understand how her husband's trauma symptoms are affecting her
- learn how to deal positively wiht grief, loss and forgiveness issues associated with her husband's PTSD
- learn how to build her own "healing place," develop her support network and know when and how to find physical safety
- understand and focus on her true identity in Christ
- learn how she can contribute to her husband's healing environment
- learn how to construct a safe, healthy environment for her children
- understand the process of moving on to a "new normal"

Available from the Military Ministry Online Resource Center at http://resources.CruMilitary.org or by calling 1-800-444-6006. Information at http://www.whenwarcomeshome.info

ISBN: 978-1-4392-0890-8   Soft cover, 284 pages
Price: US $23.99 or $15 for active duty military and their spouses

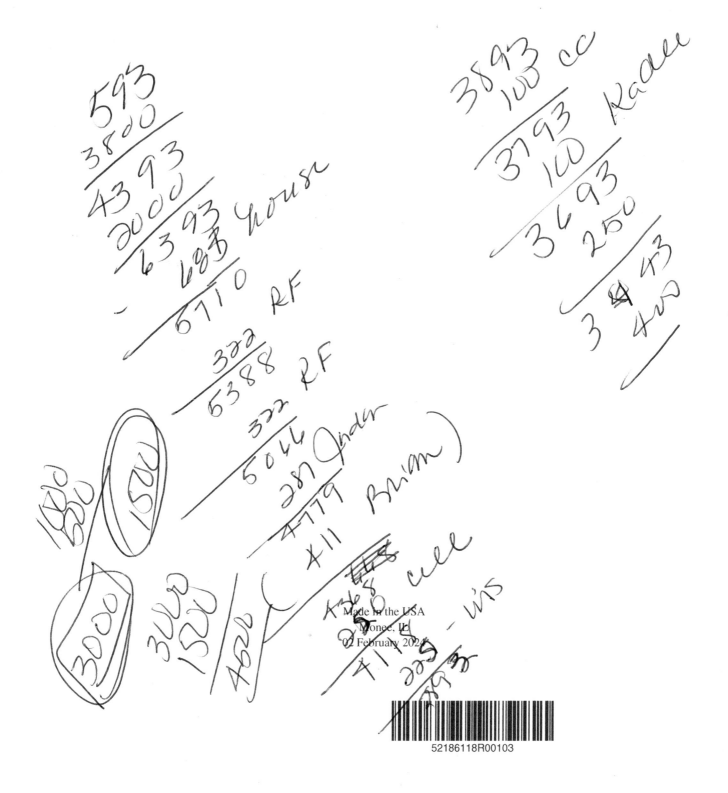